Ghosts

Ghosts

A Natural History: 500 Years of
Searching for Proof

ROGER CLARKE

St. Martin's Press
New York

*For my mother, Angela H. Clarke,
who saw a ghost*

GHOSTS. Copyright © 2012 by Roger Clarke. All rights reserved. Printed in the United States of America. For information, address St. Martin's Press, 175 Fifth Avenue, New York, N.Y. 10010.

www.stmartins.com

Library of Congress Cataloging-in-Publication Data
is available upon request.

ISBN 978-1-250-05357-2 (hardcover)
ISBN 978-1-4668-5786-5 (e-book)

St. Martin's Press books may be purchased for educational, business, or promotional use. For information on bulk purchases, please contact Macmillan Corporate and Premium Sales Department at 1-800-221-7945, extension 5442, or write specialmarkets@macmillan.com.

First published in Great Britain under the title *A Natural History of Ghosts* by Particular Books, an imprint of the Penguin Group, a division of Penguin Books Ltd

First U.S. Edition: October 2014

10 9 8 7 6 5 4 3 2 1

Contents

Contents

List of Illustrations

My Haunted Houses

O death, rock me asleep,
Bring on my quiet rest
Let pass my weery guiltless ghost
Out of my careful breast.

– said to have been written by Anne Boleyn,
in the Tower of London before her execution

There was a dead woman at the end of the passageway. I never saw her, but I knew she was there. The passage was at the top of the stairs, leading to the left, to the spare bedroom and my parents' room. The end was always in shadow. Even at the height of summer I greatly disliked it. Returning from the village school in the mid-afternoon, I was alone in the house. Every day I delayed the rise up the stairs until it became a mad dash to my bedroom, eyes clenched shut, hands cold.

We lived in a seventeenth-century former rectory, a thatched cottage with roses rambling up its west side and garden walls of great antiquity. It was the 1960s, and on the Isle of Wight it was still an England Thomas Hardy would have recognized. It was immemorially rural. The village school had a holiday for the annual agricultural show. Many of the children had parents working on farms.

At school, the dinner lady used to tell us stories. I absorbed a certain amount of them – there was the ghost of a Roman centurion in a wood on the approach to Bembridge, and a spectral horseman who foundered in the marshes near Wolverton, a place cut through by a clean-running stream where we would go on nature walks.

I began to devour books on the subject. Among the most intriguing things I learnt, as it was repeated many times over, was that there were more ghosts per square mile in England than in any other country in the world. But why should this be the case?

My mother, noticing my growing fascination with the subject, mentioned that she had seen a ghost at the end of that passage at the top of the stairs. A friend, visiting, had seen her too. The ghost had entered the spare room while she was lying in bed. At breakfast, the question was asked: 'Who is she?' Whoever she was, her energies seemed to dissipate when alterations to the house were made.

Still, she hung in my mind.

When I was fifteen, we moved to an even older building, a manor house that had once belonged to a Norman Abbey; it too was haunted. The last pagan king of the Isle of Wight[1] was buried in the woods on the hill nearby. By the pond, an old yew tree had grown against a millstone, like a finger swelling round a wedding ring. There was decayed panelling in one room. Smugglers' marks in the form of sailing ships were carved in the chalk of the medieval dovecote.

You could hear the ghosts – a man and a woman – talking inside the house sometimes; it was as if someone had put the radio on. The dogs growled at a particular spot in the kitchen. There were ghosts outside too. My father's horse shied at the chalk pit a few hundred yards away, in the lea of Shalcombe Down. A flying boat had crashed there in 1957, on the way to Majorca, full of honeymooning couples. Forty-five people died. Horses still don't like the chalk pit, I'm told. At the top, near the line of fir trees, lies a scree of twisted metal under the forest grass.

The spare bedroom wasn't a good place to sleep. Bodies from

the wreckage had been brought up via the stone steps outside, and for a day or so it served as a temporary morgue.

I thought about ghosts and ghost-hunting all the time. There were lots of books about people seeing ghosts, but almost nothing about what ghosts might be. Some ghosts seemed aware of the living, and others did not. I began to correspond with the people whose books I read with such passion.

One was the ghost-hunter Andrew Green. He believed that ghosts were either caused in the brain by electrical fields or *were* electrical fields. A humanist, he was noted for his good-hearted scepticism, and became the literary archetype of the doubting boffin assailed by genuine ghosts in which he does not believe. I also corresponded with Peter Underwood, author of dozens of books on ghosts, who ended up quoting some of my theories in his autobiography, *No Common Task* (1983). I found myself as a teenager in the acknowledgements of books by both Green and Underwood, then the two best-known ghost-hunters in England. I became the youngest member of the Society for Psychical Research when I was fourteen, proposed by Andrew Green.

I still hadn't actually *seen* a ghost, though. It was becoming tiresome.

Between 1980 and 1989 I visited four places said to be haunted: the Tower of London, Knighton Gorges on the Isle of Wight, Sawston Hall in Cambridgeshire and Bettiscombe House in Dorset, famous for its screaming skull.

The Tower of London is and was a death zone. It reeks of death, at night. The severed head of a mythical king[2] rests beneath it. The original White Tower, built with forced labour in 1077, was an edifice of malice intended to intimidate the population of London. For a large part of its history, the Tower of London was a royal residence; then it became a prison, particularly for those convicted of treason, with graded cells, from Anne Boleyn's quarters to a notorious cell called Little Ease, where you could not stand and you could not lie down. In medieval times, a husband-and-wife blacksmith team lived there; he made the torture instruments and she the shackles and manacles.

By day, it's a kitsch tourist venue of great popularity; by night, a high-security establishment guarded by members of the regular British Army. Ghost sightings are common among the small community living there. In 1957, a young Welsh guardsman named Johns saw a shapeless form on the Salt Tower at 3 a.m. which slowly bloomed out of the cold damp air with the face of a young woman. An officer from his regiment later commented, 'Guardsman Johns is convinced he saw a ghost. Speaking for the Regiment, our attitude is "All right, so you say you saw a ghost – let's leave it at that." '

There is only one book written on the Tower of London ghosts, and that book was written by a Yeoman Warder named George Abbott. Abbott spent thirty-five years in the RAF as an NCO before donning the Tudor 'undress' uniform of the warders in 1974. He wrote four books on different aspects of the Tower, the best known of which is on torture instruments, and after he retired he was occasionally to be seen sporting a resplendently long warderine beard and dropping chilling, dry facts into documentaries about torture.

One autumn evening in 1980, aged sixteen, I found myself at the Middle Tower just as the last of the hundreds of daily visitors had left and the gates were closing. George Abbott was waiting for me there, and we went in. It was dark. The Tower had a kind of airy vastness about it I hadn't expected. Without tourists, it hovered in time. Near the Bell Tower, we were challenged by a sentry to identify ourselves before entering through the heavy bolted door of the Bloody Tower. We were in a version of darkness, with no light bar that from the white phosphorescent security lights on Tower Green, which cast a magic-lantern show of trees moving in the wind against the old walls. Abbott pointed to a darkened corner where the little Plantagenet princes had lain, perhaps, before their assassins entered from the battlements. I kept looking at the door. It seemed about to open, all the time. So much of the ghost story is the anticipation.

I had the same feeling of anticipation when we were outside on one of the walkways, and Abbott showed me the spot near the Martin Tower where the ghost of a bear once rose from behind the door of the Jewel Room to confront a sentry. I gazed at it, half expecting the show to start. But nothing happened. The wind was in the trees and the pitiless lights continued, much like the floodlights of a 'killing field' sports arena, the neat grass covering a bed of mass murder. In the chapel of St Peter ad Vincula, a technician was tuning the organ. It gasped a succession of unruly notes, and the effect was one of gathering gothic intensity.

In the crypt, Abbott showed me a tomb the size of a minibus built into the side of an entire wall. Most prisoners from the Tower were taken outside to be executed, but that still left a great many disappearances unexplained. The silhouette of Abbott's beard fell against the polished stone, like the image of Ivan the Terrible in the Eisenstein movie. 'Every time someone planted a rose bush the police had to be called,' he told me. 'There were always human remains. So a while ago we decided to excavate a large area and have done with it, and the ton or so of bones they found were all gathered together here and given a Christian burial.'

Anne Boleyn, after her execution only yards away, was buried under the altar of this chapel. In 1882, a book was published by someone under the pen-name 'Spectre Stricken' which included a story of another soldier seeing lights burning in the chapel of St Peter. Rather than going in (he'd obviously heard the stories), he found a stepladder and climbed it to look down into the chapel, which he found illuminated by some kind of spectral radiance: 'Slowly down the aisle moved a stately procession of Knights and Ladies, attired in ancient costumes; and in front walked an elegant female whose face was averted from him, but whose figure greatly resembled the one he had seen in reputed portraits of

Anne Boleyn. After having repeatedly paced the chapel, the entire procession together with the light disappeared.'

In another incident, in 1864, a sentry challenged a white shape walking towards him, which was also seen by two people looking on from the Bloody Tower – luckily for him, since the sentry was court-martialled, on the charge of having been asleep on the job. As he lunged at the shape with his bayonet, he received a shock that knocked him senseless. Other sentries have been spooked by head-less women outside the Bloody Tower, and by a nameless thing following them up and down their beat from the Sally Portal entrance from the River Thames. In 1978, two were bombarded with stones from battlements which were sealed and impossible to access.

One Saturday night in October 1817, there was a dinner party held in the Martin Tower by the Keeper of the Regalia, Mr Edmund Lenthal Swifte, whose saturnine portrait by John Opie can be seen on the Tate Britain website. A Tower functionary, promoted by the Duke of Wellington, he was a former Irish bar-rister and a published minor poet who married four times and had twenty-eight children. He was also fascinated by ghosts.

That night, at what he fancifully called 'the witching hour', the three doors to the room were firmly closed and the curtains drawn as the keeper sat down in the company of his wife, sister-in-law and seven-year-old son. The room, its walls nearly nine feet deep, was said to have been the prison cell of Anne Boleyn. The fire-place projected far into the room, and an oil painting hung over it.

Swifte sat with his back to the fire and, as he raised a glass of wine to his lips, his wife cried out, 'Good God – what is that?' Hanging above the oblong table was what he described as a trans-lucent cylinder about three inches in diameter, and within it a bluish and a white colour commingled in constant flux. It moved behind his wife and she shrank away from it, exclaiming, 'Oh Christ! It has seized me!' Swifte, shocked into action, jumped up and hurled his chair towards it just as it crossed the upper end of the table and vanished into the recess of a window. He dashed out of the room and summoned the servants. 'Even now when writing I feel the fresh horror of that moment,' he wrote later. 'The marvel of it all is enhanced by the fact that neither my sister-in-law nor my son beheld this appearance.'[3]

The Tower was a focus of death and torture for a thousand years, and it is perhaps unsurprising that its fabric has drunk this in. At one point in the reign of Edward I, for example, six hundred Jews were crowded together in various dungeons, even in the menagerie. Some of the Tower's ghosts are more subtle – a baby crying; a hand on the shoulder while sitting in a bath; the smell of incense and horse sweat coming from nowhere; the sound of a monk's sandals slapping against a carpeted floor as he walks across it – but the rest make up a tableau of blood. As recently as the 1970s, screams were heard, emanating, it is suggested, from the ghost of Elizabeth Pole, Countess of Salisbury, who ran around the scaffold on Tower Green pursued by the headsman, who eventually hacked her to the ground.

Another haunted house was closer to home. At about the same time I was corresponding with George Abbott, I became very preoccupied with a site a few miles away from my home. I rode over the hills on my red Suzuki motorcycle and, in minutes, there I was at the derelict gateposts of Knighton Gorges. This house wasn't just haunted, it *was* the ghost: an ancient manorial building that had been demolished in the early nineteenth century in an act of spite.

This was the story I grew up with. Originally, the house, a Saxon hunting lodge used by Earl Godwin before the Norman Conquest, had a mossy tiled roof made from thick slabs of Bembridge limestone. It was shrouded in ivy. A tower stood at its north-east corner which contained a haunted room known as the 'Room of Tears'. It was here, in the fourteenth century, that a nobleman from a neighbouring house had died of his wounds after battling the French incursions which made the Isle of Wight almost uninhabitable during that period.

7

1. An early nineteenth-century sketch of Knighton Gorges,
showing 'The Room of Tears', the largest rectangle in the
upper part of the tower.

I loved that story, but it turned out to be not remotely true.
Knighton certainly had a history: it was originally owned by one
of the knights who killed St Thomas Becket – Hugh de Morville,
a Templar, Crusader and ex-communicant who is buried at
the Al-Aqsa mosque in Jerusalem. The estate descended to the
Dillingtons. They renovated it, and built the rusticated gateposts
topped with their heraldic lion crest, before Knighton fell into the
hands of youthful rake George Maurice Bisset in the 1780s.

Bisset became even more notorious when he ran off with the
wife of the governor of the Isle of Wight. Legend has it that when
his daughter married against his wishes, he vowed that she would
never set foot in the house again, and made sure of this by remov-
ing the house altogether. In 1821, syphilitic, mercury-poisoned
and deranged, he had his bed removed to a gardener's cottage

and called in the dilapidators, watching with satisfaction as they knocked the house down.

It's another good story, but in reality the house burned down between 1815 and 1816. It may well have received severe structural damage when a huge landslip caused an earthquake on the south coast of the island a few years earlier. It was not rebuilt. After its destruction, Bisset moved first to Shepton Mallet and then on to the Bisset family seat near Huntly, Aberdeenshire, which he had lately inherited. He was buried in the family vault in Lessendrum, and his daughters were never disinherited.

Many aspects of what most people accept as the classic story were first described by Ethel C. Hargrove, author of two guide-books to the Isle of Wight. Ethel had two experiences at Knighton Gorges – one on New Year's Eve 1913–14, when she heard at midnight 'a marvellous aural manifestation of a lady singing soprano . . . lastly came some very dainty and refined minuet airs'.

Two years later, she held the same New Year vigil, settling again at the old gates and waiting to see what would happen, with a friend who claimed to be able to see a 'square white house with ivy covering the lower part', and guests arriving, and a man in eighteenth-century dress leading a toast to the new year. Music seems quite a theme for the apparition, along with the sounds of dogs barking and carriage wheels. As it happened, the original house was never a white Georgian affair; furthermore, the main room, where any party would have been held, was on the first floor, not the ground, and there were no bay windows, as described. Whatever her companion saw that evening, it certainly wasn't the house seen in popular prints.

Two local vicars gave the story some more pep. Francis Bam-ford, who was an enthusiastic antiquarian, made up a similar story of a time-slip concerning a girl called Lucy Lightfoot, who fell in love with the statue on a Crusader knight's tomb in Gatcombe Church and, during a fearsome electrical storm, managed some-how to slip back in time to be with him. The real wooden effigy on which he based his story almost certainly comes from descriptions of the demolished medieval chantry at Knighton. The other storytelling man of the cloth was one R. G. Davies, in a paper published by the Hampshire Field Club which mentions the Room of Tears, and the tradition of phantom music.[4]

The details of the 1916 Knighton ghost sighting echo a famous ghostly experience written up by two Edwardian academics, Charlotte Anne Moberly (1846–1937) and Eleanor Jourdain (1863–1924), and called *An Adventure*, published only five years earlier. They believed they had slipped back to the time of Marie Antoinette, and gave an account of an experience at Versailles where they interacted with characters and vanished buildings. (More on this in the next chapter). The widely believed story of the Angels of Mons, in which archers from the 1415 Battle of Agincourt appeared to help the beleaguered British Army in 1914, was another kind of time-slip. The mid-war timing of the Knighton experience is also significant; as we shall see in later chapters, wartime does seem to increase a tendency towards belief in ghosts, and especially at this point in the First World War.

The story of Knighton stretched back further than 1916, however, to another writer, Constance MacEwen. MacEwen's main claim to fame was being mocked in print by Oscar Wilde for her proto-feminist riposte to Jerome K. Jerome, *Three Women in One Boat*, the story of a Thames sculling adventure featuring three ladies and their cat, Tintoretto. In 1892, she published a sickly historical romance entitled *A Cavalier's Ladye*, which purported to be a diary of an eighteenth-century individual whom she called Judith Dionysia Dyllington.

Her inspiration certainly seems to have come from the Isle of Wight. She dedicated the book to the attorney-general, who was also the local MP, Sir Richard Webster, and a day or so wandering the back lanes of the countryside near his newly built house in Luccombe may have taken her to Newchurch, to learn of the local folklore about a vanished house and its ghostly reputation, and to visit the Dillington tombs. She has a foreword entitled 'Facts' which includes details of large skeletons having been dug up in the garden of Knighton, stories of music heard, and that once a priest had come from the nearby town of Brading to exorcize the house. This was almost certainly a folk memory of the Brading cleric Legh Richmond, who wrote of his visit in *The Dairyman's Daughter*. It would have been handed down in the neighbourhood over the years and become garbled as it went from household to household and generation to generation. In later chapters, we will see this localized oral tradition at work again and again.

Knighton Gorges remains one of the few genuinely folkloric stories still active in England. Every New Year's Eve, people turn up, hoping to see the house appear. In this overgrown and abandoned spot, partly because there is so little of the modern world to intrude, there is still the room to imagine. Never mind that the house was never once recorded as haunted when standing.

For the people who turn up, this is a place where the veil between worlds is thin. The most often reported phenomenon is electrical cut-outs in cars beside the gates, followed by people hearing music and horses and seeing the heraldic lions restored to their place on the gateposts.

Much to my disappointment, I witnessed nothing at Knighton, though I repeatedly tried to offer myself up for the experience, arriving at all hours of the day and night, and in all weathers.

The year before I went to university, I finally went on a formal ghost hunt. When I was eleven years old, my father had given me a book called *Folklore, Myths and Legends of Britain*, and it almost never left my hands. I copied out the stories in longhand and in art classes would copy the etchings, wood and lino cuts commissioned as illustrations. One of the most fascinating images in it, among its wonders, was a photograph of an Elizabethan

2. The haunted bedroom at Sawston Hall – this is the picture I was obsessed with, aged eleven. Eight years later I slept there.

four-poster bed, with tapestries hung behind it in a gloomy and atmospheric panelled room. The caption claimed that this was the most haunted bedroom in England. I decided that, one day, I would sleep in it. Just a month shy of my nineteenth birthday, I wrote to the owner of Sawston Hall in Cambridgeshire. I went there one raw January evening, slept on the bed, and was, I suppose, haunted.

I didn't go alone. I contacted the Society for Psychical Research and they put me in touch with a Cambridge SPR member, Tony Cornell, a leading figure in the world of the paranormal with a special interest in poltergeists. Cornell brought a small group of Cambridge graduates with him, and that night we all camped out in the house – which was, apart from the famous bed, largely stripped of furniture in anticipation of its new life as a language school.

Sawston had been burned to the ground by Protestant forces in 1553 during the brief reign of Lady Jane Grey. They had been in pursuit of Henry VIII's Catholic daughter Mary, who had stayed there on the way to Suffolk; the house was set on fire as a punishment on the Catholic Huddlestones who had harboured her. It was rebuilt with funds from Queen Mary herself. The picture I had seen – and the bed that was still here, despite the Huddlestones having sold up, after four hundred years – was her bed. Unlike the Great Bed of Ware, it was not the bed itself that was haunted;[5] rather, it created a kind of focal point for the whole drama.

When I arrived, late that winter afternoon, a freezing damp was rising off the Cambridgeshire Fens: weather for ghosts, and the season for it too. Harry Price, Britain's most famous ghost-hunter, was of the opinion that there are more hauntings in January than at the more traditional times of Christmas and December.

Tony Cornell followed standard practice in securing the house; pranks are not uncommon out in the field when local youths get wind of a ghost hunt. All outside doors were reported locked and bolted. The house was searched and everyone accounted for. A log fire was lit in the sitting room in the vast Tudor fireplace. There was an unexpected kind of seriousness about it all, quite different from the vaudeville of contemporary televised ghost hunts. We were entering into communion with the dead.

The house felt steeped in theology, a flashpoint of Catholic ghost-belief versus Protestant scepticism. Its many priest holes had secured persecuted priests during the Protestant purges of Queen Elizabeth I; the Catholic priests would have believed in ghosts, and the Protestants who hunted them would not. By vanishing into the wainscots, these clerics were, in a sense, well on the way to becoming ghosts.

We wandered around all night, sometimes together, sometimes alone. I don't remember much about the other people there. In the Long Gallery, I set down a piece of quartz I had with me, on the instructions of a medium I had met on the Isle of Wight. In somewhat hushed tones, I invited the spirits of the hall to communicate with her using it. As I spoke, I felt very foolish, but somehow it felt like the elasticity of the air changed.

I slept fitfully, not getting into the bed but lying on top of the covers, watching the bar of light beneath the door, which was known to open and close on its own. Ghosts display a particular interest in doors and windows; for what reason, nobody knows. Once, I thought I heard the sound of a child's ball bouncing.

In the early hours of the morning, everyone came into the bedroom, and we all lay down there in sleeping bags. Its ancient central heating stood no chance against the damp chill. At first, all was calm, but at about 4 a.m. I woke up, hearing knocks – gentle taps, in orderly clusters. I turned on a tape-recorder and fell back asleep. The knocks continued, but we all slept. Among the rustle and coughs of the sleepers, other, stranger sounds later emerged when the tape was played back: not least, three notes played on a woodwind instrument.

We all parted that morning, and I never saw any of the others again. A few days later, returning home to the Isle of Wight, I took the piece of quartz to the medium, a woman in late middle age who lived in a brick house on the sunny Undercliff in Ventnor. She had already written several books on her ghostly experiences. When I had met her before she reported how a spirit had sprinkled *eau de violette* on her clothes, an aroma which succumbed instantly to decomposition, reeking of rotten vegetation within minutes. The clothes had had to be burned. After clutching the quartz for a few moments, she handed it back. It felt unusually warm, almost hot, like a cupcake from the oven; certainly much hotter than it would be from body heat alone. It seemed to crackle with energy. She took up a pen and began some rapid automatic writing.

I remember the cod-historical speech she wrote down – 'Fie, sir, unhand me!' – and the story of a maid made pregnant and then murdered by a son of the house.

In a phone call, Tony Cornell told me that the taped noises

demonstrated the sonic inversions, or ramp function, observed in some poltergeist cases – the sound wave was backwards when analysed, something impossible in nature. In the 1980s, this was cutting-edge parapsychology. But I never got to hear the recording. The subject of a paper in an edition of the quarterly *SPR Journal* of 1984, the tape is now reported to be lost.

Time passed. I began to feel a little embarrassed about my obsession and, slowly, other enthusiasms took the place of ghosts. But one Christmas – 1989 – I stayed in a house with some friends which turned out to be another one I'd read about as a child – Bettiscombe House in Dorset. It had recently been sold off by the Pinney family, who had lived in it for centuries. Almost the first thing I did when I arrived that December afternoon was to go up to the attic, where Bettiscombe's 'screaming skull' had been placed in a brown cardboard box with a Bible resting on its lid. It was said to be the head of an African, who as a slave had vowed that his spirit would not rest until his body was buried in his native country. Yet somehow the story was that screams issued from all over the house, and poltergeist activity broke out whenever the skull was physically removed from the dwelling.

After a day or so, I fell sick with flu, and one afternoon went to bed. At about four o'clock my friends came up to see me. Why was I making all that noise? They looked round the room. It sounded as if I had been moving heavy furniture – but I had been in bed all the time.

That evening, I slept in the master bedroom, where the house's new owner had seen the figures of a woman and a little girl. The whole night, I had a sense of people coming and going, a busy atmosphere. The next morning, I found out that a composer friend, Matteo, had been kept awake by dreadful crashes all night, as if, he said, someone had been trying to jemmy out a fireplace. Again I had heard nothing.

*

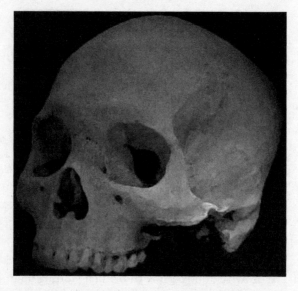

3. The screaming skull of Bettiscombe House.

And so to the here and now, and why I wrote this book.

Most ghosts are seen once and never again. Most instances of sightings are never written down or recorded. I found that there were very few genuine ghost stories with a beginning, middle and end; however, in this book, I have focussed on those that function as narratives. Often, I found I was more interested in the people being haunted than in the ghosts. It seems we have this idea that, whatever ghosts are, they seem to be trying to frighten us. We all respond very differently to fear. Maybe they aren't trying to frighten us at all. Maybe, as in the film *The Others*, they are simply locked in a world of their own making and we are shadows to them, and the encounters between us are the product of infinitely elaborate confusions.

The subject of ghosts has been degraded by the poorly informed and seekers of raw sensation. The discourse has not moved on since the eighteenth century, and most people still think, if they believe in ghosts, that to be haunted is to have an encounter with the actively dead.

But things have started to change. The chemistry of the brain is slowly being unlocked. And after ignoring the paranormal for decades, academia has found a new interest in ghost-belief and folklore, taking up where it left off one hundred and fifty years ago. The discourse is now being renewed. In this book I've included much recent academic work, including material on the flashmobs of Victorian London and the recent archive-led discoveries on the Drummer of Tedworth and the Ghost of Mrs Veal.

Discussion has drifted away – thank goodness – from efforts to prove or disprove the existence of ghosts. That idea belongs to 1880s London. In a basic sense, ghosts exist because people constantly report that they see them. This is not a book about whether ghosts exist or not. This is a book about what we see when we see a ghost, and the stories that we tell each other about them.

A Taxonomy of Ghosts

The tea-party question, 'Do you believe in ghosts?' is one of the most ambiguous that can be asked, but if we take it to mean, 'Do you believe that people can sometimes experience apparitions?' the answer is that they certainly do.

– Professor Harry Price

With ghosts there is a taxonomy – that is to say, there are many kinds of ghosts. After a lifetime spent collecting and investigating ghost stories, Peter Underwood settled on eight varieties, and this is a good place as any to start. They are as follows:

Elementals
Poltergeists
Traditional or Historical Ghosts
Mental Imprint Manifestations
Crisis or Death-survival Apparitions
Time Slips
Ghosts of the Living
Haunted Inanimate Objects

Elementals are often 'ghosts connected to burial grounds' and are 'primitive or race-memory manifestations', writes Underwood. An American ghost-hunter would probably call them demonic. Many of the ghosts of Wales and Scotland are elementals, fragments broken off from a pagan past, such as the 'kelpies' in lochs. Robert Aickman (1914–81), one of the finest ghost-story writers England has ever produced, describes them thus:

Elementals are, it is thought, exceedingly primitive entities: they squat in a single place, and to stare at one, even in the dusk (though it seems occasionally they appear in the fullest horror of daylight) is instant insanity[1] . . . A prominent British statesman who had a great interest in psychics (many will know who he was)[2] went with others to visit the Elemental that occasionally materialises in the cellar of a Somerset manor . . . one of the party looked too long, and was never the same man. The statesman never visited another Elemental.

The ghost witnessed by Edmund Lenthal Swifte in the Tower of London is in the elemental spectrum. The ghosts in the stories of M. R. James (1862–1936) tend to be either elementals connected to black magic practices, or reanimated corpses in the medieval and Scandinavian style.[3] For theological reasons, some Jacobean puritans classed all ghosts as elementals or *'larvae'*, referring to the mask or guise of human beings they sometimes adopt.

Thanks to Hollywood, poltergeists are now one of the best-known types of ghost.[4] Poltergeists present themselves as violent energies connected to a focus person, though there is some debate, according to Guy Lyon Playfair (b. 1935), the world's greatest living expert, as to whether they are 'alive or dead'. The focus is generally a teenager, usually a girl. In the 1930s, the psychologist Nandor Fodor (who we'll meet in a later chapter) advanced the idea that poltergeists were the result of repressed anger or frustrated sexual desire. The most famous modern case is the Enfield poltergeist, in the late seventies, which presented the whole gamut of phenomena.[5] The world of ghost stories is riddled with class, and the poltergeist is occasionally tagged as the 'council house ghost'. The paradigm of these stories is usually a family under siege by a host of alarming and unpleasant phenomena, perhaps the most famous of all being the immensely peculiar

Bell Witch case,[6] which took place in 1817 in Tennessee, and the Tedworth Drummer, which is described in a later chapter.

The category of traditional ghosts is straightforward: they are the souls of the dead, aware of the living and able to interact with them.

Mental imprint manifestations are those described also in the 'stone tape' theory, named after a TV drama made in 1972. Somehow, an effusion of mental energy soaks into a particular place, usually a room, and represents a psychic model of an extreme state of mind. These ghosts repeat the same actions over and over again, such as opening a door and walking across a room, and no consciousness is involved. Such ghosts also tend to be associated with a date and a fixed schedule. They often appear on anniversaries – for example, Lady Jane Grey is said to appear on the date of her execution – though, since the calendar was adjusted in the eighteenth century, this can be thought nonsensical. It is more likely that this idea is related to the sublimated Catholicism that marks English ghost-belief – ghost days are rather like saints' days. Like Anne Boleyn, Jane Grey is another villainess in the Anglo-Catholic folkloric pantheon.

Crisis, or Death-survival Apparitions have a long history, and people often see or experience someone with whom they have a close bond at the moment of their death, or at the moment they experience a life-threatening ordeal. These ghosts are common in wartime, for example when Wilfred Owen's brother Harold saw him when serving on HMS *Astraea*.[7]

Time-slip experiences became all the rage from 1911 till the end of World War One. It's hard not to read them now as nostalgia for a lost world, or perhaps one that was about to be shattered. These time slips are usually rather picturesque and decorative, almost like stepping onto a movie set, and they especially appeal to the imaginative with a sense of history.

I mentioned in my introduction the most famous time slip of all, which took place in France.

One August afternoon in 1901, two English ladies were enjoying a trip to the Palace of Versailles. After searching for the Petit Trianon, Eleanor Jourdain and Charlotte Moberly became lost. As they wandered, a solemn and heavy mood descended. Two men dressed in 'long greyish-green coats with small three-cornered hats' passed by, and directed them until they came upon a gazebo shaded by trees where a repulsive-looking man, his face marked with smallpox, stared unpleasantly at them both.

Just then someone came rushing up and warned them that they were going the wrong way. They were told to cross a small bridge, and when they did so they arrived at what they assumed to be the Petit Trianon. Here a woman was sitting on a stool, sketching. She wore an old-fashioned dress, covered with a pale-green scarf. Again, they experienced a sensation of intense gloom. Suddenly, a footman came rushing out of a nearby building, slamming the door behind him. The footman told them that the entrance to the Petit Trianon was on the other side of the building, and so they walked around the house, where they found a wedding party waiting to tour the rooms. The dark mood lifted, and nothing else unusual happened.

At the time, the two ladies were not aware that they had seen anything strange, and it wasn't until three months later that they realized their experiences did not exactly correspond – for example, Jourdain did not see the woman sketching. They soon became convinced that something mysterious had happened. Jourdain discovered that the day of their visit was an anniversary – that on that day in 1792 Louis XVI and Marie Antoinette had been taken prisoner when revolutionaries stormed the gates of the royal palace and sacked the Tuileries.

Though they kept their identities secret, the fact that these ladies were the principal and vice-principal of St Hugh's College, Oxford, gave their story weight. These were unusually well-educated and respectable people to have seen a ghost (as we'll see, the middle classes rarely admit to sightings), and many were convinced that these ladies had indeed stepped back into the world of Marie Antoinette. Miss Moberly speculated that she and Miss Jourdain had 'inadvertently entered within an act of the Queen's memory when alive'.

It was later suggested that what they had actually come across was a fancy-dress party. The advocates of the two ladies argued hotly that this would not serve as an explanation for the altered landscape, buildings and bridges they had seen. Subsequently, other people reported similar experiences, including one thirty years earlier, by the Dodsworth family in 1870. But it seems likely that what the Dodsworths saw was one of the last outings of Napoleon III's imperial hunt before the outbreak of the Franco-Prussian War.

In 1908, before the Moberly/Jourdain account was published, three members of the Crooke family also saw the sketching woman reported by Miss Moberly, who had seemed to grow out of the scenery 'with a little quiver of adjustment'. But it was the book by the two very proper ladies that set the scene for this relatively new paranormal experience.

One of the first and possibly greatest discoveries of the Society for Psychical Research was published in 1886 in two volumes called *Phantasms of the Living*. It contained 701 case studies which purported to show a phenomenon that went completely against the popular perception of ghosts, which was that they had to be dead. Some of these experiences of ghosts of the living constituted no more than a mental picture, and half-images caught between wakefulness and sleep. Curiously, the ghost-hunter Andrew Green[8] was involved in just such an incident. After he had moved house from Robertsbridge in Sussex, the family who had bought his house came to visit him in his new cottage. When Green opened the door, the daughter of the house fainted on seeing him. On coming to, white as a sheet, she said she had seen him many times in the garden of his old house.

When Green's mind was drifting, he had, it seems, been visiting an old haunt, especially the rockery he had so painstakingly created and left behind. Ghosts of the living are of especial interest to parapsychologists because they seem to suggest something of the brain function behind certain paranormal phenomena, and seem to indicate that such phenomena are actually nothing to do with the dead at all. Somehow, using ESP and the ability of the brain to generate images, some invisible signal is accessed and processed.

The final item on Underwood's list is haunted inanimate objects. It is not unusual for a bed to be haunted, or a chair where someone liked to sit.[9] The ghost moves with the item. Objects associated with death, such as a sword or a pistol, can also have an entity hang around them. Precious gems and jewels can seem to have a story, coded into their crystalline structure; there are several in the Crown Jewels, for example the Black Prince's ruby and the Koh-i-Noor diamond.[10] There is a brisk eBay trade in 'haunted furniture' and, in the United States, a strong belief in haunted toys which I haven't come across anywhere else.

Underwood only listed the ghosts of people but I would add the ghosts of animals to the list. What is striking about animal ghosts is that they are all of domesticated species – mostly cats, dogs and horses.

There are said to be a couple of phantom bears in London. Ghosts of dogs are frequently demonic, in other words, elementals, such as the hounds that haunt the country lanes of Suffolk and, in the church at Bungay, leave deep scratch marks on the door. These creatures have dramatic names: Galleytrot, Black Shuck and Barghest. The fact that they are mostly located in East Anglia and Yorkshire seems to suggest a Viking antecedent.[11]

People catching sight of a beloved and recently departed cat or dog is reported remarkably often. It's also a popular belief that pets can sense ghosts. Stories abound of cats, dogs and infants watching an invisible presence coming down stairs or moving across a room. The unencumbered mind appears to be a ghost-seeing mind.

Headless dogs and horses are a motif of nineteenth-century ghost stories. There are also folkloric animals such as birds and hares which, in the seventeenth century, were considered to be shape-shifting witches, or portents of invisible supernatural powers.[12] At the Punch Bowl Inn, in Lanreath, Cornwall, a clergyman is said to have returned in the form of a demonic black rooster.

The inhabitants of Arundel Castle in Sussex fear the appearance of a small white bird at their windows, seeing it as a portent of death.

Ghosts have changed over the years, which is why, I would suggest, there is a natural history needs to be told of them. The earliest ghosts in the *Epic of Gilgamesh*, for example, bear little relation to what came afterwards. Babylon's dead seemed to hover between the human and the inhuman. The ghosts of Ancient Greece were strange wraith-like creatures, pathetic and winged, who had no power over the living. Medieval ghosts were reanimated corpses or holy apparitions; Jacobean ghosts, demons pretending to be human.

Post-Restoration ghosts returned to correct injustices, right wrongs and supply information about lost documents and valuables. Regency ghosts were gothic. In Victorian times, ghosts were to be questioned in séances, and ghost-seeing became far more associated with women. Late Victorians embraced paranormality, seeing the ghostly as a manifestation of as yet understood laws of nature. The 1930s found the poltergeist.

So, what are ghosts seen as, now? To some extent, the idea of the demonic ghost has been re-imported to the UK by the descendants of the East Coast Jacobeans, who took the idea over to the New World with them in the seventeenth century. There are a collection of contemporary beliefs in popular culture, but people are very clear about what's possible. The overwhelming primacy is of the mood and atmosphere, having your head touched on ghost hunts, feeling a sudden breeze, falling temperatures, doors opening by themselves, then sudden noises, staccato or single words. Apparitions in plain sight are rare, but they do turn up on camera, and on digital cameras now, there are 'orbs', which, we are told, are ghosts before they dress themselves for the human eye.[13]

In one study in 1999, a group of Manchester women thought that hauntings were more to do with malign presences – in other words, a bad feeling – rather than the soul of someone who is dead making themself known.

Ghosts are no longer souls. Ghosts are now an emotion field.

The Visible Couch: A Brief History
of Ghost-Hunting

Do I believe in ghosts? No, but I am afraid of them.

– Marie Anne de Vichy Chamrond, Marquise du Deffand

I decided to pick up where I left off thirty years ago: with the ghost hunt. The man who coined the term 'ghost hunt' was the Irishman Elliot O'Donnell (1872–1965) in his book *Confessions of a Ghost-Hunter*,[1] however, it is Harry Price who is by far the best-known English ghost-hunter of the twentieth century.

Price was a cadaverous-looking man with pointed ears and an expression in his eyes described by at least one young woman[2] as 'not polite'. He twitched, he chain-smoked, had Nazi leanings and did his best to disguise his Cockney accent with a garbled form of Received Pronunciation. He was considered disreputable by fellow experts on the subject, but the public and the press loved him.

As a young man, Price would almost certainly have read the wildly popular stories of *Carnacki, The Ghost-finder*.[3] But for Price, there was no sitting around having a chat with witnesses over a cup of tea. Houses were to be staked out, recorded, scrutinized, with technology brought in. No one wanted to interview other people, they wanted to experience things themselves, first-hand; it's no surprise his ghost-hunting kit included a flask of brandy. It was a new, self-assertive way of doing things, which placed the investigator at the centre of the story.

Price was not a figure who endeared himself to the grandees and aristocrats of the Society for Psychical Research. After all, he

4. Harry Price, hamming it up.

came through the door marked 'TRADE'. All his life, he pursued a part-time job as a travelling salesman at Edward Saunders & Son in Cannon Street in the City of London, selling paper bags and tea wraps in bulk to the baking and grocery trades.

But by night, like Count Orlok, he came to life. He staged supernatural-themed spectaculars in London and Germany. He was making live broadcasts from haunted houses with the BBC seven decades before ghost-hunting shows became popular in the US and the UK.

In 1936 he conducted the first ever live broadcast from a haunted house, on 10 March, with BBC radio transmitting two investigations into Dean Manor near Rochester in Kent.[4] Among those with him was Professor C. E. Joad of Birkbeck College, London, who had some interesting ideas on the nature of ghosts.[5]

In the early thirties, Price still believed he could become respectable by disproving the antics of as many mediums as he could get his hands on. Even though this affected his friendship with men such as H. G. Wells, he promoted himself firmly and squarely as a sceptic. His close friendship with Harry Houdini was on the understanding that he was a fellow traveller, a trained conjurer who could detect fraud and hocus-pocus. In fact, as his subsequent activities came to show, Price was only a sceptic for hire.

Between his two books on Borley Rectory, known for a while as the 'most haunted house in England', you can see the change take place. It's as if they were written by different men. The first is cool and collected; the second tells people what they want to hear. The gamekeeper has quietly turned poacher and, as a result, incurred the everlasting enmity of those who cared about the new science of parapsychology.

'People don't want the debunk, they want the bunk,' Price once noted, a trifle acidly.

He wrote well – in print, at least, he was sensitive and sympathetic and rarely had a bad word to say about anyone. And he knew how to spin a yarn. Journalists recognized in Price a writer who had no qualms about the gingering-up of a story to give it colour and texture. He was, in this sense, very well connected, easily able to drop stories on the front page of national newspapers (something that didn't necessarily endear him to others in the field, who found his showmanship at worst fraudulent and at best *de trop*).

After Price died, increasing numbers of books threw doubt on his commitment to authenticity. In truth, he never had much interest in science, unless it connected to his sense of theatre or might prove useful in his desire to become an approximation of an establishment figure. His life and his creation of the instantly recognizable modern ghost hunt as a form of entertainment remain highly influential.

Clips of Price can today be seen on YouTube, where he plays the Oxbridge don in a book-lined study, rather than the tradesman from Holborn he really was. The more generous incline to think he started out well but then went wrong,[6] for all sorts of reasons, and that he was just a working-class media pioneer rather ahead of his time. His commitment to being truthful had to be bent in order to make a living – something not uncommon among the mediums he was often testing. Science, however, is rather unforgiving on the subject of faithfulness: one example of bunk means that everything is bunk, even if it isn't.

Price was a showman. But ghost-hunting began in a spirit of high seriousness. Joseph Glanvill (1636–80) might reasonably be called England's 'Ghost-hunter General', having published a succession of influential books on the subject of the supernatural, and gone out into the field to prove them. In 1662 he became the vicar of Frome Selwood, in Somerset, and it was here that he began to explore his interest in witchcraft and the occult. Though just a country parson, he was very well regarded and had powerful friends in the establishment. Intellectually, he juggled an enthusiasm for the latest experimental science with his religious beliefs, and his election to the Royal Society did raise the odd eyebrow – here was a man who believed in witches and spectres working with the most modern advocates of new rationalism. He does, however, seem to have been careful to keep these beliefs to one side when dealing with the scientists.[7]

Though the conventional Puritan line on ghosts was denial (since Puritanism held that Purgatory,[8] a theologically suspect Roman Catholic doctrine, did not exist), Glanvill believed that ghosts were the best, almost domestic, way of proving that God existed and that atheists were wrong. Ghosts may have been only a modest part of the supernatural light-show that was God Almighty, but they were still a part of it. If ghosts weren't from Purgatory, then they were from Hell, and that was just as good

Glanvill's book:[9] after all, there were ghosts in the Bible.[10] There was, at this period of English history, a profound fear of extremism, and it was thought that the wits and rakes mocking the divine in fashionable London coffee-houses were symptomatic of a general spiritual crisis. Glanvill believed that providing rational, cautiously investigated evidence of ghostly and occult activity would provide a useful bulwark in the fight against this crisis of spirituality.

Glanvill's most famous case was the Tedworth Drummer, which we shall visit in a later chapter.

Though ghosts were again of very great interest from 1762 onwards, when the Cock Lane ghost convulsed the new wave of printed magazines and newspapers of Georgian London, there were no eighteenth-century figures we would recognize as ghost-hunters. We don't encounter the breed again until we get to two very different women of the Victorian era: Catherine Crowe (1790–1872) and Eleanor Sidgwick (1845–1936).

Catherine Crowe came to public attention in 1848 with a book called *The Night Side of Nature*. An exploration of 'ghosts and ghost seers', it was a bestseller which ran through eighteen editions in six years and had the distinction of introducing the word 'poltergeist' (a word first 'found' by Martin Luther) into the English language. Crowe worked hard to sort out the many stories she heard, stripping away what embellishments she could. Her belief in ghosts was urgent and palpable. The book marked, according to one influential writer on this subject, a turning point in 'society's relationship with the paranormal'.[11] But Crowe's success and subsequent celebrity did not bring her happiness or respectability and, after a mental breakdown, she withdrew from any kind of public life.

A very different, much more respectable figure, the sister to a future prime minister of Great Britain,[12] Eleanor (or Nora) Sidgwick was one of the first administrators of the Society for

Psychical Research. She was a gifted and formidable woman who was also a very able assistant to her brother-in-law, the physicist Lord Rayleigh, in his laboratory work, which included the discovery of argon.[13] She was reluctant when given the official SPR role of investigating apparitions, because, she confessed, she did not believe in them. Logical to her fingertips, she was much troubled, for example, as to why the souls of the dead wore clothes, since clothes had no souls; this, she believed, was proof that ghosts could not be the dead returned.

In 1901, she investigated a haunted house in Cheltenham. The sightings were of a tall lady dressed in a black woollen dress that made a sound when it moved. Her face was hidden, rather spookily, by a handkerchief held in her right hand, and she had been seen by four of the sisters living in the house with their father and mother: 'There was no cap on the head, but a general effect of blackness suggests a bonnet, with a long veil or a hood.' Sometimes, she would be heard pushing at a bedroom door; sometimes, she seemed about to speak. She walked very softly, as if wearing thin-soled boots. One sister attempted to touch her, 'but she always seemed to be *beyond* me.'

There was, at this stage, very little in the way of structured surveillance within an orderly time frame. A house would be visited, tea would no doubt be poured, a cake would appear like a sugary apport (the transport of material objects without material agency), and a notebook would come out as the witness spoke. There would then be a long look at the places where any apparition had been seen, to check lines of sight, which way doors opened, and so on.

Harry Price would be the man to change all that, and his approach, especially the use and primacy of technology, is the one we see most today.

There were two other twentieth-century ghost-hunters whose differing approaches have helped shape the field.

Born in 1927, Andrew Green was a London School of Economics graduate who wrote a book in 1973 called *Ghost Hunting: A Practical Guide.*[14] It was the final democratization of the process begun by Harry Price. Green liked to use a certain amount of equipment in his investigations, right up to his best-known last hurrah, when in 1996 he spent over twelve hours surveying the Albert Hall for paranormal activity. Until his death, Green believed that ghosts were an electrical residue of emotions that became entangled in the living.

This belief came from a teenage visit to an empty tower in Ealing. Green was accompanying his father, a retired policeman who had been in charge of rehousing people whose homes had been bombed in the Second World War. The tower was the site of a murder and twenty suicides, and the teenager felt an overwhelming desire to jump from the top. He managed to draw back, but it was a near thing. He took a picture of the tower at the time and later used the photograph in some of his books. The face of a woman appears at a window, peering out at him.

Green was outlived by the other seminal figure in this field, Hans Holzer (1920–2009), an Austrian-born eccentric. His *Ghost Hunter* book of 1962 launched his publishing career and his long-running TV show. In 1977, he investigated the infamous Amityville Horror,[15] which spawned both books and films, where one of the mediums with whom he customarily worked 'channelled' the spirit of a Shinnecock Indian chief. He's generally regarded as the man who introduced the 'Indian burial ground' trope, now so familiar in ghostly popular culture[16] it feels like part of the scenery.

His obituary in the *Daily Telegraph* quoted him saying that there were 'three "dirty words" in his vocabulary: belief, disbelief and supernatural. 'Belief is the uncritical acceptance of something you can't prove' he explained. 'I work on evidence.' However, Holzer didn't believe much in the usefulness of technology. Though he studied at several universities and eventually achieved

5. Hans Holzer: he believed ghosts needed therapy.

a masters degree, he was probably more influenced by being a Wiccan high priest and vegan[17] who believed strongly in past lives.

He saw ghosts as 'a surviving emotional memory', a kind of fragment of a living person that has somehow peeled off from their mind like the rind from an orange. These ghosts often do not know that they are dead, and are confused. 'Ghosts by their very nature are not unlike psychotics,' he writes. 'They are quite unable to understand fully their own predicament.' This idea that ghosts behave like someone who is brain-damaged is a recurrent theme in the contemporary literature on the subject.

Holzer saw himself almost as a doctor for ghosts, diagnosing their taps and knocks as a doctor would a pulse. 'When a ghost tells of his woe, he also relieves the pressure of being trapped in the spot of the haunting,' he wrote. 'It is a little like psychoanalysis, except the "patient" is not on a visible couch.'[18] He felt a 'moral' duty to help out.

In the modern age in the western world, ghosts are increasingly connected with our emotional selves, and have less and less to do with providing proof of any supernatural or paranormal occurrence. Holzer was a kind of throwback. He was always searching for the story, whereas the modern ghost hunt is in search of sensation.

These days, the TV show[19] is king when it comes to the ghost hunt; it has a classless, speedy, problem-solving quality that appeals to the modern mind. There are very few formal SPR investigations these days, and almost no qualified parapsychologists out there doing fieldwork. It's best in some ways to look at what we have learned over the years, at the great stories of the past, rather than chasing round in groups for an experience of – who knows what? Access to ghosts is now of interest to the masses. It has been for some time. The crowd has moved into the haunted chamber.

The House That was Haunted to Death

A lady once asked me if I believed in ghosts and apparitions.
I answered, with truth and simplicity, 'No, Madam! I have seen
far too many myself!'

– Samuel Taylor Coleridge

In 1871, an account of a country-house haunting was published in
the *Gentleman's Magazine* just in time for Christmas. It had everything – an Elizabethan mansion, an authentic narrative, reliable
witnesses, apparitions, bumps and bangs, phantom music and
horrible groans, rattling windows: the lot.

Nowadays, Hinton Ampner is a National Trust property open
to the general public, sold very much as a garden with a house
attached. On a sunny day, all is well there. Enthusiasts wander
happily through gardens created on unpromising soil by the last
private owner, Ralph Dutton, who died in 1986, leaving his house
and its 66 acres of ground to the nation. In the guidebook to the
later neo-Georgian house, there is no hint of what went on
there two hundred years before, merely a mention in passing of
the vanished 'haunted Tudor house'.

The abbreviated version of the story goes something like this.
In 1771, a woman named Mary Ricketts, renowed for her common
sense, became so exhausted by a parade of inexplicable terrors
that she packed her bags and left her home. That home was
finally demolished after it proved impossible for anyone else to
live there.

There are many reasons why this particular story is so

fascinating. The first is why the story remained concealed for so long, the particulars recounted privately over four generations of the several families affected by it. The second is how modern the account seems, especially since it was written in an age when most people's idea of a ghost was a theatrical one based on Greek and Roman literature and Elizabethan dramaturgy. The third is the quality, quantity and consistency of the witnesses, which included a future First Lord of the Admiralty, a future brother-in-law of the King of England and a future governor of Barbados.

But perhaps most gripping of all is the possibility that this story forms the basis for Henry James's *The Turn of the Screw* and is the famous 'lost' ghost story supposedly related to James by the Archbishop of Canterbury, E. W. Benson, one winter evening in 1895.

The last embers of this story glowed again relatively recently, in literary terms. In 1968, Ralph Dutton published a book about Hinton Ampner entitled *A Hampshire Manor* (Hinton was his ancestral home). Dutton's passion was for Italian art, especially if it involved the representation of lissom youth. He loved porphyry and restful planting schemes and was known locally for his waspish lunch parties. Naturally, he was intrigued by the ghost story; the approach of most aristocrats is to see the ghost story as a form of ancestor worship. He was careful to offer no hint as to whether he believed in ghosts himself, nor did he directly address the rumour that some of their ghosts had moved to the new house built 60 yards to the south in 1793 and that noises could be heard in the early morning. But he did know the story.

Dutton mentioned that a printed account of the haunting in his possession had been amended on the page by his grandmother. She wrote, of Dutton's great-grandmother, '[Lady Sherborne] remembers when about 6 years old [c. 1786] while staying at Hinton being awoke in the night and carried down to the Rectory as the noises were so great Lady Stawell could not remain in the house.'

There is an overlooked orchard area north of the house which extends to the church of All Saints, where Dutton and his kin are buried. It's bounded by clipped yew hedges and in early summer looks overgrown, as the daffodils are allowed to die away between the blossoming cherry trees, blossoms chased by flowering apples and quinces. No one much looks at it, preferring instead the pleasures of the Philadelphus Walk or the sunken garden to the south. In his book, Dutton mentions how difficult it was to get fruit trees to grow there, because their roots are so pinched by the compacted foundations of the demolished house.

We don't know what this house looked like. There is no image of this vanished domain, no drawing, sketch or description of its exterior, and its interior is only imperfectly preserved through Mary Ricketts' account of the haunting and one bare-boned survey. In the British Library, there's a roughly sketched floor-plan. It seems it was a classically vernacular E-shaped house with a central hall, possibly medieval in origin, and parlours either side in the wings; in one wing a dining room, and in the other a breakfast parlour, housekeeper's room and kitchen. It was built of brick, possibly made and fired on site, with the edges cornered with stone from nearby Selborne. It was north-facing, typical of many houses of this era; there was an occasional belief that winds from the south bore disease and that a south-facing front door offered an invitation to continental agues.

Upstairs, we know, there was a Yellow Bedroom, especially haunted, over the servants' hall and apparently facing south, towards where the new house now stands, and a Chintz Room over the entrance hall and looking out over the gables of the porch, apparently looking north. There was a nursery and a nursemaid's room (the Red Nursery) opposite the Yellow Room, and attic or garret rooms on the top floor for the servants. A 1649 survey of the house, after it was seized and sold off by Parliament subsequent to the Civil War, shows a brewery, a mill house, a granary, a bowling green, stables and a malt house in the grounds.

Dutton has the impression, from his own practical knowledge

of the situation and, I like to think, some subliminal family memory, that the house was a cold and draughty place, set as it was on the top of a small hill, long before the tree planting that now helps protect it from the winds that come up the English Channel from the Bay of Biscay. Other storms that battered it include the 1644 battle of Cheriton, which at least one historian has coming up to the very walls of the house; it was a nasty, bad-tempered battle of rolling skirmishes. It was also a Parliamentary win, so it seems entirely possible that there were unpleasant consequences for the Royalist household at Hinton Ampner both during and after the fighting.

So this, then, was the Tudor manor house that Mary Ricketts saw when she rattled up the steep lane past the church one day in January 1765. The line of lime trees she would have been driven through are still there as are some of the oaks in the garden, now nearly 500 years old. Weather records for January 1765 in London and the south of England show bright mornings followed by fog and drizzle. The house would have seemed cold and dark after a journey from London, despite the fires having been lit in advance by their own servants from their London house, who had gone on ahead. For the first time in the history of the house, the Stewkeleys and their descendants, the Stawells, had left through choice. Lady Stawell had endured a miserable childhood there and, after the early death of her husband – who had only used it as a shooting lodge, it seems – the best thing to do was to let it out.

So here are Mr and Mrs Ricketts and their two-month-old son and heir, making themselves at home in a somewhat isolated and antiquated country house in the south of England. Mary Ricketts had met her husband, William Henry, in Jamaica, where the Ricketts family were well-known and influential, William's grandfather having been a captain in the Penn (William Penn – father of the founder of Pennsylvania) and Venables Parliamentarian force that took the country from the Spanish in the mid-seventeenth century. He rose to become a general. The Ricketts family were part of a shrewd ex-army stock made wealthy in this period by trade in the colonies, and on the verge of joining the aristocracy either through marriage or by the creation of new titles. One account also describes William Henry Ricketts as a 'bencher', or lawyer, at Lincoln's Inn.

Mary Ricketts herself came from solid Staffordshire gentry, and her father was a barrister, counsel to the Admiralty and treasurer of the Greenwich Hospital in London. Her brother John Jervis was to become a leading light in the Royal Navy and a great reformer of that institution, eventually being made an earl after his role in the Battle of St Vincent, and especially respected as a mentor to Horatio Nelson.[1]

If you had to construct a proto-Victorian character who was stoical and committed, dedicated to science and a fulsome defender of well-earned meritocracy over effeminate elected privilege, it would be John Jervis. He was not a man who tolerated any nonsense – but let's keep him in the background for now. He has yet to visit Hinton.

So to the ghosts. After the Ricketts' arrival at Hinton, it didn't take long for things to kick off. As early as the death of Edward, 4th Baron Stawell, in 1755, the house had developed a reputation among the locals for being badly haunted.

'Soon after we were settled in Hinton,' Mary Ricketts was later to write, in a private journal intended only for her descendants,[2] 'I frequently heard noises in the night, as of people shutting, or rather slapping doors with vehemence.' Mr Ricketts was sent to investigate. He assumed that these noises came either from housebreakers or perhaps the servants misbehaving, yet no trace of either activity could be found. The servants were not caught out of their rooms, and there was no evidence of a break-in. The noises continued to be heard on subsequent nights. Every lock on every door was replaced: 'I could conceive no other cause than that some of the villagers had false keys to let themselves in and out at pleasure.' It made no difference. The doors continued their slamming at the dead of night. Bam, bam, bam, BAM!

A favourite cat began to behave strangely. In the downstairs parlour, 'when sitting on a table or chair with accustomed uncon-cern she would suddenly slink down as if struck by the greatest terror, conceal herself under my chair, and put her head close to my feet. In a short space of time she would come forth quite unconcerned.' The servants gave a similar account of 'a spaniel that lived in the house'.

Summer came and, one sultry June evening, a nursemaid named Elizabeth Brelsford was sitting next to the baby in the nur-sery upstairs when she happened to look up. The door was open to the corridor to allow a cooling breeze to circulate, since the room was hot and Elizabeth was waiting for her fellow servant Molly to come upstairs with her supper on a tray. She saw a man in a 'drab-coloured suit' go past in the corridor, and into the Yel-low Room, a room, we are told, 'usually occupied by the Lady of the House'. When Molly appeared with her food shortly after-wards, Elizabeth casually asked who the man was. When they realized a stranger was in the house, both women went, with some trepidation, into the Yellow Room, but found nothing. They did not immediately tell their mistress and, when they did, they found she didn't take them very seriously: it was the lot of most servants of this period and beyond. 'I treated it as the effect of fear or superstition,' Mary Ricketts later wrote, clearly with some regret, 'to which the lower class of people are so prone, and it was entirely obliterated from my mind.'

Some months later, as autumn came, George, son of the groom, Richard Turner, happened to be crossing the great hall to go to bed when he also saw a man in a 'drab-coloured suit', which he 'took to be the butler who wore such coloured clothes, he being lately come and his livery not made'. As with the nurse-maid, the youth was not perturbed by this incident on an experiential level, since the man appeared to be corporeal and gave no hint of being anything else. But when Turner got upstairs to the servants' quarters he noticed that the butler was in bed and, consequently, the man he had seen remained unaccounted for.

In July 1767, we have another early-evening apparition, and this one is very rare, since it was witnessed simultaneously in daylight by four people.

The Ricketts had returned from London with their second son, Edward, now four months old, and relatives of theirs were staying at Hinton. It was a full and busy household. At about seven in the evening, the cook, Dame Brown, was washing up some pots and pans in the scullery, and a postilion called Thomas Wheeler, two maids and a fourth individual named Dame Lacy were sitting in the kitchen. The first thing was a noise: the sound of a woman's silk dress,[3] heavy, someone in it clearly coming down the back stairs and entering the corridor that led to the kitchen. Before they knew it, a female figure hurried into the room through the 'house door' and they distinguished a tall figure in dark-coloured clothes, but the spell was broken as the cook, finished with the dishes, suddenly re-entered the kitchen, prompting the woman in silks to vanish in plain sight.

Curiously, another male servant, making his way in from the yard outside, saw absolutely nothing. But picture it: two doors open, midsummer, two people coming in, four people sitting, and a ghost vanishing at the touch of sunlight. That's a unique scenario. It's not explicit in the account by Mary Ricketts, but there's an impression of agitation and hurry in this ghost, picked up perhaps in a drawing of the incident included in Harry Price's *Poltergeist over England* of 1945, in which a stippled figure in old-fashioned garb, with a gash for a mouth, rushes past the servants.

The noises 'continued to be heard occasionally', records Mary Ricketts. The maid of one of her visiting relatives, Mrs Poyntz, saw the ghost in the kitchen, and the maid of another relative, a female cousin, a Miss Parker,[4] was 'terrified by the most dismal groans and rustling round her bed'. But Mary was preoccupied by her third pregnancy, and a daughter was born in 1768.

In November 1769, William Henry Ricketts was called back to the family estate in Jamaica on various family and business matters, including the purchase of twenty-four slaves[5] for a relative and the building of a family mausoleum. (A feature of the various slave rebellions in Jamaica was that the graves of the white settlers were often desecrated, and so William had the task of having a new tomb built and supervising the removal of his family's remains to a more isolated spot.) It was decided that Jamaica was no place for the children. Mary Ricketts decided to stay behind at Hinton Ampner with her Swiss butler, Lewis Chanson, and six others – Mary's personal maid, Ann Sparks; Ann's husband, John Sparks the coachman; housemaid Lucy Webb; the cook, Dame Brown; nursemaid Sarah Horner; and John Horner, the new 16-year-old postilion (the postilion who had seen the ghost in the kitchen had since died).

Mary was now sleeping in a bedroom above the kitchen, later called the Red Nursery, to be closer to her children. The ghosts prowled in the corridor outside. Mary found herself constantly searching the cupboards for whoever kept walking in there and whoever it was whose silks rustled against the door – not the gentle rustle of softly falling fabric but 'so loud and of such continuance as to break my rest'.

At about this time, she was also told a local tale by an old man from the poorhouse in West Meon who had known a carpenter who had worked on the house in the time of the Civil War. He had taken up the floorboards of the dining rooms in order for Sir Hugh Stewkeley to conceal a box beneath them; Sir Hugh then ordered the carpenter to reseal the boards.

For whatever reason – perhaps they had just had enough – Mary's staff began leaving. Her maid and coachman resigned; a brief attempt at replacing Ann Sparks with one Ruth Turpin did not end well when, as Mary tells it, she 'being disordered of mind continued with me but a few months'. No doubt the groans, footsteps and apparitions didn't help. Eventually, the woman who would help her dress and so forth was replaced by the sister of a local grocer, but then the Swiss butler too took his leave. By this time, none of her original staff was left.

Mary was in the Yellow Bedroom when she heard the footsteps. It was summer again, the dog-days favoured by the Hinton ghosts. She had been in bed for only half an hour when she distinctly heard the heavy footfall of a man walking right up to the end of her bed, as if he could see in the dark, and her alarm was so great that she fled the room. A later account says that the sounds were preceded by the sound of someone jumping from the window-seat, suggesting that someone had climbed in through the first-floor window. The nursery maid helped Mary in her search – but, needless to say, nothing was found. 'This alarm perplexed me more than any preceding, being within my own room, the footsteps distinct as I ever heard, myself perfectly awake and collected.' It says a great deal about Mary Ricketts that she went straight back to bed in the same room, refusing to be intimidated or frightened.

However, by November, she had moved bedroom, this time to the Chintz Room over the hall. Here, she was convinced she heard music once or twice and, on another occasion, three very heavy and 'violent' knocks on the front door, which were sufficiently alarming for her to ring the bell beside the bed and initiate another – fruitless – search. The splintering crashes she heard were so ferociously loud, she was convinced that someone was trying to force open the front door.

Soon after Christmas, the murmuring began. It was a deep susurration. People were talking; lots of people. It was a noise in the back of the house's throat. 'I was frequently sensible of a hollow murmuring that seemed to possess the whole house,' Mary wrote. 'It was independent of wind, being equally heard on the calmest nights.'

On 27 February 1770, the evening after the old housekeeper was interred mere yards away in the church at Hinton, Mary's new maid, Elizabeth Godin, was 'never in her life more terrified' than by the 'dismal groans and flutterings' around her bed in the deceased housekeeper's room. The housekeeper had retired and died away from the house, and only Mary Ricketts was aware of the coincidence of the burial. She resolved not to mention this to Elizabeth Godin, not wishing to make the situation worse.

It seems to have been a rather melancholy period. Mary Ricketts' husband was building a family mausoleum thousands of miles away, her brother raising a monument to a recently killed family friend in a chapel in Gibraltar – and then the letter sealed with black wax had arrived: Mary's father was dead at the family home in Staffordshire. And poor Elizabeth Godin wasn't flourishing at all: come April, she was lying in bed with a fever. She was awoken by her mistress ringing her bell at two o'clock in the morning. Could she see, cried her mistress through two closed doors, anyone in the corridor outside? Mary Ricketts had been listening, for twenty minutes, to someone walking up and down, the door creaking, as if someone was trying to push it open. For the first time, she could make out more than one person prowling between her door and the nursery.

As they searched the area, checking the window and the fireplace, looking under the couch, the door behind them into the Yellow Room suddenly moved, and carried on moving, 'as if played to and fro by a person standing behind'. They rushed into the nursery and rang the bell connecting to the male servants' sleeping quarters; the new butler, Robert Camis, came to investigate: nothing was found and nothing was out of place.

Weeks passed. By 7 May, Mary felt that the susurration was growing in volume: 'the murmur was uncommonly loud,' she complained, and it was stopping her from sleeping. She described how she restlessly moved around the house, sleeping for an hour with the children in the nursery, then back to, presumably, the Chintz Room, for she was roused again by great crashes hammering the front door – and she jumped out of bed and craned to look down at the porch, since it was now dawn, with the grey light on the white lawn, hoping to see the cause. The door was examined and found to be locked and bolted.

She confessed herself 'harassed and perplexed'. A servant was now sleeping with her to keep her company and, no doubt, to act as witness, for by this point Mary was deadly keen to have everything written down and rigorously witnessed. 'After Midsummer the noises became every night more intolerable.' They would last until daybreak, sometimes slightly beyond. She could now distinguish different people talking. There was a woman with a shrill voice, and two others, men, one with a deep tone. One night, it seemed as if someone was brushing past the curtains of her four-poster bed. There were sounds, like music but not music, a 'vibration of harmonious tones'; there was walking, talking, knocking, opening, slamming of doors repeated every night.

When Mary's brother came to stay, she was unsure what to do, knowing full well that he was a no-nonsense type. She had confided in some clerical friends, the Revd Mr and Mrs John Monk Newbolt (he was rector of St Maurice in Winchester), four months earlier – but now a sympathetic ear simply wasn't enough. One morning, she could bear it no longer and blurted out, 'I was afraid that last night my servants would disturb you, and rang my bell to order them to bed.' Her brother was puzzled. He had heard nothing, he replied. But at least the subject of the nocturnal noise had been raised.

Hours after John Jervis had taken his leave for Portsmouth, Mary encountered the most frightening incidents of her entire six-year residence. Evening fell. She went to bed. At three o'clock in the morning, Mary was roused. 'Good God! Did you hear that noise?' she exclaimed to Elizabeth Godin, who lay in the same room on a truckle bed. Nothing. She asked again. Elizabeth made a few faltering noises. She was paralysed by fear. At that moment, outside the bedroom, it happened – 'the most loud, deep tremendous noise which seemed to rush and fall with infinite velocity'. It then devolved into 'a shrill and dreadful shriek . . . repeated three or four times, growing fainter as it seemed to descend, till it sank into the earth'.

Hannah Streeter,[6] in the nursery with the children, heard it also, lying in a state of shock for nearly two hours. She described it as sounding like someone being dragged to Hell.

John Jervis was delayed in Portsmouth. Mary now had a bad chest cold and a slow, enduring fever. She must have worried for her sanity. The noises continued to plague her and the household. When her brother strode in one day after a ride out from Portsmouth, she attempted to hide her desperation, but her brother was, we know from his correspondence, deeply shocked by her tired and haggard appearance. She held off for another few hours. 'However desirous to impart the narrative,' she recalled later, 'yet I forebore until the next morning.'

It was the first week of August 1771.

That next morning, she told him everything. He was a sceptic by nature, but he must have seen that the household was falling apart. It seems from her correspondence that she had the Newbolts to breakfast to verify what they could of her story for him. Just as she finished her account, a neighbour named Luttrell came to call, and by the end of a second recollection of the story, both Luttrell and Jervis had resolved to stay up that evening and catch out the impostor, since imposture it must be.

Captains Luttrell and Jervis (by this point, Jervis had his own command, HMS *Alarm*) prepared themselves for an evening showdown with what they assumed would be local rogues who had somehow managed to gain clandestine access to the house. Jervis and his own valet or batman, John Bolton, methodically examined the house that evening, searching every cupboard and place of concealment, before making sure the house was secure, locked and bolted. Having done so, Jervis retired to his bedroom clearly expecting nothing to happen, with Bolton and Luttrell in the Chintz Room nearby resolved to take watch and rouse him should anything happen. 'My brother was to be called on in any alarm.' The two men armed themselves with pistols. They were taking no chances.

Every bedroom on that floor was occupied that night. The children were in the nursery. Mary Ricketts was in Elizabeth Godin's room. 'I bolted and locked the door that opened to that floor from the back stairs, so that there was no entrance unless through the room where Luttrell kept watch.'

In other words, they had secured an area of the house in a manner which would, many years later, become standard for the investigation of hauntings, and indeed remains common practice now.

They didn't have to wait long.

There was that silken rustling again, just outside the door of the room where Mary lay. It was elusive at first. She ordered Elizabeth Godin to sit up a while and, if the noise continued, to go and tell Luttrell about it.

Shortly afterwards, Elizabeth 'heard it and instantly Mr Luttrell's room door was thrown open and we heard him speak'.

Luttrell had also heard footsteps, it turned out, and opened the door, saying 'Who goes there?' as 'something flitted past him'. This woke Jervis, who in turn heard the footsteps continuing towards the Chintz Room, nearer and ever nearer. Luttrell, Bolton, Elizabeth Godin, Jervis and Mary Ricketts were now all hearing the same thing: a woman walking towards the Chintz Room. 'Look against my door!' shouted Jervis loudly as he heard the footsteps draw near.

As the men came out into the corridor, they found it empty,

the door to the staircase just beside the room being used by Mary Ricketts locked and clearly undisturbed. There was a dash up to the attics to check the servants were in their rooms – which they were; silence seemed to descend after the visitation, but Luttrell and Jervis stayed up in Luttrell's room till daybreak, when Jervis finally returned to the Chintz Room.

As Mary records: 'About this time, as I imagined, I heard the Chintz Room door opened and slammed with the utmost violence, and immediately that of the hall chamber opened and shut in the same manner.' Mary mentioned to Elizabeth how shocked she was that her brother would do such a thing, since he was 'ever attentive not to alarm or disturb the children'. An hour later, the front door to the house opened and slammed so fiercely that the fabric of the house shook. But Luttrell had had a very different experience. 'I assure you Jervis made not the least noise; it was your door and the next I heard opened and slapped in the way you describe.'

Jervis had heard nothing. But he did rather sheepishly admit that when he had first gone to bed he had heard other noises he could not account for – including 'dreadful groans'.

At breakfast, Luttrell boldly declared that the house was 'unfit for habitation for any human being'. Jervis, who had experienced the least, remained sceptical, but it was agreed that the landlady's agent should be contacted.[7] That morning, Mary wrote to her friend, the Revd Mr Newbolt. 'My brother authorises me to tell you that neither himself nor Capt Luttrell can account for what they have heard from any natural cause.' She confesses that she derives 'satisfaction in my reports being fully accredited'.

Every night the next week saw Jervis sit up, waiting and watching, no doubt angry and disturbed. 'In the middle of one of these nights,' wrote Mary, 'I was surprised with the sound of a gun or pistol let off near me, immediately followed by groans as of a person in agonies, or expiring, that seemed to proceed between my chambers and the next, the nursery.' Yet neither the nurse with the children nor, one assumes, the children, nor Jervis stand-ing guard, heard it.

'Several instances occurred where very loud noises were heard by one or two persons, when those equally near and in the same direction were not sensible of the least impression.' In other words, people in the same place at the same time were not hear-ing the same sounds. This is similar to the kitchen experience, where not all the servants saw the same thing, depending on where they were. This cognitive puzzle, incidentally, is common to more modern accounts, but was unknown in writings of this period.

Since Jervis was staying up all night, he was now sleeping dur-ing the day and, one afternoon, when Mary was reading in a downstairs parlour and the children were out on a walk, she heard the bell to his room ring very violently. She found her brother uncharacteristically dishevelled. He had heard a noise of shocking loudness in his own bedroom – hearing 'an immense weight fall through the ceiling to the floor just by that mahogany press'. No one else had heard anything, not even his man, Bolton, sitting with another servant in the room beneath. If Jervis had doubted the situation, he no longer did so.

He didn't know what was going on, but he *did* know that he didn't like it, and that Mary should leave the house and he would help her leave; if he was suddenly called back to Portsmouth, he would send over a lieutenant from the Royal Marines, a Mr Nichols, to look after her. He had decided to escalate the matter and acknowledge there was a crisis.[8]

Jervis immediately wrote to William Ricketts in Jamaica.[9] He knew Ricketts well, but it was still a difficult letter to write. It was a matter of a 'delicate nature' but there was no way of dressing it all up:

> *I therefore proceed to tell you that Hinton Ampner House has been disturbed by such strange and unaccountable noises from the*

2nd April to this present day, with little or no intermission, that
it is very unfit your family should continue any longer in it. The
children, happily, have not the least idea of what is doing, but
my sister has suffered exceedingly through want of rest, and by
keeping this event in her breast too long.

He then goes on to apologize for not resigning his commission
and staying with his sister, but he was at that time engaged with
transporting the king's brother, the Duke of Gloucester, to Italy,
and there was no possible way he could get out of it.[10] He coun-
sels his brother-in-law that there is no need to hurry back from
the West Indies – she is 'harassed, not terrified, by this continual
agitation' – but that he was putting a scheme in motion. Intriguingly, Mary herself adds a note to the end of this letter, claiming
that 'since my brother saw me, I am so extremely recovered
both in health and spirits that there is no longer room for apprehension.' She also got the Revd Newbolt and his wife to sign in
confirmation – further reassurance.

Apart from general sleeplessness and dealing with the various
forms of panic and upset with the servants, Mary Ricketts was
doing pretty well. What was giving her most cause for anxiety
was her children, who, almost incredibly, were the only inhabitants of Hinton Ampner who had experienced nothing of the
hauntings. Curiously, she also noted in passing that, when the
noises were so loud as to wake the entire household, her young
postilion also slept through them. Anyone in the household aged
eighteen or younger was not plagued. Mary was dreading the
moment when her children would hear or see the ghosts, who
were most active in what they called the 'lobby', outside the nursery. It could be very bad when it finally happened, and it would
happen. That bubble of calm around them was only a bubble.
Why were the ghosts leaving them alone?

In a letter to his sister dated 11 August (now in the British

Library and not previously published) and sent from HMS *Alarm*, then anchored in Spithead, Jervis intriguingly shows some doubts about the trustworthiness of Luttrell (one account has each of them arguing that the other was causing the noises) but he nevertheless pronounces himself 'very happy by your removal from such a scene of terror'.

He has made enquiries and has already uncovered a very strong Hampshire tradition of the haunting at Hinton. He had been talking to a member of the Portsmouth Guard, John Blondon, the brother of the cook, Dame Brown. 'He related to me many accounts of noises similar to those now made, which he had heard his father and mother mention.' The soldier mentions 'Luke Stent who lived with Lord Stawell and afterwards kept the White Hart at Waltham. Blondon declared whenever Stent was prevailed on to describe the disturbances at Hinton House he shed tears of agony and distress in the relation which he has often been witness to.' This seems to indicate that the house had been badly haunted even when Lord Stawell was in residence – the haunting predates both Lord Stawell and his sister Honoria.

There followed days of beautiful weather. Jervis was becalmed off Lymington, one of those dream-like days in the summer months when the Solent is smooth as a mill pond. He dashed off a note to his sister, dated 16 August: 'The more I consider the incidents, the stronger I see the necessity of the decisive step, and I almost think there will be propriety in giving up the house etc at Christmas.' He concludes, of the house, 'I beg you never to enter it again' once she has been able to leave. He remains careful when it concerns the nature of the disturbances, and quite why she should leave, preferring instead to stick with practical matters: it's making her ill – she should leave.

Two days afterwards, Mary wrote to her husband, 'I omitted to mention there are several people will prove similar disturbances have been known at Hinton Ampner many years past.'

If there were concerns about their legal position in leaving the house, they soon evaporated. Lady Hillsborough[11] released the Ricketts from their rental agreement without the slightest objection. Dutton mentions that Lady Hillsborough had known all along that the house was haunted. Whether she had experienced it or not herself first-hand, she knew at least the local tales that her father, Lord Stawell, haunted the house, and her aunt, Honoria. A couple of things seemed linked to 2 April: Lord Stawell is said to have died of a stroke in the parlour room on this date in 1755; and Jervis mentions that the final episode started on the same date. Lady Hillsborough's gouty but loyal agent, a Mr Sainsbury, pinned a notice to the door of three local churches offering a reward of 50 guineas – which was raised to 60 and then 100 – to anyone who could give details of any plot to create the noises that had been experienced throughout the summer at Hinton. The final amount, offered jointly by William Ricketts and Lady Hillsborough, was nearly three times the annual income of a semi-skilled worker of the period, but no one ever came forward to claim it.

September 20, 1771. Whereas some evil disposed person or persons have for severel Months past frequently made divers kinds of noises in the Mantion house occupied by Mrs RICKETTS, att Hinton Ampner. This is to give notis that if any person or persons will Discover the Auther or Authers thereof to me, such person or persons shall Receive a reward of Fifty Guineas, to be paid on the Conviction of the offenders, or any person Concerned in making such Noises Will Discover his or her Acomplice or Acomplices therein, such person shall be pardoned, and be intitled to the same Reward, to be paid on Conviction of the Offender.

Ralph Dutton comments: 'There is no record that any attempt was made to exorcise the house, and it is surprising that Mrs

Ricketts, who had an extensive acquaintance amongst the bench of bishops, did not call in one of these heavyweights to attack the ghosts.[12]

Yet the clergy did come to Mary Ricketts' rescue. There are letters to her in the archives from her neighbour John Hoadly, a minor dramatist and literary figure who was also a chancellor of Winchester Cathedral and a chaplain to the Prince of Wales. He tells her off for leaving Hinton in such haste, and the affectionate nature of these letters shows how highly Mary Ricketts was rated by clever men; she has 'the clearest head and the best heart in the world'. Hoadly was a sceptic when it came to the subject of ghosts – the *Dictionary of National Biography* records, 'He himself, along with Garrick, who was a great friend and correspondent of Hoadly's, and Hogarth, once enacted a vulgar parody on the ghost scene in Shakespeare's *Julius Cæsar*.' His protective stance towards Mary is touching. He deplores the 'villainous attempt to make you feel uneasy' and wonders 'that you did not . . . pay off every servant in your house'.

Mary left the house early and went to stay with her friends the Newbolts, while another more august friend, the Bishop of Winchester, arranged for the whole family to move to the bishop's old palace at Wolvesey Castle. When she was to leave Winchester, the Bishop of St Asaph[13] offered her his house in turn, in London. Mary Ricketts was very friendly with the higher echelons of the Anglican Church; though she began with a mere rector, within three months of leaving Hinton she had stayed with two bishops and a canon. While staying with the canon she was visited by Lord Radnor and Lord Folkestone – 'very desirous to see the lady that came from the haunted house', as she herself records. Word was getting round, in certain circles, at least.

Mary sent the children ahead to Winchester, finally out of harm's way, and lingered a while in Hinton, staying with the everfaithful Camis family in the village and visiting the house only to arrange for her things to be packed and moved. Her brother had warned her not to go back. But she did. The house sent her on her way with one last grandstanding performance. In some ways it's the spookiest incident of all, precisely because, this time, the details are so vague.

'When I returned to the mansion I was soon assailed by a noise I never heard before, very near me, and the terror I felt is not to be described.' This is a very rare admission of fear from the redoubtable Mary. Whatever she heard was so bad that she decided it was better not to record it at all. It's as if the act of describing it would somehow preserve it. That sound would remain locked inside her until she died.

When she was old – and she did live to a great age[14] – she did not readily talk on the subject. However, she did record in one of the several narratives written down for her grandchildren – a sheaf of papers now in the British Library – how she told the Bishop of Winchester the following: 'I related that Robert Camis had been thrice called at the window by a voice he well remembered, that of the steward of Lord Dartmouth,[15] said he would have conjured him by the Father, Son and Holy Ghost . . . this steward stole his Lord's gold buckles, and was much suspected of other dishonesty.' Ah yes, the ghost at the window: the ghost of the dishonest steward at the window of the house.

This snippet was first made known to the general public in 1943 in Sacheverell Sitwell's *Poltergeists*, in which he reproduced much of the extra documentation around the case. It's the clue to the Hinton Ampner story being the inspiration behind *The Turn of the Screw*; the only people who would have known the detail of the steward at the window were members of the Ricketts and Camis families, and senior members of the Church of England. In *The Turn of the Screw*, the approach of the corrupting ghost of the dead servant Quint to the window of Bly is one of the key scenes.

Furthermore, there is some evidence that the clergy were

retelling the story to others of the cloth; we turn to the diaries of Frances Williams Wynn,[16] in which she tells the tales in the aristocratic oral tradition. In her several pages on what she calls 'The Ricketts Ghost Story', written on 15 November 1830, she mentions how 'Mr Strong, who was chaplain to Shipley, Bishop of St Asaph, had, when at Twyford and in its neighbourhood, frequently learned the legend told in the same manner.'

In other words, that same Bishop of St Asaph who lent Mary Ricketts his London house was perfectly happy relating the story to his chaplain. It is not surprising that such a story, related by a brace of bishops, should end up being whispered in the ear of the Archbishop of Canterbury some decades later. Benson also had long connections with Winchester, travelling there once a year to visit the grave of his son, and his wife also retired there shortly after his death. During his visits to Winchester, it is perfectly plausible that he stayed in the Bishop's Palace, where Mary Ricketts had lodged all those years before.

Safely installed in Winchester, Mary was still in contact with the Camis family, who were keeping an eye on the mansion house until the lease ran out. Robert Camis reveals in one letter that Mr Sainsbury, Lady Hillsborough's agent, came round and questioned his mother closely about 'the noises'. Sainsbury subsequently organized a watch at the mansion house one night. We do not know what they found or heard, but the haunting continued in broad daylight.

On one occasion, Mary Camis and her daughter Martha were in the Hinton kitchen at midday when they heard a 'dismal groaning very loud', apparently from the next-door housekeeper's room. Again, one day at eleven o'clock in the morning, Martha was doing needlework alone in the kitchen when she heard a 'rolling clap like thunder' that made the windows rattle. The noise was coming from the Yellow Room. The kitchen was situated beneath the nurseries.

By 8 March 1773 the noises were in abeyance, and Robert Camis, behaving almost as a family member, relates one of his mother's dreams to his employer. It's a strange and fascinating piece of writing, a rare insight into the subconscious mind of a working-class individual involved in an eighteenth-century haunting:[17]

> She [has] dreamed three nights after one another that she was upon the great stairs up at the landing place that leads to the gar-rots [attics], and was troubled in her dreams, and was rambling about a great way, but att the end she was always there. One of the nights she dremed she was in the road from C—, and found a large pair of stuff shoes laced with silver very much, and a pair of gloves with a great deal of lace upon itt, and she brought itt to you, and shewed itt to you, and then she carreed itt to the top of the great stairs.

At some point between the Ricketts quitting the house and Lady Hillsborough re-taking possession, a Ricketts cousin, Lieutenant George Poyntz Ricketts (the future governor of Barbados), was walking with another family member in the pastures beside the house. One reason the Ricketts were unwilling to move too far away is because they had bought a good deal of cattle as an investment, leasing a farm at Hinton. As the cousins walked past the house on the southern paddock side, 'a great noise was heard within it, upon which one of them said, "they are at their tricks again, let us go and see."'

Since Mary Camis had left the windows open to air the house, the youths climbed through one of them and searched, looking for ghosts. 'No living creature was to be found in it, neither was there any appearance of anything that could have been moved so as to occasion the sounds they heard.'[18]

After a year, Lady Hillsborough managed to let out the house again, to another family, the Lawrences. They seem to have known exactly what they were taking on; their servants were given an injunction, on pain of dismissal, that the subject of ghosts must never be raised. Then an apparition of a woman was said to have been seen, by a housemaid, in the corridor outside the Yellow Room. And no one raised an eyebrow when the Lawrence family suddenly decamped in the middle of the night without explanation, after only a year.

In 1793, the new Lord Stawell had the house demolished, and built a new Georgian hunting lodge in a more sheltered place – a cube made out of yellow brick below the knap of the hill. It may have been because the house was too haunted, or it may just have been that it was uncomfortable and unfashionable. For whatever reason, no one wanted to live in it any longer.

But the old house had one more trick to play. During the demolition a box was discovered – one account has it beneath the floorboards of the corridor outside the Yellow Room, another on the ground floor. In it was found a small skull, rather ape-like, but perhaps of a human baby. Also found were a good deal of papers, concealed.[19]

Against all expectations, we find Mary Ricketts back in the village of Hinton Ampner, now living in the parsonage. On 7 July 1772, she decides to end this chapter of her life. She sits down to write – and the handwriting hints at speed, emphasis and agitation – a long explanation of events. It is pointedly addressed to her children. Her motives for writing it down are not completely clear, but it seems most important to her that, if her children are going to hear stories as they grow up, they need to know that their mother conducted herself in an entirely rational and upstanding way. She especially gives thanks to God and 'the peculiar mercy of Providence' that preserved them from the 'affright and terror' that was surrounding them, and she goes to great lengths to emphasize her own native probity, even speaking in the third person, as people of probity do, claiming that 'according to the testimony of that excellent person Chancellor Hoadly she was truth itself.'

This document and several others remained in the family for a very long time, and were added to when possible. For example, we find, in 1818, that Mary's granddaughter Martha Jervis has been on the case, visiting the village of Hinton to glean the last possible witness accounts from those who experienced the haunting before they died. 'I called on old Lucy Camis at the farm,' she writes. Lucy has been to visit the equally ageing former nurse-maid Hannah Streeter. Another incident emerges, fifty years on. Lucy asked Hannah whether she remembered it. They had both been sitting in the pantry one night after the servants had gone to bed when there was a very loud sound, which they thought was like an 'iron brazier' falling through the room with a strange, cyclonic impetus – 'it went Twirl! Twirl! Twirl! Till it sank in the ground.' Lucy was so terrified that she would not venture all the way upstairs to the garrets that night to sleep. She also remembered sleeping in Mrs Ricketts' room one night when they both awoke to hear music, and the 'steps of someone moving stately to it'.

Another narrative with the family papers is one transcribed by Osborne Markham, who married Martha in 1821. It must be assumed that this was written at some point in the 1820s:

The first appearance of anything being seen or heard was before Mrs Ricketts took possession of Hinton Ampner, which did not come to her knowledge till some time after the disturbances had been seen in the house. Joseph Sibley (the groom) then being one of the servants left in occupation of the house, and being in bed in the garret, the moon shining brightly into the room, and being clearly awake, saw a man in a drab coat with his hands behind him, in the manner his late master held them, looking steadfastly upon him.

Let's look at this ghost in detail. He's seen after the death of Lord Stawell in 1755 by one of his servants; the groom only knows it is the late Lord Stawell by his posture, but assumes it's him, leaving aside the question of why he'd be in the servants' quarters. He's perceived as wearing a drab or snuff-coloured coat, which is more usually associated with the uniform of servants in this period, at least in the less formal countryside. It could be simply that the ghost was fading a bit, as happens in other hauntings, where the colours bleach out of a full-figure phantom over the years. Hence, when George Turner sees the figure in the hall some years later, he assumes it is indeed a servant. By the time he's seen again, by the nursemaid, going into the Yellow Room one summer evening, it's just a man dressed in brown. And certainly no male servant would go into a room which was customarily the bedroom of the lady of the house, which is what the Yellow Room was. Unless, of course, it was a male servant who had somehow risen beyond his station.

Lord Bute, who edited the Ricketts documentation for the *Journal for the Society for Psychical Research* in April 1893, certainly thought that this was the case. He notes that when Lord Stawell died, of a fit of apoplexy in the downstairs parlour, 'his cries to be bled were not complied with, as if those around him wished him to die.' One of the first to be dismissed by Mary Stawell after her father's death was the steward (or butler) named Isaac Mackrell. 'He is spoken of as dishonest,' notes Lord Bute, echoing Mary Ricketts' view. 'If such dishonesty were, as indicated, notorious, his impunity seems strange, and looks as if he has some hold over Lord Stawell.' Bute also comments that 'Isaac Mackrell . . . was also recognised by his voice by Robert Camis.' The three sightings of the snuff-coloured man all sound like Isaac Mackrell.

When Lord Stawell's wife died in the 1740s, his sister-in-law, Honoria, moved into Hinton Ampner. She was young and unmarried; it was said that Lord Stawell then had an illicit affair with her, that she gave birth to Stawell's baby and that Isaac smothered him to save the family from scandal. It is also said that he hid the body under the floorboards, summoning a carpenter to aid him in his task. Some people allege that it is this baby's skull that was found when the house was knocked down in 1793.

Certainly, the wills of both the unmarried Honoria Stewkeley and Lord Stawell have Isaac Mackrell as witness. It was a curious business, in that day and age, to get a servant to witness the will of a baron. But he did. And once the wills had been read, Lord Stawell's daughter Mary, who five years earlier, had married Henry Legge, fourth son of the 1st Earl of Dartmouth, dismissed Mackrell almost instantly. Her actions seem significant. If, as Lord Bute suggests, Mackrell was involved in some kind of cover-up and had made himself rich on the proceeds, her distaste for him and his hold over her father may have been acute. It's not clear when Isaac Mackrell died. He's not buried in Hinton Church, as are most of the players in this story. He left no will.

In *The Turn of the Screw*, a governess is sent to a large country house, Bly, in the southern counties of England. She is hired by a bachelor at his house in London to teach his young nephew and niece, Miles and Flora, whose guardian he now is after the death of their father, in the country; he impresses her as 'such a figure who had never risen, save in a dream or an old novel, before a fluttered anxious girl out of a Hampshire vicarage'. The governess is under no circumstances to bother him about the children, and she has total charge of the business of their welfare. There's a mystery about Miles: he has been sent down from his public school for an undisclosed offence. But the governess is smitten by both children, and much is made of their innocence.

Then she sees the devilish Quint. First, he is on a tower looking down at her; then nearer, as he draws in on his prey. It's a rainy Sunday afternoon. Quint is dead, but there he is, with his white face and curls of red hair, peering through the dining-room window, like a fox scanning a henhouse for chickens. The house-keeper, Mrs Grose, identifies him from the description. He's at the window, just as in the description of Isaac Mackrell at the window of Hinton. As with the ghost in the drab-coloured coat, there's some mystery as to who he is, because he's wearing his master's clothes. Henry James seems to have built this confusion of identity into the fabric of *The Turn of the Screw*: a servant wore his master's clothes in an inversion of social custom. 'He never wore his hat but he did wear – well, there were waistcoats missed,' says Mrs Grose to the governess. Mackrell, you may recall, stole his master's gold buckles.

Mackrell appears again in the Gloucester archives in August 1750, signing agreements between his master, Lord Stawell, and a Mr Gatehouse over land leases. He seems to have something resembling power of attorney.

Then, in *The Turn of the Screw*, there's the ghost of the former governess, Miss Jessel, who formed some kind of unholy sexual alliance with Quint, which seems to have extended to the children. Her ghost starts appearing. The governess becomes obsessed with the idea that Quint and Miss Jessel have come for the children in some unspeakable way; these are predatory, paedophile ghosts. She is convinced that the children can see them, when they say they can't. Finally, the craziness reaches such pitch that little Miles expires – his heart fails – as the governess submits him to extreme psychological pressure to confirm that he can see the ghost of Quint at the window.

Honoria dies in 1754 and is followed within a few months by Lord Stawell, in 1755. His daughter dismisses the steward; we don't know how much she lived in the house subsequent to that, but, with her husband busy with matters of state, it seems unlikely they were much in Hampshire. She may have heard the local stories that her dead half-sister lay entombed beneath the floorboards. It must have been especially distasteful since her brother, Stewkeley Stawell, had died aged eleven. There's a plaque to him in Westminster School, dead of smallpox only two months after first attending, on 15 August 1731.

After many decades, the story was fading in the bosom of the Ricketts and the Stawells. But it was about to resurface in the public sphere.

On 15 November 1830, traveller, writer and society hostess Frances Williams Wynn, daughter of a Welsh grandee, wrote of the tale in her diary, which became widely read when it was published in 1864:

> Mrs Hughes told me the other day she was writing the particulars of the Ricketts ghost story, as she had heard it related in her infancy by Mrs Gwyn, who had been an eye, or rather an ear witness. The story was alluded to; her aunt stopped the speaker, and begged she would wait till the child was gone to bed. She was not to be put off, and when the orders for bed were issued she contrived to conceal herself behind the curtain: there she remained undiscovered till the tale had advanced to the hoarse voice, when her terror was so highly excited that it totally overcame her dread of punishment, and she rushed from her place of concealment, falling flat on her face.

This is the same Mrs Hughes who related the story to a sceptical Walter Scott, who published it in his *Letters on Demonology* in 1830, and the same Mrs Hughes who also related it to Richard Barham, author of the *Ingoldsby Legends*. This triple source of the public version of the story was a writer in her own right, Mary Ann Hughes. She was the wife of the vicar of Uffington[20] and the grandmother of the author of *Tom Brown's Schooldays* (her husband, Thomas, was also at one point canon of St Paul's in London, as was Barham).[21]

Having no inkling of the Ricketts documentation, Scott loftily dismissed the tale as servants' chatter, though he was also shocked to discover John Jervis's role. Rather patronizingly, he wondered 'whether Lord St Vincent, amid the other eminent qualities of a first-rate seaman, might not in some degree be tinged with their tendency to superstition'.

Mary Gwynne seems to be the extra-familial source of the Hinton ghost as oral history. There was another version of her tale that slipped out in 1870, published in *The Life and Letters of Richard H. Barham*. The details have become highly coloured by this stage; names are misspelt and basic facts are wrong. Here, Mrs Gwynne hears the sounds as of floorboards being ripped up made by the poltergeist, and runs to Mary Ricketts' aid on the occasion when Mary hears the sound of footsteps in her own bedchamber. As with the Williams Wynn version, there's a mix-up of names and generations (both finger the 'atrocious libertine' Henry Legge as the villainous squire of the story, when all evidence points to his father-in-law, Lord Stawell). Another very typical elision is taking the seventeenth-century story of the Stewkeleys hiding a box under the floorboards and applying it to the rutting aristocrats of more modern times, and the wicked and conniving butler who did the dirty deed with their illegitimate child. The Stewkeley box of documents was now the coffin of the baby, and the sounds heard those of the floorboards being ripped up to hide the crime. Never mind that it doesn't make sense to hide a body under floorboards – the folkloric story had arrived.

However, it seems the descendants of Mary Ricketts were aghast at the way in which their private family tale was being raked over in public. They knew the real story, since it had been, no doubt, read over at family gatherings, borrowed and mulled over, quietly and with care.

Mrs William Henley Jervis, great-granddaughter of Mary Ricketts, finally made a public intervention after the story was told in book form for the third time. Along with her aunt, she possessed one of the two copies of the Mary Ricketts account, and so reasonably felt she was the guardian of the true story. She contacted the *Gentleman's Magazine*. The month was November 1871, one hundred years and three months since her great-grandmother had fled the ghost-thumping tinderbox and spectral lantern show that was Hinton Ampner.

The Turn of the Screw was published in 1898. Since the apparitional aspect of the Ricketts haunting was secondary (and only the servants actually saw anything), and it was assumed that the male ghost was Lord Stawell rather than his steward, nobody made the connection between the Ricketts haunting and Henry James's novella. Since its publication, the source has always been a great mystery, despite James having hinted that the origins of the story lay in an ecclesiastical palace, both in his diaries and in the preface to the book.

The Archbishop of Canterbury died before the novella was published, and his wife and his son, E. F. Benson, claimed they had never heard their father tell a ghost story that resembled it in any way.[22]

The general scholarly view is that *The Turn of the Screw* is not based on any known story but, in fact, the story recounted one January evening at the Archbishop's house in Addington, south London, tallies in some key respects with some dark goings-on in Hampshire in the 1770s. Since senior members of the royal family knew about it, and knew people who had witnessed the haunting, it doesn't seem all that surprising that this is a story the Archbishop of Canterbury might know, too.

Henry James was, after all, writing fiction and not a supposedly real ghost story – especially as the essence of *The Turn of the Screw* is that it is never clear whether the ghosts exist outside the mind of the governess. It's possible too that James knew elements of the story even before the Archbishop told it to him: his brother

William was a pioneer in parapsychology, founding the American Society for Psychical Research, and it seems likely that brother Henry would have had access to the account of the Hinton ghost published by Lord Bute in the *SPR Journal* of November 1892, only twenty months before that dinner with Archbishop Benson.

But maybe we can venture at the story the Archbishop told. It would have featured the ghost of a man and the ghost of a woman in the undertow of a sex scandal, and another woman who leaves a handwritten account of their predation. Every night, it seems, they are at the door of the nursery. She desperately tries to shield her children from the frightening influence being exerted upon them. The servant prowls at the windows. A ghost of a woman treads on a lake of silk.

What would a modern analysis of the hauntings show these days? Both Sacheverell Sitwell and Harry Price regarded it chiefly as a poltergeist story, but it doesn't completely conform to the spectrum of known poltergeist hauntings. There's no record of objects being moved, translated through walls, or of objects appearing from nowhere. There are no classically occurring spontaneous fires or water leakages. The children – all under ten – were too young to be considered standard poltergeist foci, and since the servants were replaced, no single young servant would qualify either. Indeed, to have a poltergeist and for the children to be unaware of what is going on is pretty much unheard of, though this may suggest, of course, that the focus was Mary Ricketts herself.

There seem to be four things at work here: the two apparitions, never seen together; the footsteps; and the other, more mysterious sounds. The apparition of a woman is clearly connected to the sound of rustling silk and footsteps, both on the staircase and in the corridor outside the main bedrooms. Her apparition is only ever clearly seen in the late afternoon, in the servants' hall. The apparition of a man is seen in the front hall, a bedroom

and the servants' quarters. The footsteps that appear without the
rustling of silk are his.

The woman is assumed to be Honoria Stewkeley, who died in
December 1754. The man is assumed to be either Lord Stawell, or
his servant Isaac Mackrell – or perhaps both, wearing similar
clothes. Stawell was buried on 17 April 1755. Despite extensive
searches, nothing has come to light as to when Mackrell himself
died and was buried. The sounds of two men speaking to a woman
are assumed to be the triangle of Stawell, Mackrell and Honoria.

There's the music, once. And that haunting susurration. Mostly,
the noises are loud and mysterious – slamming doors, groans, the
house shaking, the sound of shots, the sound of cannonball, of
catastrophic heavy weights coming through the ceiling. Looked
at objectively, it's hard not to wonder whether these sounds could
have originated in 1643, at the siege of Cheriton. You hear the
twirl twirl of feathering and descending artillery shot; the sound
of the front door being forced open; of a room-by-room search;
of a man shot and the agonized groaning of that man. It sounds
like an incursion into the house by Parliamentarian troops searching for the king's men. An ancestor of Lord Stawell happened to
be one of those captured, though not in the house, as far as we
know. And who was there at Hinton at the time?

In an uncanny pre-echo of Mary Ricketts' tenure, the recently
widowed Sarah, Lady Stewkeley, wife of Sir Hugh Stewkeley, was
in the house at the time of the battle, with her three young children, the eldest boy in both cases six years old. 'From the windows
of the house the unfortunate Lady Stewkeley would have had a
grandstand view of the battle which began at ten in the morning
of 29th,' wrote Ralph Dutton. The early-April date of the beginning of the hauntings every year has always been linked to the
death of Lord Stawell (which was actually in the second week of
April), but it seems more likely to be related to the anniversary of
the battle of 29 March.

Maybe it wasn't Honoria but her grandmother doing the

rounds. Sarah was an arch-Royalist. Two years after the siege, she married Sir William Ogle, who at more or less the same time as the battle of Cheriton, held Winchester for the king. She might have been upstairs. The children were probably upstairs too. From the Chintz Room, she would have seen much of the battle. It's said that Lamborough Lane ran with blood; though, of the 20,000 combatants, there are thought to have been fewer than 2,000 casualties. The battle put an end to Charles I's hope to march on London.

The Ricketts children never heard the sounds of battle because Sarah was protecting them, in her ghostly way, as she protected her own children. But, all the same, they were the great-grandchildren of a Cromwellian officer, and nobody else in the household was going to be spared.

So what of the fate of those who experienced Hinton Ampner?

Captain Luttrell of Kimpton (later the 3rd Earl Carhampton, after the death of his brother, a demonic figure in the history of Irish emancipation) had a sister, Anne, who secretly married the Duke of Cumberland, George III's brother, in October 1771, just weeks after he conducted his ghost hunt at Hinton.[24]

Captain Luttrell was later a member of Parliament. He disapproved of governmental policies towards the American colonies and consequently seems cut from a different cloth to his brother, whose feud with John Wilkes is one of the most notorious battles in British democratic history. Luttrell's presence at Hinton Ampner that morning in 1771 has always been something of a puzzle, until you remember that Captain Jervis was taking the Duke of Gloucester off to Italy for an asthma cure. Eight weeks after his ghost watch at Hinton, Luttrell and the Duke of Cumberland became related via the clandestine marriage in Mayfair. Perhaps he was bringing news of the impending nuptials to the also secretly married Duke of Gloucester.

It was Luttrell who told the world that Hinton was unfit for human habitation, and Luttrell who both heard the ghosts and briefly saw one flit past – the only above-stairs witness to do so. Jervis was involved in trying to blockade the French Fleet in the Channel during the American War of Independence, which was in part brought on by another of our players, Lord Hillsborough.[25] When Mary Stawell married him on 11 October 1768, it's interesting to note the location: Lambeth Palace – the home of the Archbishop of Canterbury.

And what of the three children? There's a letter from Hoadly in the archives remarking on meeting the boys, Edward and William Henry, when they were about town as schoolboys at Winchester in the 1770s, and complaining light-heartedly, about the length of their hair, which he notes was the fashion among unkempt boys at Harrow also. There's another letter from Hoadly dated 12 May 1773, asking after the inoculation of Mary's 'little boy'.[26] By this time, Mary had moved with her family to a permanent home not all that far from Hinton, at Longwood, where she lived much of her life.

The elder boy, named William Henry after his father, arrived at Hinton aged just two months; he married in 1793, but divorced his wife by Act of Parliament in 1799 after discovering she had committed adultery with a captain of the Lancashire Fencibles. He had several children with another woman, but died before he could marry her, drowned in a naval accident in 1805. Younger brother Edward married in 1790 and also divorced by Act of Parliament, in 1798, after his wife ran off with a Mr Taylor of Cavendish Square (whom Edward sued successfully for £5,000). In an age when there were about ten divorces a year for the whole United Kingdom, and when they were hugely expensive to finance, this is an unusual percentage for a family. Edward later inherited from his uncle, including the title, which eventually died out.[27]

Having joined the Navy at the age of thirteen, John Jervis ended up as Admiral of the Fleet. His reforms included the mechanization of the Portsmouth docks. He was also a ferocious disciplinarian; he instigated the swabbing of decks before sunrise, and Sunday executions of mutineers and sodomites.[28] But he's probably best known for giving his flagship, HMS *Victory*, to Admiral Nelson for use in the Battle of Trafalgar. This is not a man who saw spooks behind drawing-room doors.

It rankled with him that the 'mystery' of Hinton was never solved. Up until now, it's been assumed that he took a straightfor-wardly sceptical line, but a previously unpublished letter in the British Library states, 'I think it is an indisputable duty to bear testimony to the innocence of the servants and my belief of the improbability of any trick from without doors. As to the rest I give no *publick* opinion whatever are my real sentiments.' The word 'publick' is inserted by Jervis as an afterthought.

Well after his sister had moved out of the house he was press-ing her, in a note from Pisa in 1771: 'HRH is master of the Hinton ghost and in addition to my own interested feelings I in his name desire all and every particular.'[29] The following year, he's writing, 'The Duke of Gloucester frequently asks if I have heard any more of the Hinton mystery, and interests himself greatly in your suf-ferings, which I ardently wish may soon be put at an end to by a manifest discovery of the cause of your disturbance.'

But it was not to be. It's a curious thought as to what extent the experience of Hinton influenced his personality, and whether his later, almost incandescent hatred of disorder and mutiny had any-thing to do with the unsolved mystery preying on his mind.

It is said that, in later years, he 'flew into a rage' whenever the ghosts of Hinton were mentioned.

A Kind of America

Ghosts are people, or part of people, anyway, and thus governed by emotional stimuli.

– Hans Holzer

In February 1665,[1] Joseph Glanvill arrived at the Warwickshire mansion of Lady Conway. He was much admired by a new Restoration establishment; the clever son of Plymouth puritans.[2] She was the sickly daughter of a former speaker of the House of Commons. Her brothers were powerful establishment figures in London. But the horse-trading of Whitehall did not interest her. What interested Lady Conway was ghosts.

Among the other guests gathering in the house and, more importantly, the library[3] at Ragley that February were the Cambridge philosopher and Neoplatonist Henry More, and the chemist and father of modern experimental science, Robert Boyle. We do not know how often this group met; it may have been no more than once, followed by a great deal of correspondence. Yet this little-known gathering was to shape the English attitude to the supernatural for many years, and Glanvill's book, *Saduscimus Triumphatus*, which arose from it, was to contribute in no small part to the witch trials in Salem, Massachusetts, in 1692.[4]

Anne Conway is one of the forgotten figures of her age; she was, in her time, a well-regarded philosopher. She was born some months after the death of her father, just weeks before Christmas in 1631, in the Jacobean brick house that later, when it passed into royal hands, would be renamed Kensington Palace.[5] Lacking a father figure during her childhood, she had been very much spoilt by her solicitous elder brothers. Unusually for the time, Anne was allowed to educate herself in whatever manner she chose, perhaps because her health was so bad that she was often bed-bound for months.

At the age of nineteen, Anne married Edward, 3rd Viscount Conway. Their rolling estate, with its woodlands, was not far from Stratford-on-Avon, and Edward fully encouraged her intellectual pursuits and her correspondences with some of the great minds of her age. He also spent a small fortune on doctors and faith-healers from Ireland, England and mainland Europe in the hope that they would cure her brutal migraines.[6] Probably during her adolescence, she was examined and treated by her kinsman William Harvey,[7] one of medicine's iconic figures. (Incidentally, his scepticism of witchcraft had been instrumental in leading to the dismissal of most of the charges against the Lancastrian Pendle witches in July 1634.)[8]

When he first met her, Glanvill would have seen a woman marked by the smallpox that had killed her only son. She was pale from too long spent sitting in silent and darkened rooms, etiolated through nausea, one eye slightly sunken in from the hammer-blows of constant neurological trauma. His hostess's interest in the supernatural and the apocalyptic had been sharpened by the sheer horror of her medical condition.

She had been corresponding with Glanvill's friend Henry More for two years. Despite the difference in class and gender, Conway had become close to the Cambridge academic. She received the equivalent of doctoral training through this correspondence, which had to be done discreetly, via a postal address using a house in Bow Lane. She already knew about Glanvill and his interest in ghosts.

The man Anne Conway met was well turned out and slightly dandyish, with an easy and engaging manner. He had a square face with large features more like a farmer's than those of an intellectual, his eyebrows slightly quizzical. A querulous half-smile

6. Joseph Glanvill, England's Ghost Hunter General.

plays about his lips in the engraved portrait of him (above) that is his best-known likeness today.

Glanvill's exposure to the Ragley circle firmed up his intention to publish on his interest in ghosts and witches.[9] Between 1665 and 1666, he was corresponding with More and Boyle and busy collating ghost stories from various sources he considered credible, while Lady Conway collected stories for him from Ireland. What the Ragley party[10] wanted to hear was his own supernatural experience: the story of a reliable man schooled in theology who had seen a ghost. His ghost story had taken place a few years earlier.

When he moved to Frome, Somerset, Glanvill became friendly with Robert Hunt, a local justice of the peace who had been unusually active in his prosecution of witches since the 1650s. And when Glanvill heard that there was a haunted house on the Hampshire/Wiltshire border not all that far from his parish, and that the haunting had been initiated by an act of witchcraft, he made efforts to get himself invited to see all this for himself.

In March 1661 a local landowner and militia officer, John Mompesson, had intervened in the case of William Drury. Drury had used forged papers to get money from the local constable, and had been causing a nuisance generally by using a drum to busk for money. Mompesson interviewed him personally, and an unintimidated Drury continued to insist that his papers were genuine, despite the fact that Mompesson knew that the signature, supposedly of a Colonel Ayliff, was a forgery. (He knew the colonel and was familiar with his signature.) His business as militia officer dispensed, Mompesson handed Drury over for prosecution. For various procedural reasons, the tinker's drum ended up in Mompesson's house at Tedworth, where he lived with his wife, three children and widowed mother. It was a circumstance he would very soon come to regret.

On his return from London in April, he found that his house had been turned over in what appeared to have been a straightforward burglary. Three nights later, Mompesson was awoken by persons unknown knocking angrily on the wooden cladding of the house and, more alarmingly, knocking from inside the building. He armed himself with a brace of pistols and rushed downstairs, flinging open the door even as it was being knocked at. There was no one there, and immediately the rapping moved to another door. Mompesson found himself, again and again, led from door to door, only to find nobody behind any of them. Puzzled, frustrated and upset, he returned to bed, but heard a noise like a drum coming from above the house, which then seemed to fade away, as if it was ascending into the night sky.

This was to become a notable feature of the case: drumming apparently from the skies just above the roof. It's the source image of the famous contemporary engraved illustration by W. Faithorne showing the devil in winged ascendancy above the house, surrounded by eight demons, with drumsticks twice as big as the chimneys.

7. An explicitly satanic appararition hovers over Tedworth House: even Christopher Wren came to hear it drumming.

Throughout the following month, the drumming seemed timed to disturb the household within a few minutes of their bedroom lights being extinguished, 'whether early or late', according to Glanvill, and seemed to be concentrated on the room where the drum lay. The sounds would inevitably be prefigured by a kind of rush through the air above the roof, and despite Mompesson lying in the room with the drum on many occasions, presumably armed, he failed to find any human agency behind it. The drumming tended to last for about two hours.

Mompesson's wife had a baby, and on the night of the birth and for three weeks afterwards the noise ceased completely, as if the newborn had temporarily offered some level of psychic protection to the household. But then it returned, according to Glanvill, 'in a ruder manner than before'. It now seemed to concentrate on the children, banging and shaking their bedsteads and scratching beneath their beds as if it had 'iron tallons'. Sometimes, the children would levitate. They were not even safe when put to bed by day in the attic.

On 5 November, the mysterious agency began prying the boards loose in the children's room – whether the wainscot or the floor isn't quite clear – and when challenged by a servant, in front of Mompesson and a group of people, the boards moved with snake-like intent upward towards him, and he pushed them back, twenty times. He was told off by his master for provoking the phenomena, and the response to Mompesson's heated words was the sudden arrival of a sulphurous smell in the room. A waft of sulphur is, of course, the signature scent of Satan. That evening the local minister, Mr Cragg, came to pray at the children's beds with a group of Mompesson's neighbours. But as soon as the prayers were over, the assembled party looked on agog as chairs started to dance around the room and the children's shoes flew through the air. A bedstaff was thrown at the priest, but it hit him, in classic poltergeist fashion, without any force, 'so favourably that a lock of wool could not have fallen more softly'.

'It was noted, that when the noise was loudest, and came with the most sudden and surprising violence, no Dog about the House would move, though the knocking was oft so boisterous and rude, that it hath been heard at a considerable distance in the Fields, and awakened the Neighbours in the Village, none of which live very near the house.'

Whatever it was then moved its interest to the servants, plaguing one in particular, pulling off his sheets and blankets as he slept. It reacted to a light-hearted comment by one visitor that the sounds and noises were the work of fairies, and fairies should leave money, by creating the additional, mocking sound of jingling change. This also confirmed Mompesson's feeling that they were under surveillance, possibly by a witch. On Christmas Eve, an unknown entity assaulted Mompesson's young son as he rose to go to the lavatory, driving a nail from the door into his ankle; and the next day it threw a Bible into the hearth and buried it in ashes.[11]

There was often a feeling of heaviness and paralysis in those who were attacked. In January 1662 members of the household heard the sound of singing in the chimneys, and strange lights were seen about the house, one of them blue, which caused 'great stiffness in the eyes of those that saw it'. As at Hinton Ampner, there was sometimes the rustle of silk, as if someone walked invisibly near the children's room, and 'one morning Mr Mompesson rising early to go on a journey, heard a great noise below, where the children lay, and running down with a Pistol in his Hand, he heard a voice crying a witch a witch, as they had heard it once before.'

One night, in one of the most alarming moments, something invisible went under one of the daughter's beds, lifting it up as it moved from one side to another. Observers tried to stab at it with a sword (it was considered such actions would wound the witch who had sent the demon), but it 'still shifted and carefully avoided the thrust, still getting under the Child when they offered at it'. The next night it returned, panting like a dog under the bed, making the room very hot and filling it with 'a bloomy noisome smell'.

Ashes strewn about the room deliberately to catch impressions were found next morning to bear the imprint of a claw, besides many other circles and scratches.

At about this time in the progression of the haunting, Glanvill paid a visit and stayed overnight. At eight o'clock, the children were sent to bed. The maidservant putting them to bed rushed down to tell their father and Glanvill to come up immediately, so they went up the stairs to the room. The image before them was of two demure little girls aged between seven and eleven neatly tucked up in bed with their hands outside the blankets, but it was the scratching sound that Glanvill first noticed: a scratching on the wall behind their heads, 'as with long nails'.

Glanvill acted immediately, thrusting his hand down 'behind the bolster', from where the sounds were coming. The scratching stopped, but resumed as soon as he withdrew his hand. He was impressed by the little girls' lack of fear: they were, by now, he thought, used to the situation. (The lack of alarm experienced by children during poltergeist activity is another regular feature of such cases through the ages, and very different to the scenario presented in films, where fear, we are told, feeds the power of the demon. However, their lack of fear in real-life accounts leads to the suspicion that the children are playing tricks.)

Glanvill then used his fingernail to scratch the bedlinen – five, seven and ten times. The scratches returned the numbers. By this point, Glanvill had become convinced that this was no trick but the noise of some 'daemon or spirit'. Shortly afterwards, an impression in the feather mattress looked as if something small was lying there beside the children. 'I graspt the Feathers to see if anything living were in it.' It appeared to be *inside* the mattress.

Then the panting started, but not any old panting. It was so loud it shook the room with every laboured breath. During this time, Glanvill noticed that a linen bag tied to one of the beds was moving around as if there was a rat inside it.[12] He plunged his hand inside, only to find nothing. He left the room after half an hour, and the being, whatever it was, was still panting as he left, the windows shaking with every puff.

He says he slept well that night, but something peculiar happened in the early morning. 'I was awakened . . . by a great knocking just without our Chamber door. I askt who was there several times, but the knocking still continued without answer. At last I said "In the name of God, who is it, and what would you have?" To which a voice answered, "Nothing with you."' An enquiry a few hours later drew a blank – no servant had been to his bedroom door.

On preparing to leave, Glanvill discovered his horse was in a sweat, 'as if it had been ridden all night' – 'hag-ridden', in the vernacular. Nobody could explain the horse's condition, and after a mile or so riding from the house the animal went lame, dying two days later. Glanvill did not believe this was a coincidence, especially when he heard from Mompesson of another of the drummer's tricks: in April, he had found his favourite horse lying in some distress on the stable floor, its hind leg stuffed into its mouth. It took 'several men to get it out with a Leaver'.

There were other incidents, including money turning black in a man's pockets, a metal spike inserted in Mompesson's bed and a knife in his mother's, and also:

> On another night strangers being present it purr'd in the Children's Bed like a Cat, at which time also the Cloaths and Children were lifted up from the Bed, and six Men could not keep them down. Hereupon they removed the Children, intending to have ript up the Bed. But they were no sooner laid in another, but the second Bed was more troubled than the first. It continued thus four hours, and so beat the children's legs against the Bed-posts, that they were forced to arise, and sit up all night. After this it would empty Chamberpots into their Beds, though they were never so carefully watcht.

Mompesson also wrote to Glanvill claiming he was 'several nights beset with seven or eight in the shape of Men, who as soon as the Gun was discharged, would shuffle away into an Arbour'.

On 31 March 1663, Drury's case came up at the Gloucester assizes. Among other charges, he was found guilty of stealing two pigs and sentenced to transportation to the New World.[13] (Coincidentally, this was also the day on which More first wrote to Lady Conway about the case, quoting Glanvill.) Drury managed to escape from the barge in which he was being transported to, eventually,

America, found his way back to Wiltshire, bought a new drum and was rearrested. Mompesson had gone to the trouble of travelling to Gloucester, and had learned that, while in custody there, Drury had claimed responsibility for the haunting at Tedworth. Mompesson consequently had Drury indicted under a Jacobean witchcraft statute, but a trial in August of that year in Salisbury failed to convict him, though Drury remained guilty of the other charges. It seems that, on this occasion, his transportation to America was successful, and his descendants may live there still.[14]

Mompesson did some investigating into Drury's background. He had been a soldier in the Parliamentary army under Cromwell, and he hailed from the hamlet of Uffcott in the parish of Broad Hinton near Swindon. He was also described as a tailor, though it seems he 'went up and down the Countrey to show Hocas pocas feats of activity'. Essentially, he was what used to be called a tinker; a traveller existing on the fringes of society and occasionally indulging in petty criminality. He had spent some time in his youth in the service of a vicar whose name had been associated with witchcraft, and had read the clergyman's 'gallant books', as books of spells and sorcery were then called. Centuries later, the men who travelled the country lanes offering magic-lantern shows were called 'gallantee men'.

Glanvill returned to Tedworth that November, when it seems that the drummer had been banished. But Mompesson was still having to entertain an expensive stream of visitors, including the diarist John Aubrey and Christopher Wren. Aubrey was droll about the hours the devil kept – all quite civilized. Wren suspected one of the maidservants. A little-known writer named John Beaumont recorded a rumour that 'it was done by two Young Women in the House, with a design to scare thence Mr Mompesson's Mother.' Certainly, it would not be the first or last time that servants had been involved in hoaxes on their employers. The Stockwell poltergeist of 1772 was judged to be the work of a disgruntled maid named Ann Robinson.

Many assume that our forebears were universally credulous, but in fact there was a great deal of scepticism about the Tedworth Drummer. It was said that Mompesson was trying to make money out of his visitors, or that he was renting the house and trying to get the amount he paid down. In fact, he was plagued by visitors, and the grander ones required a fairly high standard of food and hospitality. He also discovered that his servants were becoming quite insolent, knowing that, if they left, the tales of the haunting would make it very difficult to hire anyone new.

When word of the curious business at Tedworth was relayed to Charles II, he sent down two courtiers to investigate. The earls of Chesterfield and Falmouth spent some hours there, during which time nothing at all happened. Pepys records Lord Sandwich, another sceptic, in June 1663, noting that the demonic drummer, who would copy any tune played to it, was confounded by one especially complex rendition, clearly suggesting a human agency at work.

Soon there was a story abroad that the king himself had summoned Mompesson, and that he had admitted the whole story to be false. A scathing attack appeared in print in John Webster's *Displaying of Supposed Witchcraft* (1677). In 1716, Joseph Addison produced a sceptical play about the whole case called *The Drummer, or the Haunted House*, and Hogarth mocked it in a print that also mocked the Cock Lane ghost: a barometer measuring popular ghost mania is inscribed 'Tedworth' and has a death's-head drummer at the top.

That the whole incident was a hoax remains the standard position to this day. Charles Mackay confirmed this opinion in 1841 in *The Extraordinary Popular Delusions and the Madness of Crowds*, although it is only in 2005 that the full story was finally told, drawn together from diaries, letters, state papers and books.[15]

In 1668, Glanvill first published *Saducismus Triumphatus*, including his account of the Tedworth visit: it made him famous. Glanvill was to revise it in later editions, the best-known published

8. The frontispiece to Glanvill's *Saducismus*: ghosts and witches were proof of supernatural power, and thus proof of God himself.

after his death, in 1682. Some of the early flippancy and light-heartedness was edited out after over a decade of attacks on his integrity. In the 1681 edition, he added testimonials from Mompesson stating that he stood by the story of witchcraft and had never confessed to the king that he had made the whole thing up.

It seems likely that Drury's itinerant friends did their best to exact revenge, perhaps with the help of someone in the house, possibly a lower servant. That Mompesson immediately concludes that the seven figures in his garden are ghosts, and that they shrink away at the sight of a pistol, is bizarre, since it appears this incident happens only a few days after Drury's appearance at the Gloucester assize. It is a classic example of an individual in a heightened state of mind ascribing supernatural causes to quite explicable incidents. The presence of a knife in Mompesson's mother's bed and a metal spike in his own is a criminal warning sign as old as the

Camorra. The initial incident that triggered the whole thing off was a burglary, and it seems entirely possible that the 'haunting' was an attempt by Drury's fellow-travellers to steal back his drum, which he regarded as a 'tool of his trade', a powerful concept in British common law. Mompesson's retention of it was probably seen as a monstrous injustice. It's interesting to note that, even though the drum was burned in a field outside the house while the haunting was in full swing, the drumming continued.

However, there are aspects of the case that could point to the paranormal. Many events happened before several witnesses and involved the moving of furniture – most of it the heavy oak of the era (a very different proposition to the horse-hairs used by the servant Ann Robinson to jerk crockery off the shelves in fake ghostly activity in Stockwell). In Tedworth, children floated and couldn't be kept down. Some sounds simply couldn't be accounted for. That the dogs didn't bark seems also a significant detail. Dogs please themselves, and bark they certainly would at strangers lurking outside. There were simply so many people involved in visiting and watching over a twelve-month period that it seems unlikely that an elaborate conspiracy could have gone on undiscovered.

Most observers were sceptics, and Mompesson soon grew tired of their demands to pull up the floorboards and their treatment of him as the architect of an imposture. The mockery of the court drifted all the way from London, in part encouraged by no less a figure than the poet and libertine Lord Rochester, yet Mompesson was unable to earn a living for fear of leaving his family on their own.

We know this enraged Glanvill, because he addresses it in the 1682 edition of *Saducismus*:

I have been asked a thousand times, till I have been weary of answering, and the Questionists would scarce believe I was in earnest when I denied it. I have received Letters about it from known Friends and Strangers out of many parts of the Three Kingdoms, so I have been haunted almost as bad as Mr. Mompesson's House ... Most of them have declared that it was most confidently reported, and believed in all the respective parts, that the business was a Cheat, that Mr Mompesson had confessed as much, and I the same: so that I was quite tired with denying and answering letters about it.[16]

By 1682, both Anne Conway and Glanvill were dead. The posthumous 1682 edition of *Saducismus Triumphatus* has a notable omission. Glanvill has dropped his suggestion that the Royal Society investigate the 'land of spirits' which is 'a kind of America'.

Anne Conway expired in February 1679. Over the years, she had tried every cure available, finding succour only in the treatments of the Irish faith-healer Valentine Greatrakes, whose breath was so refined it was said to smell of violets. Another doctor who came to treat her – the iatrochemist and cabalist Francis Mercury van Helmont – never left. He was with her when she died, and arranged for her body to be embalmed for her husband's return from Ireland. She floated in spirits of wine in a glass-lidded coffin placed in the library, her face finally free from pain, in the very room where she had held her psychic salons. Her request for a Quaker burial was ignored.

Lady Conway's husband did, however, go on to found 'a kind of America'. Moved by Anne's conversion to Quakerism before her death, it was he, as Secretary of State and Lord President of the Committee of Trade, who signed off the creation of the state of Pennsylvania with its special dispensation for Quakers in 1681.

William Penn had been another regular at Ragley, as had Quaker George Keith, which is one of the reasons that Conway became a well-known name[17] in the nascent US (and that of a borough in Pennsylvania). How different America would have been had it been largely colonized by, say, the Diggers, who believed in no afterlife whatsoever. It was the Quaker schismatics, the Shakers, who were to pave the way for the nineteenth-century séance, which was then imported back to England – so not only did Anne Conway's headaches lead to Salem, her darkened sick-room was to lead to the Victorian séance.

There was simply no possibility that the Royal Society was going to get involved in ghosts, as Glanvill had hoped. Not even Isaac Newton dared reveal his deep interest in the occult and prophesy. And though he had contributed the story of the Devil of Mâcon[18] to the book, Robert Boyle, another Fellow of the Royal Society, was also circumspect in broadcasting his interest. There is, though, a family story[19] that, after Boyle's sister had seen the ghost of their brother Lord Orrery, he told her, when the ghost returned, to ask him some metaphysical questions. 'I know these questions come from my brother,' said the ghost flatly. 'He is too curious.' The scientist subsequently admitted to the possibility of 'an aerial body', but declined to explore the concept any further.

In 1666, Glanvill was appointed rector of the Abbey Church in Bath, and he remained there for the rest of his life. He also became chaplain-in-ordinary to Charles II in 1672, and would probably have been made a bishop had he not died in his mid-forties.

As Glanvill's theology gathers dust, he is now studied as a key prose-writer, a transitional figure who brought plainness and clarity back to British writing. His books were quoted by Edgar Allen Poe and in Aleister Crowley's *Diary of a Drug Fiend*, and Matthew Arnold used one of his stories as the basis for *The Scholar Gypsy*. There's something too of Glanvill in the narrators of the stories of M. R. James:[20] the scholar brought to a startling realization by an encounter with a supernatural entity with more than a touch of the diabolic about it.

When Glanvill attended the funeral of his former mentor the Provost Dr Rous at Eton College in 1659, he would have been sitting in the stalls where, some centuries later, M. R. James would take evensong before winding his way back to the lodgings to read his stories to the schoolboys, as always, at the end of the Michaelmas Half.

The Devil of Mâcon

'I like annoying you.'
'Where do you come from?'
'The graveyard.'

— Guy Lyon Playfair talking to the Enfield poltergeist

Another story certainly recounted at Ragley was that of the Devil of Mâcon. Robert Boyle corresponded with Glanvill about it, and it remains the earliest extensively documented poltergeist case. Robert Boyle heard it first-hand as little more than a schoolboy; shortly after leaving Eton, where he was educated, he embarked on the Grand Tour, and in 1644 was in Geneva on the way home from visiting Galileo in Florence.

There he the met French Calvinist François Perreaud, who for two months in 1612 had been subjected to an unremitting attack from a malicious and unseen entity. Perreaud was from a respectable family and was raised in the Pays de Vaud, a Savoyard area of Switzerland with a long reputation of witchcraft and werewolves. A third-generation minister, whose grandfather had been swayed to Calvinism by Calvin himself, Perreaud moved with his new wife, Anne Farci, to take up a post in Mâcon in what seem to have been his late thirties. His account of the haunting was later published in England by Boyle, who paid for its publication himself and also brought it to the attention of Glanvill in a correspondence.

On 19 September 1612, Perreaud had returned home to Mâcon after an absence of five days to find his domestic space in uproar: his wife and her maid had been plagued in bed by something that tore back the curtains of the four-poster and ripped off the bed-sheets. Pots and pans were thrown around the kitchen at night, with the door locked from inside the room, where no one could subsequently be found.

Despite Perreaud's attempts to secure the house, chaos again came to the kitchen at night, and on one occasion when a physician came to call in broad daylight, the sheets of a bed disordered themselves before their eyes. Once, when Perreaud was trying to read, a noise resembling a 'fusillade of muskets' sounded from beneath the floorboards. In the stable, he found the mane of his horse twisted into knots, and his saddle turned back to front.

By the third week of November, one evening, alarmingly, the poltergeist had learned how to talk. The voice was hoarse and seemed to hang in the air in the middle of rooms. 'Minister, minister!' it rasped at Perreaud. He shouted out: 'Yes I am a minister and a servant of the living God before whose majesty you tremble,' to which the spirit replied with a sly assurance: 'I'm not contradicting you!' It then began to recite garbled versions of prayers and psalms. It also revealed details of Perreaud's private life, including the fact that his father had been poisoned, and named the man who did it and where the deed was done. Significantly, the spirit claimed that it hailed from Pays de Vaud, a region so steeped in fear and people acting on fear, it is where all subsequent European laws against sorcery have their origins.

The Calvinist church elders rallied round their cleric, and a cadre of 'watchers' was set up with the dual purpose of detecting imposture and, if the haunting was proven genuine, to provide witness to the wiles of the Devil. The spirit responded to these watchers with some enthusiasm, mimicking them and their family members, recounting private conversations and private facts. It also seemed to mock their Protestant faith, on one occasion suggesting they get a Catholic around to exorcize the house.

Fairly soon, and inevitably, some suspicion fell on the maid, who seemed relatively unworried by the spirit's activities and comments in her local dialect until she became fed up with its habit of untidying rooms she had tidied. The suspicion, however, was not of faking but of witchcraft, and Perreaud believed the maid came from a family who practised the dark arts. When it seemed she might leave, the spirit attacked her replacement as the maid was training her up, beating her soundly and throwing water over her as she slept.

It then pretended to be a ghostly valet fallen on hard times, on one occasion saying it was on the way to Chambéry, where, according to Perreaud, he did later discover that in the household of a famous lawyer in that town, a disembodied voice had demanded exotic food for its 'master'. The lawyer was then treated to a seventeenth-century radio show of bawdy songs, fairground cries from quack doctors and the huzzahs and halloos of a hunt in full fig and flight through the countryside.

The voice, variously wheedling and threatening, promised a hidden fortune of gold in Perreaud's house before bursting into angry insults. Its final flourish was two weeks of lithobolia, or stone-flinging, in the two weeks leading up to Christmas; then, on 22 December, a large viper was caught slithering out of Perreaud's house, like Satan from Eden. The dead snake was paraded through town. From that date, nearly all the phenomena ceased.

However, 22 December was also the date when the previous owner of the house, who had been ejected to make way for Perreaud after he petitioned the town council for a better residence, appeared in court to explain her actions. She was resentful and angry at having been removed from her house, and had been found one day exhorting the Devil to enter Perreaud's house via the chimney. It was, in his opinion, this woman who had bewitched him.

There are thousands of poltergeist stories in the canon, including examples from India and China, but there is something irreducibly Teutonic in their origin and in their evolution. Catherine

Crowe first noted this in the chapter 'The Poltergeist of the Germans' in her *The Night Side of Nature*, published in 1848. This was the intellectual moment when poltergeists were identified as a separate species to the common-or-garden ghost. Martin Luther, surprisingly enough, was the first to use the word. The moniker of 'rumbling' or 'noisy spirit' comes from the verb 'poltern', to cause a disturbance, and the noun 'polter', a rowdy individual; 'geist' means ghost. One of the earliest recorded examples, around AD 500, is the stone-throwing haunting of a doctor in Ravenna, one Helpidius, physician to the Germanic Gothic emperor Theodoric the Great, as it has some aspects of poltergeist activity (although, uniquely, it was cured by the application of holy water).

Yes, the *heimat* of the poltergeist is Germany. Some years earlier than Perreaud's poltergeist, or so Jacob Grimm, in his *Deutsche Mythologie*, would have us believe, Bingem-am-Rhein had been host to an event which for the first time has all the hallmarks of a modern poltergeist story. More recently, the Rosenheim case in Germany in 1967, in which the 19-year-old secretary Annemarie Schneider became the focus – or should that be locus? – of uncanny events, remains, of all the stories, and by common consent among the informed, the most evidential, partly because both the police and electrical engineers became involved. There are signed statements from local Bavarian policemen, physicists from the Max Planck Institute and engineers from Siemens concerning the wealth of ghostly phenomena – bizarre and physically impossible multiple phone calls to the speaking clock, phones ringing simultaneously, exploding and swinging lights, drawers opening by themselves, and so on. State-of-the-art equipment, including something called a Unireg machine, was used to work out how the speaking clock could be called forty-six times over a fifteen-minute period, something impossible on an old dial telephone using an analogue system (it took seventeen seconds to be connected each time).

There are also accounts of early poltergeist activity in England.

St Godric, in his Finchale hermitage, was bombarded with stones and drenched in wine in the year of his death, 1170, and Giraldus Cambrensis writes of a poltergeist at the home of one Stephen Wiriet in Pembrokeshire in 1190, where 'foul spirits' threw dirt, and – the first time this is ever mentioned – a voice manifested, telling tales of the local people and their embarrassing secrets. Shortly afterwards in that same year, at the tiny village of Dagworth in Suffolk, at the home of Sir Osborne of Bradaewelle, a similarly indiscreet entity held forth.

The strangest aspect of the Enfield poltergeist investigated by Guy Lyon Playfair in the 1970s involved some hoarse vocalizations coming from the little girl at the heart of the business, and these vocalizations happened also in the Bell Witch haunting in America in 1817, and in an 1889 case in Denmark.

The first instance of a clear human female focus at the centre of a poltergeist case[1] involved the haunting of a nun at the nunnery of St Pierre de Lyon in 1526, in which a young sister, Anthoinette de Grolée, endured levitations, and rappings which followed her around (although these were perceived by the Catholic orthodoxy to have been brought about by a spirit back from Purgatory, and involved a former nun of the nunnery being exhumed and reburied to rest her knocking spirit – no Lutheran demons here).

Sacheverell Sitwell considered that some of these stories were the result of faulty observation and hysteria. He also had firm views on Nazi Germany. 'Adolf Hitler is the perfect type of medium if ever there was one,' he told the *Guardian* in 1941. 'We could readily believe that this remarkable person, did he feel so inclined, could displace objects and move them about in oblique and curving flight; or rap out equivocal answers; or cause lighted matches to drop down from the ceiling.'

Another commentator and writer[2] on this subject went even further. 'There are extraordinary points of resemblance between the records of Poltergeist hauntings and the Nazi movement.

Both are manifested in a subconscious uprush of desire for power. Both suck like vampires the energies of adolescents; both issue in noise, destruction, fire and terror.'

The discourse was no longer of a kind of externalized form of Tourette's exhibited in the presence of teenaged girls. The *Sturm und Drang* of this ancient Germanic infestation had become a way of life, and a way of war.[3]

Entering the Epworth Scale

My mother tells me a very strange story of disturbances in your
house. I wish I could have some more particulars of you.

– Samuel Wesley to his father

Nearly half a century after the poltergeist at Tedworth, a mother
sat down and wrote to her son:

> 'This evening we were agreeably surprised with your pacquet,
> which brought the welcome news of your being alive, after we
> had been in the greatest panic imaginable, almost a month, think-
> ing either you was dead, or one of your brothers by misfortune
> had been killed.'

Samuel Wesley was the eldest of a large and fractious family,
and grew up in a Lincolnshire parish where the locals so hated his
clergyman father they tried to burn down the family house –
twice. His mother and father were notorious for their feuding,
even separating for a while over their disagreement over whether
the new king was the legitimate sovereign. But what makes this
story so interesting is that his younger brother John was later to
start up a new kind of evangelical christianity that was to shape
the next century, Methodism. Methodism's early involvement
with ghost sightings was to prove highly contentions.

As the 25-year-old teacher at Westminster read on, he could
scarcely believe what his mother was writing.

> On the first of December, our maid heard, at the door of the dining

room, several dismal groans, like a person in extremes, at the point of death. We gave little heed to her relation, and endeavoured to laugh her out of her fears. Some nights (two or three) after, several of the family heard a strange knocking in divers places, usually three or four knocks at a time, and then stayed a little. This continued every time for a fortnight; sometimes it was in the garret, but most commonly in the nursery, or green chamber. We all heard it but your father, and I was not willing he should be informed of it, lest he fancy it was against his own death, which, indeed, we all apprehended.

As at Tedworth and Hinton Ampner, the initial suspicion must have been that a human agency was involved, such as the villagers having come back to burn the Wesleys's house down.

But when it began to be so troublesome, both day and night, that few or none of the family durst be alone, I resolved to tell him of it, being minded he should speak to it. At first he would not believe but someone did it to alarm us; but the night after, as soon as he was in bed, it knocked loudly nine times, just by his bedside. He rose and went to see if he could find out what it was, but could see nothing. Afterwards, he heard it as the rest.

In other words, he was now tuned into the noises that everyone else was hearing.

One night it made such a noise in the room above our heads, as if several people were walking, then ran up and down stairs, and was so outrageous that we thought the children would be frighted, so your father and I rose, and went down into the dark to light a candle. Just as we came to the bottom of the broad stairs, having hold of each other, on my side there seemed as if somebody had emptied a bag of money at my feet; on his, as if all the bottles under the stairs (which were many) had been dashed into a thousand pieces. We passed through the hall into the kitchen, and got a candle, and went to see the children, whom we found asleep.

As with other poltergeist cases, not everyone heard the same thing. The following evening, a sombre Wesley sent for reinforcements in the shape of Joseph Hoole, the rector of the neighbouring parish of Haxey. They sat up until two o'clock in the morning, around the fire in the matted chamber beside the nursery, listening to the knocks. One of the new noises was the sound of a carpenter planing a piece of wood, 'but most commonly it knocked thrice and stopped, and then thrice again, and so many hours together.'

On a night just after Christmas, the family pressed Wesley to speak to the spirit. One dark evening, about six o'clock, he walked into the nursery and heard several deep groans then a knocking. 'Then he questioned it as if it were Sammy, and bid it, if it were, and could not speak, knock again, but it knocked no more that night, which made us hope it was not against your death.'

At the time, the Wesley family at home consisted of seven daughters, with a manservant and a maid in attendance. Thirteen-year-old John was a schoolboy and, as was not unusual at the time, was spending the holidays at school. The distance between Lincoln and London meant that relatives could go for weeks without knowing the whereabouts or welfare of their loved ones.

The correspondence that January in 1717 between a concerned Sammy Wesley and his parents is one of the most interesting exchanges on paranormal phenomena of the eighteenth century. He was about to leave his lodgings in the dean's yard and catch a coach from the Red Lion in Aldersgate to Doncaster when a letter arrived from his father saying the phenomena had ceased. In a model of diligence that would do any modern ghost-hunter proud, Samuel Jr continued to collate information on the case.

On 19 January, he replied with measured scepticism, asking for further details and suggesting all manner of natural causes. 'Those who are so wise as not to believe in any supernatural occurrences, though ever so well attested, could find a hundred questions to ask about those strange noises.' Were there rats? A new servant, playing a trick? 'I expect a particular account from every one,' he ended firmly.

On 24 January, his sister wrote. Sammy and Sukey, or Susannah, were clearly close. Susannah added a bit of colour and playfulness to the account, claiming that the maid's hair stood up and her ears stood out during the incident of 1 December. 'But, to lay aside jesting, which should not be done in serious matters; I assure you that the first to the last of a lunar month, the groans, squeaks, tinglings, and knockings, were frightful enough.'

Their experience was also centred around the dining room, where Susannah was with their sister Nancy, hearing someone come in from the garden door and then move around upstairs. Later, all were sitting in their bedroom, when they heard thumps beneath them; then some kind of electricity seemed to play about with the metal fittings and features of the room, trembling around the latch and warming pan.

The night that Revd Hoole visited was a horror. As her father sat downstairs with his fellow clergyman, all hell was breaking loose in the nursery, with loud, bed-shaking retorts on the wooden headboards of the younger girls, and a new manifestation: 'I heard something walk by my bedside like a man in a long gown,' claimed one of the girls. The knocks eventually drew the men upstairs.

Then an interesting detail: knocks were heard at family prayers, but only when Revd Wesley asked for blessings on the king – in other words, this was a spirit with the same Jacobin views as his wife.

'Do not say one word of this to our folks, nor give the least hint,' concluded Susannah. A secret letter, then, a keeping of confidences away from the battling parents.

On 25 January, Mrs Wesley wrote back to her eldest son. They had indeed hired new servants on Martinmas (11 November), so

9. Epworth Rectory: genteel without, seething within.

about three weeks before the disturbances began, but since they had been in the room with them when many of the noises occurred, and the maid in particular seemed terrified to distraction, Mrs Wesley did not see how they could be responsible. Their man, Robert Brown, had run down the stairs from the attic almost naked on one occasion, to escape the ghosts. The servants always attended family prayers, and that was when the noises were worst.

'All the family, as well as Robin, were asleep when your father and I went down stairs, nor did they wake in the nursery when he held the candle close by them, only we observed Hetty trembled exceedingly in her sleep, as she always did, before the noise awaked her.'

Mrs Wesley also mentioned her belief that encounters with ghosts would be far more common 'did not our lapse into sensuality prevent it'. In other words, modern morals were to blame. If people weren't wallowing in their own filth, 'frequent intercourse' with 'good spirits' would be common, a position that William Blake would later explore with his doors of perception.

In a letter written on 12 February, Samuel Jr was becoming quite frustrated; the details from his sister and mother were so vague he couldn't even establish whether the haunting was still going on.

'Have you dug in the place where the money seemed poured at your feet?' he asked his mother. This was an ancient idea from classical texts, that ghosts were often messengers revealing the spots of buried bodies or treasure. And his father had still not deigned to correspond. 'I have not yet received any answer to the letter I wrote some time ago,' complained Samuel Jr. 'I am sure I am a party concerned.'

And the letters cross: here is one from Revd Wesley dated 11 February, saying the disturbances have ceased, and rather making light of them. 'It would make a glorious penny book for Jack Dunton,' he observes. Since the bookseller John Dunton (1659–1733) appears to have been his brother-in-law, the reference seems surprisingly dismissive. It's clear that neither does he hold much faith in the ability of the female members of the family to relay the unadorned truth. 'Your mother had not written you a third part of it,' he says. 'When I see you here you will see the whole account, which I wrote down.'

Years later, John Wesley himself asked his sisters Molly, Nancy and Emily to write down their own versions. One of the longest accounts comes from Emily, fleshing out some of the details.

Just after the clock struck ten I went downstairs to lock the doors, which I always do. Scarce had I got up the best stairs, when I heard a noise, like a person throwing down a vast coal in the middle of the fore kitchen, and all the splinters seemed to fly about from it. I was not much frighted, but went to my sister Sukey, and we went together all over the low rooms, but there was nothing out of order.

Our dog was fast asleep, and our only cat in the other end of the house. No sooner was I got up stairs, and undressing for bed, but I heard a noise amongst many bottles that stand under the best stairs just like the throwing of a great stone among them, which had broke them all to pieces. This made me hasten to bed; but my sister Hetty, who sits always to wait on my father going to bed, was still sitting on the lowest step of the garret stairs, the door being shut at her back, when soon after there came down the stairs behind her, something like a man, in a loose night gown trailing after him, which made her fly rather than run to me in the nursery.

Her father reacted to their story with gentle amusement, and their mother, insists Emily, considered the whole issue a matter of rats. This is not a frightened household. Emily appears to be saying that she is the sole person in Epworth who believes in the supernatural origins of the sounds.

I believe it is witchcraft, for these reasons. About a year since, there was a disturbance in a town near us, that was undoubtedly witches; and if so near, why may they not reach us? Then my father who had for several Sundays before its coming preached warmly against consulting those that are called cunning men, which our people are given to; they had a particular spight at my Father.

Something like a badger was seen by the mother under the bed of one of the children; its head was in shadow. It was observed again sitting by the dining-room fire. Then a creature resembling a white rabbit was seen in the kitchen, 'which seems likely to be some witch'.

By 27 March 1717, Samuel Jr's mother is writing, 'I am quite tired with speaking or hearing of it, but if you come among us, you will find enough to satisfy all your scruples, and perhaps may hear, or see it for yourself.'

Revd Wesley, meanwhile, was keeping a diary of events. He heard nothing at all until 21 December, when he was woken by nine knocks that seemed to come from the room beside his bedroom. Thinking there were people breaking into the house, and no doubt wary of the locals, the next day he went out and got himself a 'stout mastiff'. The day after Christmas, the ghost announced its arrival with, the Revd learned from his daughter, a familiar noise 'like the strong winding up of a jack'. This strange, clicking, abrasive sound was later described by others as like a windmill turning. There follows a cluster of events – the dog being frightened, the tapping out of knocks to see if it will answer, and a noise as if the poltergeist was trying to gain energy to speak 'a little louder than the chirping of a bird'. Uniquely among the people in the house, Samuel was physically attacked, pushed by an invisible force a total of three times. We also know that he challenged the entity out loud, that Boxing Day night. Bellowing out that it was a 'Deaf and Dumb Devil' and demanding that it meet him in his study, he bade it cease annoying his family.

Though the mastiff barked vigorously on the first day it arrived, from the day after, it did little but whine miserably.

Years passed. In August 1726, the young John Wesley, as mentioned earlier, asked all his family to write down their accounts of the events he had missed out on experiencing. His interest in the everyday miraculous was already pronounced; he must have wished he had been there that Christmas, tapping back, and seeing and hearing marvels. In the way of things, details were still being added. The ghost was called by the family Old Jeffrey. His first arrival had been 'long before' the Christmas events, after a sharp quarrel between one of the Wesley boys and Sukey, 'at which time . . . the door and windows rung and jarred very loud, and presently several very distinct strokes, three by three, were struck.'

Robert Brown initially believed the groans were from a Mr Turpin, who sounds like a neighbour who may have had some kind of medical emergency at Epworth, since 'he had the stone and used to groan so.' Other odd phenomena included the gobbling noise of a turkey cock, and Robert seeing, at the top of the garret stairs, a hand mill for grinding malt and corn whirring on its own, which seemed to be the source of the grinding noises. It says something about their general state of mind that he lamented the ghost was turning the mill with nothing in it, when it could have saved him some work. When he saw the rabbit creature in the kitchen, he was feeling sick, and was half asleep.

My favourite detail comes from sister Molly, who had been 'ordered' to light her father to his study one night. 'Just as he had unlocked it, the latch was lifted up for him.'

Several clergymen colleagues, including, one assumes, Revd Hoole, urged him to leave the rectory, to which he replied, 'No, let the Devil flee from me: I will never flee from the Devil!'

The one thing that is missing from this documentation is anything by Hetty (Mehetabel), who, we know from other family members, was committing her version of events to paper. It was she whom the noises followed round the house, she who stirred so in the throes of REM sleep, she who is generally assumed to be the focus. It seems pretty clear that John Wesley suppressed her version, for reasons we can only guess at.

Samuel Jr went on to be much like his father: staunchly Anglican, and given to the composition of indifferent poetry. John went on to found the Methodist Church, and when he was barred from his own church in Epworth, after he took over the living, he preached sermons from the churchyard outside – on his father's grave. Though it was later dropped, ghost-belief was an early key element of this religion. There is evidence that John Wesley had some misgivings over publishing any of the more intimate details of family life at Epworth, but he believed so strongly in the moral value of the story that he published it in *The Arminian Magazine* in 1784, when he was over eighty years old and looking back on his life.

Though a belief in ghosts was never formally introduced into the mainstream of Methodism, Wesley's journal, which was published in instalments during his lifetime, made no bones about his personal convictions. In the early 1760s, he read Baxter's *Certainty of the World of Spirits* during a journey to London, and observed with great interest how 'it contains several well-attested accounts'. When elsewhere asked about his views on the spirit world, and whether he had seen a ghost, he replied:

> No: nor did I ever see a murder. Yet I believe there is such a thing; yea, and that in one place or another, murder is committed every day. Therefore I cannot as a reasonable man deny the fact: although I never saw it, and perhaps never may. The testimony of unexceptional witnesses fully convinces me both of one and the other.

By the end of the eighteenth century, ghost-belief was common among proselytising Methodists and even Anglican clergymen with evangelical tendencies, as in the case of the Cock Lane ghost (see 'Miss Fanny's New Theatre' for more on that).

Interestingly, just as Roman Catholicism was returning to British public life after centuries of banishment, the Methodists were choosing to distinguish themselves from establishment orthodoxy with a similar belief. For centuries, to believe in ghosts had indicated Roman Catholic tendencies; now, it could also mean that you were at the other end of the scale.

There is an intriguing connection between the Tedworth and the Epworth cases. In the journals of John Wesley, written in 1768, we find a mention that his elder brother, Samuel, had been at Oxford University with one of the Mompessons. At the time; Samuel had asked him whether the whole business had been a trick.

'The resort of gentlemen to my father's house was so great, he could not bear the expense,' Mompesson told him. 'He therefore took no pains to confute the report that he had found out the cheat; although he, and I, and all the family, knew the account which was published to be punctually true.'

Hetty (1697–1750) may well have been the most gifted of all the

Wesley brood. Now the object of some academic interest, she is known to have eloped on at least two occasions, before being forced by her parents to marry a plumber[2] – someone with whom she had no intellectual connection. They ended up running a business in Frith Street, Soho, her health eventually wrecked, possibly by exposure to the extensive use of lead in her husband's business.

In 1726, John Wesley publicly upbraided his father in a sermon for his treatment of Hetty after, it seems, she had given birth to an illegitimate child. That was also the year that John Wesley started asking his family for their accounts; perhaps there was even some renewed activity at Epworth, since we are told the ghost manifested itself during family tension.

Technically, with its brief efflorescence and with a pubescent girl at the centre of it, this is a classic poltergeist haunt. That the entity responded to verbal cues referencing this quarrel lends it an unusual specificity; it means the poltergeist wasn't only linked to the daughter, but to the mother also. Hetty would have been four or five when this quarrel took place, and it may have had a profound effect on her.

Another interesting aspect of the case is the ringing of metal fittings in the room before phenomena happen, which to a modern eye points to low-frequency sound waves. Its effects remain unproven. Some work has been done – some of it by NASA – on the physical effects of infrasound on the human body, especially round about the 19-hertz level.

During a piano concert at Liverpool's Metropolitan University in September 2002, infrasound pulses were sent out at certain points – unbeknown to the concert-goers. Asked to complete a questionnaire on leaving, people reported a variety of effects, including tingles on the back of the neck, 'strange feelings in the stomach' and heightened emotions. Being exposed to a sound wave of 19 hertz can create a kind of ripple in the eye, which in turn will give the anomalous impression of movement on one's peripheral vision. In short, a low hum makes you feel uneasy and think you see things moving that aren't in fact there. When psychacoustics engineer Vic Tandy, who teaches at Coventry University, was working for a company that manufactured life-support systems, a cleaning lady told him that the place was haunted. One night he happened to have his fencing foil with him and it started to vibrate and move on its own; to cut a long story short, he found the culprit was a newly installed exhaust fan in the basement.

The use of infrasound to create altered states seems to have been familiar to our forebears; there's some indication that some Neolithic buildings were specifically engineered for acoustics. So-called 'standing wave' effects can be produced at many enclosed monuments in the Celtic world, including Camster Round in Caithness and Maeshowe in Orkney, initiated either by ritual drumming or chanting. However, this does not explain all the phenomena at Epworth; even if some of the disturbance was caused by infrasound, there remains the question of where it came from.

Samuel Taylor Coleridge suggested that the Epworth haunting was a contagious hallucination; the poet laureate Robert Southey thought it demonic. Could it be that travelling sorcerers and cunning men were again involved, as they were at Tedworth, ranged against the big man in the big house who was trying to take their trade away from them? There certainly seems to be a local animus against Revd Samuel Wesley Sr wrapped up in this haunting.

He did not serve his family well, and it is interesting that the Methodist establishment prefers to shine a light on John Wesley's mother as the true moral authority in that household. High-minded and aloof, Samuel Wesley turned his local congregation against him and even spent time in jail for debt. His neighbours, perhaps even members of his congregation, destroyed his property and maimed his cattle. He was furthermore perfectly able to leave his wife Susanna for five months in 1702 because they disagreed on a point of principle. Susanna would not say 'Amen' in prayers for William of Orange, who she considered a usurper, and it was only on the death of King William and the accession of Queen Anne that the Wesleys were finally reconciled.

In 1991, a Dr Murray Johns of the Epworth Hospital in Melbourne, Australia, came up with a formalized sleepiness scale that is now the medical standard for describing sleep disorders. He named it after the hospital he worked at as a specialist in apnoea and hypopnoea, which, in turn, being a Methodist foundation, is named after the rectory in Lincolnshire where the founder of Methodism was raised. Hence that measured area between wakefulness and sleep is now named after one of the most well-known poltergeist cases of the last few hundred years, the Epworth poltergeist.

As you fall asleep, slowly and surely, you are entering the Epworth Scale.

The Ghost of Mrs Veal

I was asked the other day by a very great person if I had heard
anything of the story you showed us in your letters about the
apparition in Canterbury.

– Dr John Arbuthnot to John Flamsteed

It flourished in the long night drawing in from All Hallows'
Eve, when fires were lit and lanterns blazed against the coming
darkness. This was the time when, according to Mayhew, the travelling tinkers and traders would set aside their knife-sharpeners
and usual wares in favour of the magic lantern, setting it up in
public houses and village halls to project a creepshow of painted
spooks and ghouls[1] – the witch of Endor raising the ghost of
Samuel, for example – shrouded figures, skeletons, burning tapers
and bearded men standing in cabalistic circles as the dead, hunched
and cold, moved closer in.

The literary ghost story: England's great gift to the world. It
reached its apogee, as did English children's literature, in the late
Victorian and then Edwardian eras. The early stories were
steeped in gothic melodrama, with a pronounced sense of madness and derangement. The narratives usually involved someone
being put in a haunted room not generally in use, and then, after
a night of terror, identifying the spectre from the family
portraits.

A good example of this is Walter Scott's 'The Tapestried
Chamber', first published in a literary winter annual called *The
Keepsake* in 1829 and which M. R. James mistakenly identified as
the first English ghost story.[2]

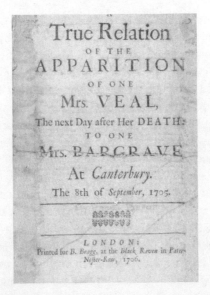

True Relation
OF THE
APPARITION
OF ONE
Mrs. VEAL,
The next Day after Her DEATH:
TO ONE
Mrs. BARGRAVE
At *Canterbury.*
The 8th of *September,* 1705.

LONDON:
Printed for B. *Bragg,* at the *Black Raven* in *Pater-
Noster-Row,* 1706.

10. England's first ghost story: Daniel Defoe's mix of fact and fiction was to become impossible after a tax change in 1712, and so the ghost story faltered even as it began.

But, as it happens, the first formal English ghost story is not hyper-real, hallucinatory and alarming. It is quietly domestic: a ghost comes round for 'tea'.

A True Relation of the Apparition of one Mrs Veal, the Next Day after her Death, to one Mrs Bargrave, at Canterbury was published anonymously in 1706. Its author, Daniel Defoe,[3] was adept at spotting a gap in the market: what people wanted was a real ghost story, the more mundane the better, because it made it more likely to be true.

On Saturday 8 September 1705, a Mrs Margaret Bargrave was sitting alone in her small house in Canterbury situated near St George's Gate. The clock had just struck noon.

Thinking she heard the rustle of a dress, Margaret looked up to see her dear old friend, Mary Veal. She had not seen her for two years, and was both delighted and surprised by her sudden, entirely unannounced, arrival. At the time, she did not particularly notice nor care that Mary Veal was in her nightclothes, wearing a hood, and had a silk handkerchief tied beneath her neck. Margaret rose to embrace her – but her friend, clearly in some kind of a hurry, slipped quickly past and sat down in an armchair.

At first they talked of familiar things, including their happy time living together in Dover, but after a while the conversation took a more serious turn. Mrs Bargrave confessed, sadly, that there was marital discord in the household, and that she was not happy with her life. Mrs Veal, for some reason best known to herself, comforted her Canterbury friend with the assurance that this unhappiness would pass, that all unhappiness passes. After a while, the conversation took a third turn, which was their shared love of reading. Mrs Veal had noticed a book lying on the windowsill and was pleased to discover it was a copy of Charles Drelincourt's *Discourse against the Fear of Death*, of which Mrs Veal had a firm opinion: that it was full of truth.

Mrs Veal finally asked Mrs Bargrave if she might oblige her by writing some letters to various of her family members, including her brother. She wanted him to give some of her jewellery and rings to such and such, and from her purse in her cabinet she wanted two gold pieces to be given to her cousin Watson.[4] For some reason, Mrs Bargrave did not seem to think this request an odd one.

After nearly an hour and three quarters, Mrs Bargrave accompanied her friend to the door, said goodbye, then watched her walk down the street until she turned a corner and was gone.

The next day, she discovered from a local undertaker that Mrs Veal was in fact quite dead, indeed had died from a fit at exactly noon on Friday, when Mrs Bargrave had first set eyes on her. The body was already going cold as Mrs Bargrave spent a pleasant afternoon warmly chatting to the ghost of Mrs Veal.

The first version of this story appeared in *The Loyal Post* on

Christmas Eve in 1705, a single-folio publication of local and foreign news printed on both sides. Recent archival work has produced a fuller picture. A letter dated 13 September 1705 gives a first indication of the excitement and the gossip doing the rounds. This letter tells us that Margaret Bargrave was the wife of a lawyer, and that Mary Veal, while alive, had been a close childhood friend from Dover. Mary Veal was unmarried and aged about thirty when she died, and she looked after her brother William, who had a senior appointment at the Dover customs house.

But while Mary's situation had improved since their childhood, Margaret's life was firmly on the way down, thanks almost entirely to the behaviour of the man she had married. Her husband was a mean drunk who had been fired from his job, as a result of which they had been forced to move away from Dover. In Canterbury, under a cloud and strapped for cash, they had rented a house on a considerably reduced income.

There's one especially telling detail in this letter, which is that on the day that Mrs Bargrave said she had seen the ghost, her husband returned home drunk and abusive some hours later and then locked her out. She spent Saturday night sitting on the steps outside her front door, unwilling to expose his bad behaviour, and in consequence contracted a fever and had to go straight to bed on Sunday.

The ghost seemed to have an old-fashioned moral purpose: to ensure that her bequests were correctly followed, since she didn't trust her brother William to do so; to ensure that the correct burial ritual was followed, since Mary Veal's parents still didn't have a headstone[5] on their grave; and, finally, to comfort her old friend with the knowledge that she wouldn't have to put up with her unpleasant husband for very much longer. When interviewed years later in 1714, Mrs Bargrave specifically identified the encounter as some kind of precursor to her husband's death in 1707. When offered a cup of tea, the ghost declines, because she assumes the husband has destroyed all the usable china in one of his inebriated rages.

Ghosts that worry about funerary ritual and bequests go right back to classical literature, as does the detail of the ghost appearing at noon. Everyone knows that ghosts appear at midnight, but not so many know that the same applies to midday, and that, traditionally, ghosts are summoned by the extreme transitional stages of the clock. You are as likely to see a ghost before lunch as you are after going to bed. In later years, this tradition died out, since it seemed ghosts were inalienably connected to the night. Indeed, the whole nature of the ghostly at this period was linked to the vapours exhaled by the earth when the world turned dark.[6]

On 9 October 1705, we have another personal letter in the archives, this time from a Lucy Lukyn, daughter of a prominent Canterbury notary. Lucy was about twenty-five years old and lived in St Mary Bredin. She also knew the Bargraves' landlords, the Oughtons. According to Lucy, Mrs Bargrave recalled that the spirit had 'the strangest blackness around her eyes she had ever seen'. She was 'very pale'. Lucy also confirms that the Bargrave household was not a happy one, and adds some details of the personal bequests, which now included giving a best gown and petticoat to a cousin.

By Halloween, the story was already being circulated at a high level in society. On 31 October, we have Queen Anne's own private physician writing to John Flamsteed,[7] founder of the Greenwich Observatory and the first Astronomer Royal. Dr John Arbuthnot was elected to the Royal Society in 1704, and was a friend and colleague of the likes of Isaac Newton and Jonathan Swift. He asked Flamsteed to send copies of the letters to St James's Palace so, in a curious turn of events, on the eve of All Souls, Queen Anne is asking her doctor for ghost stories.

In fact, the matriarchal interest from the queen suited the gender-wars aspect of the story quite well. What is striking about this tale is the female solidarity of the woman Mrs Bargrave and the ghost Mrs Veal, and how the letter writers seem to show it was mostly women who discussed the case in the locality.

It didn't take very long after the story broke for the men in the lives of the two protagonists to step up to the calumny. By 8 September 1706, Defoe's account was already on its fourth edition and, in a copy housed in the British Library, the story is already being added to in handwritten annotations by the unknown owner.[8] These notes record that the two men who come off so badly in the account are now conspiring to undermine the credibility of the female witnesses. 'Mr Veal does what he can to stifle the matter,' it claims. 'Since the death of his sister he never went near Mrs Bargrave and some of his friends report her to be a great Liar.'

In the year that had passed, William Veal claimed that there never had been any ghost of his sister, because when he opened the cabinet as requested there were no gold pieces to be found inside it. He furthermore acidly observed that nobody else had witnessed the ghost in the street at two o'clock in the afternoon that Saturday, when Mrs Bargrave said goodbye and saw her friend walk away. He had some reason to feel aggrieved – the ghost had implicitly accused him of being unfilial and vaguely untrustworthy, unable to tend family graves and unreliable when it came to bequests. Since he held a revenue-gathering post for the government, such stories could even be professionally damaging. William Veal also claimed that his sister's friend had made a dubious habit of always 'seeing' ghosts, which, according to one modern commentator on the matter, 'was in fact a misunderstanding provoked by the adulterous exploits of her wayward spouse'.[9]

The Queen was so interested that Flamsteed had discreetly recruited an investigator in Canterbury to keep tabs on the story, indirectly for the queen herself. Part-time scientist Stephen Gray, despite some work at an observatory at Trinity College, Cambridge (proposed by Isaac Newton, no less), had been obliged to return to the family silk-dyeing business in Canterbury. He was later to become known for his work on the nature of electricity and was finally elected to the Royal Society in 1732, but at this point in his life, knee-deep in vegetal colour, he was keen to preserve this one intellectual lifeline by being as diligent as possible in service of the astronomer.

It was in one of these letters that Gray, having nosed around the district, told his patron and friend of the words being whispered against the integrity of Mrs Bargrave by her own husband, and by William Veal. The reason Veal thought that Margaret Bargrave imagined ghosts everywhere makes a heartbreaking story. One evening, Margaret went in search of her husband, who had not come home, and eventually found him some miles outside Canterbury, carousing in a public house. Not only was he drunk, but when she went round to the garden area she saw a woman making a hasty exit over the wall.

Not wanting to believe what she was seeing – a prostitute vanishing from the embrace of her own husband – she initially thought it to be an 'apparition'. Gray notes sourly that her husband did nothing to disabuse her of this fanciful notion, 'being Glad of the opertunety of soe Pretty a Delution to Conceal his Roguery'. Mrs Bargrave, it seems, believed in a ghost because the reality was too painful to bear.

Both unknown letter writer EB (almost certainly a woman) and Lucy Lukyn expressed great sympathy for the plight of the impoverished and unhappy Mrs Bargrave and, if nothing else, the story showed up her shameful treatment at the hands of her husband. What reads so strangely now, however, is the religious nature of the apparition. Defoe was keen to make it an apparition rather than a ghost, since the word 'apparition' wasn't just the upper-class word for a ghost, it lent the possibility that the visitation was at least in part angelic.

Knowing that Mrs Veal was in part being viewed as an angel, EB mentioned that Mr Bargrave viewed his wife's experience as 'discoursing with ye Devil' – in other words, his wife was a witch. It was a perfectly respectable Protestant position, but it didn't play well at Canterbury, which, after all, was the seat, hub and spiritual home of the Anglican Church.

Publishers did well out of the whole episode. One used the opportunity to package the story alongside the religious book mentioned in it, Drelincourt's *Defence against the Fears of Death*, and by 1732 *The Universal Spectator* was accusing the author of *A True Relation* of fabricating the story for his own gain. The Stamp Act of 1712 had made the difference between fact and fiction paramount, simply for tax reasons (news items were taxable), but Defoe's setting of the scene, his careful description of clothing and speech, brought a sense of narrative to the events which simply hadn't existed before. It came at the key point where Defoe was moving from journalism towards the outright fiction for which he is so well known. *Robinson Crusoe* is based on the real-life adventures of Alexander Selkirk, and its main character is not unfamiliar with thoughts on the subject of ghosts.[10]

The archaic aspects of this story make it surprisingly universal. Take this undated story from Japan.[11] The wife of a priest at the Kori temple was working alone in the kitchen when she heard footsteps approaching. She had heard that the daughter of a tofu seller had been horribly burned in an accident and was near death, but to her surprise the door opened and there she was, dressed in a new kimono and not at all looking like someone at death's door. She invited the tofu seller's daughter to stay for tea, but when she returned from the kitchen with the cups, the girl had vanished. 'At this moment a man came from the city and brought the news that the tofu seller's daughter had just died.'

It's worth noting that this kind of ghost was the conventional ghost of the period – appearing like a person fully alive and seen by day. It is also a death-bed or crisis apparition of a kind much written about by the Victorians – a man fighting for the empire in some distant part of the world would appear to a relative back in England.

In his book *Satan's Invisible World Discovered*, the Glaswegian mathematician George Sinclair told of an incident in Marlborough, Wiltshire, on a November morning in 1674. A weaver named Thomas Goddard was walking on the road that led out of town to Ogbourne Maizey when he happened to see his father-in-law, Edward Avon, leaning against a stile. Avon greeted him as he approached.

What was wrong with this scenario was that Avon had died six months earlier. Despite his fear, Goddard talked with the ghost for a while on family matters, before it asked him to give the daughter he had neglected twenty or thirty shillings. Goddard declined and fled. But the ghost was not finished with him.

> The next night, about seven o'clock, it came and opened Goddard's shop-window, and stood in the same clothes as before, looking him in the face, but saying nothing. And the next night after, as Goddard went forth into his back premises, with a candle-light in his hand, it appeared to him again in the same shape; but, being in fear, he ran into the house, and saw it no more then. But, on Thursday, the 12th instant, as he came from Chilton, riding from the hill between the Manor-House and Axford Farm-field, he saw something like a hare crossing his way; at which his horse, being frighted, threw him in the dirt. As soon as he could recover his feet, the same apparition met him again in the same habit and, standing about eight feet before him in the way, spake again.

To escalate the matter, the ghost began confessing to a murder. It began issuing instructions. Goddard was to bring his brother-in-law – a shoemaker called William – and his sword, and come to a designated wood near the village of Alton Barnes.[12]

> Then Goddard, laying down the sword upon the ground, saw something stand by the apparition like a mastiff dog of a brown colour. Then, the apparition coming towards him, Goddard

stepped back about two steps, and the apparition said to him, 'I have permission to you and commission not to touch you.' And then it took up the sword and went back to the place at which before it stood, with the mastiff dog by it as before; and, pointing the top of the sword to the ground, said, 'In this place lies buried the body of him which I murdered in the year 1635, which is now rotten and turned to dust.' Whereupon Goddard said, 'I do adjure thee, wherefore did you do this murder?' And it said, 'I took money from the man, and he contended with me, and so I murdered him.'

Later, brother-in-law William gave his version of the encounter with the ghost. He had heard Goddard speak as if to someone and some kind of distorted reply coming from somewhere; yet had seen no figure. 'He heard his voice and understood what he said, and heard other words distinct from his, but could not understand a word of it, nor saw any apparition at all . . .'

The weaver was so disturbed by the week of incidents that he gave a sworn deposition to Mayor Edward Lypiatt and Joshua Sacheverell, Rector of St Peter's in Marlborough, on 23 November.

It's interesting to find just how common daylight apparitions were in former times. For example, there's another in John Aubrey's *Miscellanies*. In 1647, a gentleman named Mohun was killed in an ambush on his way to a duel in Chelsea at 10 a.m.; he was seen at exactly this time by his mistress in James Street in Covent Garden, as he lay dying in what is now Ebury Street. She saw him 'come to her bedside, draw the curtain, look upon her and go away', without replying to her questions. In another incident, in 1693, Lord Coningsbury's brother-in-law appeared to his own sister in Fleet Street at the moment he was being murdered in Hereford.

In December 1706, a Norfolk vicar entered an almost identical incident in the Brisley Church register. On 21 July of that year, a Mr Shaw was in his Oxfordshire study with his pipe, reading, when, near midnight, in came a former fellow of St John's who had been dead for four years. Curiously, Shaw was not much frightened to see his old friend, and they talked for two hours. Asked whether any of their acquaintances were with him in the afterlife, the ghost responded in the negative, but said that 'Mr Orchard would be with him soon.' Asked whether he would call again, the ghost responded that, since he was rather busy on a three-day leave, he would not. Mr Orchard, we are told, died shortly afterwards. Mr Shaw had been known to the vicar, Robert Withers, and Withers believed the story to be entirely true. It took place on 12 December, just a few days before the Mrs Veal story was published in the *Loyal Post*, and represents another example of the Christmas ghost story.

Along with folk traditions and the burying of Catholicism in an unquiet tomb, classical literature had a profound influence on the development of the fictional English ghost story. Although Charles Dickens was essentially, like Walter Scott, a sceptic, he remained irresistibly drawn to the genre. His best story is 'The Signalman', but his best known is *A Christmas Carol*. It draws on a story that had been doing the rounds for thousands of years.

In letter 7.27 Pliny writes to his friend Lucius Lucinius Sura, a patron of the poet Martial and right-hand man to the Emperor Trajan. He enquires as to whether Sura believes in ghosts, in a slightly sceptical way, and then relates three stories of different kinds of ghosts. One of them takes place in his own household, where slave boys complain that a phantom barber is coming through their bedroom window at night and treating them to a haircut, probably the first instance in written literature of a long tradition in which servants are clearly winding up their masters with ghost stories.[13] Another concerns a prophetic ghost, 'larger than human and more beautiful', embodying the spirit of Africa, who appears to a Roman nobody, Curtius Rufus, predicting his eventual governorship of her realm. The third, and longest, contains the first true modern ghost story.

In Athens, there was a 'large and roomy house' that had a 'bad reputation and an unhealthy air'. People who stayed there could hear the sound of chains, approaching as if from a distance. A phantom of an old man then appeared, 'an old man, emaciated and filthy, with a long beard and unkempt hair', shackles on his legs and chains on his wrists. He liked to shake his wrists; he liked to make a noise. Inhabitants of the house grew ill from lack of sleep; some even sickened and died. Even when the phantom was nowhere near, he preyed on their minds. Finally, the house was put on the market and left empty.

Athenodorus, writes Pliny, 'read the advertisement, and when he heard the low price, he was suspicious and made some enquiries'. Far from being deterred by the story of the ghost, he decided to investigate it himself. One evening, he set himself up with his books and writing equipment, ready for a few hours of study, and sent his servants to the 'back of the house' (rather than giving them the night off, as is usual in later, similar tales).

He made the decision to study, 'lest his unoccupied mind produce foolish fears'; so we have this scenario of a scholar working in a library waiting for the ghost to arrive. It's an image that would be familiar to M. R. James or Sheridan Le Fanu: a scholar or clergyman absorbed in his writing as the candle flickers and the shadows rise around.

At first, all was silent, and then the sound of the chains was heard, from a distance, and then approaching. As the din grew louder, Pliny is keen to emphasize, the philosopher made a point of ignoring it. 'The din grew even louder: and now it was heard at the threshold – now it was inside the room with him!' Athenodorus turns to look at the ghost and, unfazed, returns to his work. The ghost beckons. The philosopher makes a dismissive gesture, telling him to wait. The ghost, outraged, moves closer and rattles his chains above the head of the philosopher. Turning again, Athenodorus looks at the ghost and sees him still gesturing.

With an air of irritation, he rises, takes the lamp and follows the ghost, who makes a painfully slow progress to the courtyard of the house, where he vanishes. Athenodorus marks the spot with 'some grass and leaves'. In the morning, he fetches a magistrate, who orders a hole to be dug in the courtyard – and, of course, a human skeleton is found, complete with corroded chains. 'These bones were gathered and given a public burial. After these rites had been performed, the house was no longer troubled by spirits.'

The haunting of a house because of a body – buried, usually, in the cellar – occurs again and again; we see it with the Fox sisters in nineteenth-century New York State, and the British Andover poltergeist of 1974, and in the events at Borley Rectory.

According to D. Felton in *Ghost Stories from Classical Antiquity*, 'ghosts bearing chains do not appear elsewhere in the surviving literature from Greece and Rome,' and yet the idea has been up there with ghosts in sheets as the proper form for them to take until very recent times. In the eighteenth century, the dragging of chains was considered a most unlikely thing for a free Englishman to do. The antiquarian Francis Grose (1731–79) wrote, 'Dragging chains is not the fashion of English ghosts; chains and black vestments being chiefly the accoutrements of foreign spectres, seen in arbitrary governments; dead or alive, English spirits are free.'

Marley's ghost in Dickens' *A Christmas Carol* has a very long and elaborate chain, and when Scrooge first hears it he remembers that 'ghosts in haunted houses were described as dragging chains'. As in the Pliny original, Scrooge hears the ghost from far away first approach the room and then enter it. Scrooge is at first sceptical, as was Athenodorus, putting his ghostly vision down to a poor digestion. Here the chains enrobing Marley are explicitly symbolic – linked to them are 'cashboxes, keys, padlocks, ledgers, deeds and heavy purses wrought in steel'. They are Marley's sclerotic miserliness, weighing him down in the afterlife. In Pliny, they help identify the ghost when the bones are dug up; there's some talk among folklorists about the ancient use of iron to 'bind' spirits, that Pliny's ghost had been bound, maybe after death, to stay his restlessness.

Oscar Wilde also had his take on it, in his comedic fable *The Canterville Ghost*. The American Mr Otis has gone to bed in his creaking old British house. He's awoken by the clank of metal. He lights a match and looks at the time: one o'clock. He feels his pulse: he is not at all feverish. The strange noise continues. He gets out of bed and puts on his slippers. From out of a dressing-case he takes a small phial. He goes to the bedroom door and opens it. In the dark corridor, there is the ghost – his eyes red as burning coals, long, grey, matted hair falling over his shoulders, his garments antique, soiled and ragged, and from his wrists and ankles hang 'heavy manacles and rusted gyves'.

Then comes the joke:

'My dear Sir,' said Mr Otis. 'I really must insist on your oiling those chains, and have brought you for that purpose a small bottle of Tamany Rising Sun Lubricator . . . I shall leave it here for you by the bedroom candles, and will be happy to supply you with more should you require it.' With these words the United States Minister laid the bottle down on the marble table, and, closing his door, retired to rest.

Reason, sense and modern life lay the spirit to rest.

The Ritual of the Ghost Story

Every now and again the query haunts me: are there here and there
sequestered places which some curious creatures still frequent, whom
once upon a time anyone could see and speak to as they went about
on their daily occasions . . .?

– M. R. James

Much has been written about the house party at the Villa Diodati
in 1816, but what is less well known is that house party's meteoro-
logical connection with Charles Dickens. In that 'year without a
summer', Byron and the Shelley entourage retreated from the
foul weather with the reading of some ghost stories from a Leipzig publisher. The rain fell like drops of lead outside on Lake
Geneva and the June temperatures plummeted, bringing the
prospect of universal crop failure. We now know that the atmosphere had been plunged into a chaos as a result of a vast volcanic
eruption in the remote Dutch East Indies.

In 1815, Mount Tambora had become active. An 800-megaton
explosion took place, funnelling particulates and sulphur com-
pounds into the troposphere in one of the largest volcanic events
of the last two thousand years.[1] The effects were to last decades,
framing most of Dickens' childhood. Thus the whole iconography of snowy greetings cards comes from an atypical Regency
weather event; its trigger, a naturally occurring nuclear winter,
the eruption of a volcano that set loose the first literary vampire
story ('The Vampyr', 1819) and Frankenstein's monster in the air
drifting west from tropical Sumbawa.

In 1588, Noël Taillepied wrote, in his *Treatise on Ghosts*, an angry denunciation of the then recent Protestant denial of Catholic Purgatory: 'all those writers who have drunk of the muddy and stinking waters of Lake Geneva incline absolutely to deny apparitions and ghosts . . . you will continually find it stated in the books of these heretics and ignorant ethnic bigots that the spirits of the dead cannot and do not appear.' The waters, it seemed, were never far away from the issue of ghost-belief in Europe. But it was Protestant writers who took the extremities of Catholicism and turned it into fiction: the modern ghost story arose from Lake Geneva.

The gothic novel, which arrived almost in tandem with the Catholic Relief Act of 1778, was a literary genre written largely by gay men and asthmatic women. *The Castle of Otranto* (1764) was a phantasm composed by Horace Walpole, who was at once the son of the prime minister and the man who went hotfoot to experience the Cock Lane ghost for himself. The novel purported to be a rediscovered ancient manuscript concerning an 'ancient Catholic family', with supernatural events including a portrait that comes to life.[2] As with the vastly richer and equally feline William Beckford in *Vathek* (1786), he wrote heraldic stories to populate an architectural fantasy.

The novels of the reclusive Mrs Radcliffe (1764–1823)[3] – including *The Mysteries of Udolpho* – were popular, though M. R. James deplored the 'exasperating timidity' in which all her ghostly events were eventually explained away. The wealthy son of a Jamaican slave-owner, like Beckford, M. G. Lewis (1775–1818) wrote the bestseller *The Monk* (1796), an adaptation of which also became a big hit on the London stage. With its lurid sense of horror and homoerotic charge festering in the cloisters, M. R. James was greatly fearful of it, describing it as being 'odious and horrible without being impressive'. But the key thing about *The Monk* is the way in which it incorporates the influence of German literature. (Lewis was fluent in the language and travelled there, meeting Schiller and Goethe.)

It was a book of German short stories, *Das Gespensterbuch*, that was being read at the Villa Diodati, and the Teutonic influence was to reach its apogee in British culture only a few decades later when Catherine Crowe's two-volume *The Night Side of Nature* (1848) was to be found on nearly every bookshelf in the land. She was a fluent German speaker, and the book is suffused with a Germanic sensibility and folkloric style.

Many writers[4] have argued that a deep strand of Roman Catholic tradition ran just below the surface of English culture for hundreds of years – despite a state religion and an officialdom which is quite clearly Protestant. For centuries, establishment figures bemoaned the continuing essential Catholicism of the working classes, especially on the subject of ghosts.

Many believed that only a Catholic priest could exorcise a ghost[5] – Protestant efforts to dispel troublesome spirits tended to involve the long and tortuous singing of psalms rather than any formal ceremony, and a banishment of the demon, for demon it must be. Even in modern cases this seems to be the rule – in the 1940s story on which *The Exorcist* was based, the Lutheran priests failed to control the demon and the Catholics had to be sent for. The ringing of church bells on Halloween is a hangover from Catholicism that continued for many years into the Protestant orthodoxy, to the fury of those in governance.

It is hardly a surprise that the process saw the decriminalization of Roman Catholicism in the United Kingdom; important first steps were a Canadian Act of 1774 and the Relief Acts of 1778 and 1782. The acquisition of Quebec as an English territory in 1763 brought a large, new Catholic population under the rule of the Crown, and it is only a year after that that we get our first Gothic novel, by Horace Walpole. The acts granted Catholics the right to have their own schools and bishops; reaction to this slowly evolving legislation was violent, erupting in disorder in Scotland in 1779 and the London Gordon Riots of 1780, for example. Given that the publication date of *The Monk* is 1796, although the novel is notable for its Germanic elements, is can also be read as an exploitation tale pandering to a British fear of resurgent European Catholicism – the idea of a monk undone by carnal desires and selling his soul to the Devil. Its sinister nuns herald their return to British soil, at least in spectral form; such figures are still being seen a hundred years later in Borley Rectory, for instance, and The Lanes in Brighton.

The novel was also popular in Dublin, where it quickly went through several editions, and many of its elements were picked up in *Melmoth the Wanderer* (1820) by Charles Maturin. Maturin, a Protestant clergyman of French Huguenot descent, found his advancement as a clergyman damaged by the notoriety of the novel, which concerns a scholar who sells his soul to the Devil.

But it was the son of another Protestant Huguenot cleric, Sheridan Le Fanu (1814–73), who was to have a defining effect on the English ghost story, if nothing else for the impression he made on a young M. R. James reading his work as a boy in his father's rectory at Livermere in Suffolk. In Le Fanu's stories, the dead are a malignancy never far away, through a membrane of perception so thin it can be pierced by even a mild intoxicant such as the eponymous green tea of one story; his tales tell of necrophilia (*Schalken the Painter*) and lesbianism (*Carmilla*). More or less penniless, living a life circumscribed by writing for magazines and with a sickly, neurasthenic wife, he can perhaps be seen as Ireland's Edgar Allen Poe.

Unlike his genre forebears and descendants, M. R. (Monty) James was a serious-minded academic – he was one of the greatest manuscript scholars of his age and an expert on the Apocrypha. A clever and bookish boy, he received a scholarship to Eton, went on to King's College, Cambridge, where he became dean and provost, before ending up back at Eton, where he stayed until he died, again as provost. The cloisters claimed him at an early age.

The ritual of his ghost stories at King's[6] on Christmas Eve have become part of the fabric of a British Christmas. From 1903 onwards,

11. An owlish portrait of M. R. James circa 1900. James's tales had a
knack of taking recognisable places and everyday experiences and
weaving them into the fabric of his ghost stories. Because they
felt credible, they became unforgettable.

it would take the form of afternoon tea with the choristers, fol-
lowed by the service in the chapel and dinner in the Hall; then
Monty and friends might spend an hour or so in the 'Combination
Room' (the common room for senior members of the college),
where a game of cards might be played, before an adjournment to
Monty's rooms. Oliffe Richmond describes a typical reading:

> We sat and waited in the candlelight, perhaps someone played a
> few bars at the piano, and desisted, for good reason . . . Monty
> emerged from the bedroom, manuscript in hand at last, and blew
> out all the candles but one. He then began to read, with more con-
> fidence than anyone else could have mustered, his well-nigh
> illegible script in the dim light.

In a piece of writing published after his death, 'A Vignette', James recalls a childhood experience of reading a Le Fanu story. He was upstairs in his room in the Suffolk rectory.

> The words were quite enough to set my own fancy on a bleak track. Inevitably I looked and with apprehension, to the Plantation Gate. As was but right it was shut, and nobody was on the path that led to it or from it . . . there was in it a square hole giving access to the fastening; and through that hole I could see – and it struck me like a blow on the diaphragm – something white or partly white. Now this I could not bear, and with an access of something like courage – only it was more like desperation, like determining that I must know the worst – I did steal down and, quite uselessly, of course, taking cover behind bushes as I went, I made progress until I was within range of the gate and hole. Things were, alas! worse than I had feared. Through that hole a face was looking my way. It was not monstrous, not pale, fleshless, spectral. Malevolent I thought and think it was; at any rate the eyes were large and open and fixed. It was pink and, I thought, hot, and just above the eyes the border of a white linen drapery hung down from the brows . . . Do not press me with questions as to how I bore myself when it became necessary to face my family again.

For many years, M. R. James's best-known story was 'The Casting of the Runes', about a man who is the subject of a curse from an occultist. It was the basis of one of the best British films from the 1950s, *Night of the Demon*, and was most recently incarnated in the Japanese J-horror *Ringu* (which, by the by, also appears to reference *School Story* and *The Wailing Well*, about demons that come out of wells to grab people; *The Mezzotint* and *The Haunted Dolls' House*, in their reanimated record of a supernatural crime; and *The Diary of Mr Poynter*, in which a face covered by hair is the pursuant ghost). But 'O Whistle and I'll Come to You, My Lad' is James's masterpiece. It was published in his first volume of stories in 1904,

Ghost Stories of an Antiquary, only two years after his real-life discovery of an ecclesiastical manuscript led to excavations in the abbey of Bury St Edmunds, where the lost graves of several abbots were found.

It proceeds as follows. A stuffy bachelor academic comes to stay in a seaside town; his name is Professor Parkin and he seems keen to play some golf on the links. But while walking on the windblown and largely deserted East Anglian beach, he seeks out the overgrown site of an old Templar preceptory, where he picks up a metal whistle sticking out from the ground with the Latin inscription '*Quis est iste qui venit?*'[7] It's a rare use by M. R. James of Latin as a pivotal plot point, and a wonderful pedagogic caution to study hard in your lessons or else be grabbed by a ghoul; this academic is an 'ontography' specialist, a word specially invented by M. R. James for this story but now an accepted term for the relationship between a landscape and those organisms which live on it. Parkin is rusty in his Latin, he admits, but thinks the inscription translates as '*Who is this who is coming?*'

The whistle has a strange and mysterious timbre. A Latin scholar would know that *iste* was a pejorative term, that whoever was coming is unpleasant or, indeed, not exactly human. It should be translated as '*What is this revolting thing coming towards me?*'[8]

This story introduces the archetypal protagonist of such stories, the somewhat self-absorbed and sceptical scholar who comes face to face with the supernatural. And the scholar's fall from reason is vivid, as, despite having been warned specifically about the whistle's Roman Catholic provenance by his golfing partner, a colonel, he blows it and in so doing disturbs an entity whose doglike devotion is most unwelcome.

Anyone who has spent a night in a hotel with an unused single bed beside them will know the power of such an imaginative idea, of a figure that rises up in the bed at night, with an 'intensely horrible face of crumpled linen'; in M. R. James's case, a direct recall of the face surrounded by linen that gazed on him as a boy at the Livermere rectory.

Indeed, a passing local boy in the story is terrified by the ghost waving at him from a window in broad daylight.[9] We know James wrote letters from the Red Lion Hotel at Wareham and the County Hotel at Canterbury, but perhaps it was his sojourn at the White Lion at Aldeburgh that most suggested this story to him. Otherwise, the golf-playing, slightly effete fusspot Professor Parkin is most definitely not the self-portrait some have suggested: it is a study of the half-educated.

Had he been a proper Latin scholar, he never would have blown the whistle.

As the classic tolling of the bell both at noon and at midnight was a token of the arrival of the ghostly, so was M. R. James equally attentive to both midsummer and midwinter.

In a letter[10] of 25 July 1927, he mentions: 'Tomorrow it is proposed that the Lower Master takes me by car to Worbarrow Bay in Dorset where the Scouts are in camp – it is further proposed that by the camp fire I should read them a story of a terrible nature, which I have made – contrary to my expectation.'

Worbarrow Bay is on what is now called the Jurassic coast, where Dorset meets the sea on the Isle of Purbeck. It is an isolated, numinous place in the Tyneham valley, a photograph of which was published on a half-page of *The Times* two summers later in August 1929 as a perfect example of unspoilt England. It depicts a horse-drawn harvester working against a silver sea, on land that gave up the rocks and stones that dressed most of the churches of London.

'Wailing Well' is a highly personal and unusual story for James, because he is a character in it, at least at the beginning, and the first few pages are full of humorous flourishes designed to appeal both to schoolboys of the period and these Etonians in particular. To get to the beach and the cliffs nearby where the scouts appear to have made camp, on land belonging to the Bond family (who had been there since 1683, mostly in the Elizabethan manor house), James would have been driven up past the Flowers Barrow Iron Age fort and down into the valley in time for tea.

It seems likely that James drew his inspiration from the maps issued to the boys, which had, marked in red, areas in which they were not to stray, for whatever reason. So he describes these maps in the story and weaves a tale out of them, portraying the boys lying on the hillside one balmy summer afternoon and noting that one area of forbidden woodland is of particular interest. One boy becomes intrigued by a clump of fir trees in the valley below. Though it is clearly within the red-ringed area designated out of bounds, and a local shepherd, purveyor of local lore, warns them off it, the boy goes anyway. From the distance, his friends watch in horror as he is first stalked then pounced on by two skeletal figures.

> Stanley struck with his can, the only weapon he had. The rim of a broken black hat fell off the creature's head and showed a white skull with stains that might be wisps of hair. By this time one of the women had reached the pair, and was pulling at the rope that was coiled about Stanley's neck. Between them they overpowered him in a moment: the awful screaming ceased, and then the three passed within the circle of the clump of firs.

The boys would not have known this, but the detail of the skull with the wisps of hair on it was taken from James's own experience.

In November 1909, when the tomb of Henry VI, the founder of Eton and King's, was opened in Windsor Castle, James was invited in his capacity as Provost. He had revived the tradition of Founder's Day at Eton on 6 December soon after his arrival there as provost. One of his duties was to record and help rebury the remains of the king, and James wrapped up the bones in a new white silk shroud before they were reinterred. To one of the pieces of skull, we learn, there was hair attached, brown in colour, except in one place, where it seemed matted with blood.

James concluded the story with more than customary relish, and a wink at his audience. Now, he said, the skeletons at the clump of trees, the clatter of their bones and the wailings heard at dusk at midwinter, were joined, when next observed, by another. According to James's obituary in the *Eton College Chronicle* (July 1936), we find that 'the scene of the story was quite close to Camp . . . with the result that several boys had a somewhat disturbed night.' The landscape has barely changed since that day, and the clump of trees may well be Rooks Grove, or the Withy Bed (out of bounds, and reachable only across some marshy ground) to the side of Balkington Farm. The whole area still remains out of bounds.

In 1943, the whole parish was requisitioned by the army. Rehearsals for D-Day are said to have been practised in the bay. On 19 December, the Bond family and all the villagers left. The Bonds were never to spend another Christmas in their ancestral home.[11] On her way out of the village, Mrs Bond stopped to pin a note to the church door: 'Please treat the church and houses with care. We have given up our homes, where many of us have lived for generations, to help win the war to keep men free. We shall return one day and thank you for treating the village kindly.' A Home Office committee in 1948 decided to keep the area under army control. Tyneham House was demolished in the 1960s; during the war it had been lived in by the women of the WAAF.

Now the whole area is an artillery range and tank park owned by the Ministry of Defence, and off limits during the week. (The valley and beautiful pebble-heaped bay is just down from the haunted landscape of Chesil Beach.) The village is called a 'ghost village' in most of the literature. In the schoolhouse, the names of the children remain beneath the coat pegs.

And the artillery range? One March morning in 1967, two 14-year-old boys from Stoborough, near Wareham, were killed by tank fire when they strayed on to the East Holme range. It is now delineated on the maps with red lines similar to those described by James as surrounding the 'Wailing Well', and, it goes without saying, you would be well advised not to venture within them.

Miss Fanny's New Theatre

But if a form should appear, and a voice tell me that a particular man had died at a particular place, and a particular hour, a fact which I had no apprehension of, nor any means of knowing, and this fact, with all its circumstances, should afterwards be unquestionably proved, I should, in that case, be persuaded that I had supernatural intelligence imparted to me.

– Dr Johnson

Late January, 1762. A media circus, the first one. On the wind is news of England's latest war with Spain, and a tempest, the worst in twenty years, roars across London. Boats on the Thames are smashed to smithereens, roofs lift from walls, rain drives down the narrow gully of a street behind St Sepulchre's.

In a number of well-publicized séances, the ghost of a dead woman is tapping out accusations of murder against her surviving husband. Drawn by the scandal of it, the *haut ton* strain to hear supernatural gossip. The clergy presses for news of the afterlife. Outside, in Cock Lane and Hosier Lane, crowds gather, frightened, gin-soaked and restless. The newspapers are warring, stealing writers from each other, running exclusives, deploying an early form of cheque-book journalism by paying for stories and poaching star writers from other publications. The artists are scratching out their satiric etchings, meticulously detailed, mocking the credulous, through candle-soot; the street-hawkers are selling doggerel. All is hubbub, all is noise. En route to the 'reigning fashion',[1] Horace Walpole quips that the ghost is an 'audition' rather than an 'apparition', because the ghost makes sounds and never deigns to materialize. It was as if the Cock Lane ghost was a monstrously amplified manifestation of eighteenth-century slander, drunkenness and delusion.

The lane is quiet now, a forgotten conduit in a busy part of London, too insignificant to be covered by Google Earth, still dark, and with a steep slope on the west side down to what used to be the shores of the Fleet River. The house itself was demolished in the sixties. North is the historic Smithfield Market, and to the south the Old Bailey marks the spot of Newgate Prison. As soon as you turn into Cock Lane, it feels as if you are falling into the crack of an ossuary.

Below, as excavations in the nineties have shown, lie ancient conduits from Smithfield Market, Roman inhumations, bones of domesticated animals, the debris of affiliated butchery trades, shreds of leather and leather shoes. The soil is still nitrate-rich from cattle blood and scattered with the dead seeds of plants, such as celery-leafed crowfoot, which grew by the gutters of the shambles. At the east end is St Bartholomew's Hospital, which is said to be haunted by its founder, Rahere, a twelfth-century travelling entertainer who turned to God, still occasionally glimpsed by sleepless cancer patients in Rahere ward.

In 1759, an apparently respectable couple took lodgings with the working-class Parsons family in Cock Lane, just outside the old walls of the City of London. William Kent and Fanny Lynes had a secret: they were living in sin. Both were impulsive and reckless, both from middle-class mercantile families in Norfolk. Fanny had eloped to be with Kent.

Kent had inherited a bit of money and had bought a house in Clerkenwell, but the renovations were dragging on. Some days earlier, they had been evicted from their lodgings after Kent had quarrelled with the landlord; now Fanny was pregnant, and they were facing a crisis over where to stay. They happened to talk with amiable parish clerk[2] Richard Parsons as he showed them to a pew at St Sepulchre-without-Newgate one Sunday morning and, within days, they had moved into the cramped, low house at what was to become 21 Cock Lane.

Kent, in a rush of gratitude, lent his landlord a sum of money. The haunting began in the very month this loan became due, and it was the default on it, and the threat of blackmail, that led, eventually, to a lawsuit.

Richard Parsons was a type – not an especially bad man, but a man who drank too much and was subsequently always short of money. He was married with two daughters, one of whom, Betty, was to become the star of Miss Fanny's New Theatre, as one satirical pamphlet was to dub the Cock Lane ghost.

Cock Lane wasn't a restful place. The smells and the sounds of Smithfield, then the largest cattle, poultry and swine market in Great Britain, were ever-present, and on Tuesdays and Fridays drovers would bring hundreds of animals into town from the outskirts of London, sometimes taking a wrong turn down Cock Lane. In *Oliver Twist*, we read that Smithfield is thronged with 'unwashed, unshaven, squalid and dirty figures', and in *Great Expectations* Pip feels sullied by his proximity to it – 'the shameful place, being all asmear with filth and fat and blood and foam, seemed to stick to me.'

The groans and din of Newgate, the expiration of the sick and wounded in St Bartholomew's (a matron from there was to host one of the public events held at which the ghost was questioned and the knocks interpreted), the spurt and slaughter of Smithfield, the tocsin for the condemned at St Sepulchre's . . . The aural and sensory effluvia must have been overwhelming.

The pub at the end of Cock Lane, the Wheat Sheaf, was Parsons' local. It seems he was there a great deal. Looking at all the evidence centuries on, it's pretty clear that the Cock Lane ghost was a pub joke that grew out of control, a boozy prank that grew exponentially in the year that followed. Alcohol plays a very big part in this story; this is the London of Hogarth's Gin Lane, in which a whole generation of Londoners were suddenly and permanently drunk on cheap distillations. Parsons was drunk. The mob out-side his door was drunk. The séances, it seems fairly clear, were drunken sport, boisterous shadow-plays, with the Parsons family relishing their roles at the centre of a phantasmagorical soap opera.

After moving into Parsons' house, Kent often left Fanny, alone and unhappy, in Cock Lane while he went off on business. It's on one of these occasions that the ghost of Cock Lane was first heard. Feeling miserable on her own at night, Fanny had asked Betty Parsons, then aged about twelve, to keep her company in the first-floor bedroom. Fanny Lynes was delicate, a passionate thing whose letters to Kent, whom she had helped through the death of his wife – her sister – and then the death of his two-month-old son, nevertheless betray obsessive tendencies.

Soon Fanny was disturbed by knocks and scratches. We shall never really know why Betty Parsons began to make these noises, but they were almost certainly attention-seeking. Her wee-small-hours petitions to Richard Parsons seem to betray the roiling projections of a feverish, over-active sensibility. There's no evidence that she was unhinged – indeed, considering the pressure she was under much later in the year, she seems quite level-headed.

Richard Parsons at first acted pretty much as anyone would under the circumstances. He investigated the noises rationally, searching out both the presence of rats in the wainscoting and the tapping of his cobbler neighbour. But Fanny wouldn't have any of it. Why would the cobbler be working on a Sunday? This initial haunting, which Fanny believed was by her dead sister Elizabeth, come back to upbraid her for running off with her husband, lasted several weeks. Whether the ghost was still active when William Kent finally lost patience with Parsons, in January 1760, is not clear, but lose patience he did, as the first payment on his 12-guinea loan fell three months overdue. Parsons declared he had no intention of paying Kent the money; indeed, if he persisted in asking for it, he would expose the situation between Kent and Fanny. Under canon law, because Kent had had a child with her sister, he could not marry Fanny. Their own child would be illegitimate.

The unceremonious ejection of William and Fanny onto the cobbled street at Cock Lane with their clothes and personal belongings proved a catastrophe for Fanny, who promptly caught smallpox and died just a few weeks later. From what little information we have about her, it is clear that Betty Parsons had formed an attachment to Fanny. Everything that happened subsequently can be laid at the door of this attachment, especially her infantile anger at Kent, whose behaviour had taken Fanny away from her. All she had left of Fanny was the knocking of her dead sister Elizabeth and, eventually, in a strange case of emotional morphology, Fanny's voice calling for justice.

For most of 1760, the ghost remained identified as Elizabeth. Fanny was dying not far away. Parsons was up to mischief, deciding to play a prank on the superstitious landlord at the Wheat Sheaf. James Franzen was abnormally, pathologically fearful in the presence of what he thought were spirits – indeed, at the later trial, he remained paralysed with fear just at the recollection of his experiences, even as the fraud was being exposed before his very eyes.

One evening, Parsons persuaded Franzen to come round to 21 Cock Lane. When Franzen was installed in the kitchen, Mrs Parsons having told him her husband was out, the clerk of the parish ran up the stairs covered in a sheet. Betty's involvement in this practical joke – physically preventing Franzen from following the ghost – and Mrs Parsons' pretence that her husband was not in the house, proves, if nothing else, that the family were happy to ginger up the story. Profoundly agitated and genuinely frightened, the phasmophobic Franzen left in a great hurry. Only minutes later, Parsons burst into the Wheat Sheaf kitchen, to which the ashen-faced Franzen had retreated. His demand for a large brandy, as he too had witnessed the ghost, makes it pretty clear what he wanted to get out of it. A drop of free booze would do the trick very nicely.

On 2 February 1760 Fanny Lynes died painfully and unpleasantly, and for the rest of the year the knockings and scratchings at 21 Cock Lane persisted, often with great violence and intensity. At this time, Betty began to suffer convulsive fits. It's an incidental detail, but an important one. It seems plausible that Fanny's death had deeply unsettled her. She was close to her father, but she must have known that it was her father's ejection of Fanny from Cock Lane that had led to her early death.

A new lodger was driven out by the disturbances, and a neighbour also complained. Parsons had a carpenter round to tear out the wainscoting, which suggests he still had no idea who or what was behind the noises. Time passed. The ghost became well known in the locality, the story no doubt fuelled by Franzen, who probably bent the ear of every drinker who came into the Wheat Sheaf. Then there was a long lull.

Why did the ghost kick up again? It was now almost two years after Fanny and William had left Cock Lane. The ghost had carried on for a while without them, and then faded away. All fingers point again to the profound and abiding agitation of Betty, now a teenager. The teenaged girl is a persistent trope in any 'poltergeist' case of note, and puberty and guilt are a powerful combination. Perhaps the answer to the resurgence of rappings lies in a piece of information learned by the Parsons family in early November 1761. They discovered that William Kent had remarried and that Fanny's brother was also suing him over a financial matter. The antipathy towards him was suddenly stoked up again.

When the Parsons family discovered these new details, which, for some reason, agitated them, reinforcing their dim view of the man, the noises returned. Franzen, on a visit to the haunted house, was informed by the Parsonses that the ghost was actually Fanny, and not Elizabeth at all. The family, perceiving some complicated slight, and following the dictum that we never forgive the people we wrong, had found the opportunity to do Kent

12. The former bedroom where the ghostly Cock Lane 'auditions' took place, painted many years later.

some damage, albeit in an incoherent and unplanned way. What were the loud noises heard by the students at the charity school opposite? Were they perhaps the conscious crashes and blows of a young girl who believed her friend had been deserted in death by her detestable husband, or were they the terrible motorized thrashings of an epileptic fit?

The noises were now being noticed by a new class of person. The Revd John Moore gave sermons at St Sepulchre's and would have known Richard Parsons, although only as a servant. Moore had connections with the church charity school in Cock Lane and, when he heard about the ghost in the house opposite, he was immediately seized by great curiosity. He visited 21 Cock Lane and asked the family about the ghost. It was at around this point that Parsons expounded his theory – that Fanny Lynes had been poisoned by her husband, and her ghost had returned to earth, seeking revenge. Never mind that she hadn't died at Cock Lane. Betty was her intermediary.

This piece of information electrified the 'Ordinary of New-gate' (Horace Walpole's description of Moore was a rapier-sharp witticism – the real Ordinary of Newgate was one Stephen Roe, and *The Ordinary of Newgate's Accounts*,[3] with its lurid record of criminal confessions, was a bestseller every year). It didn't take long for Moore to lose all sense of proportion and self-preservation. There were specific cultural reasons why he appears to have been quite so credulous. Moore was, despite his appointment as a vis-iting rector to one of the oldest churches in London, something of a modern thinker. He tended towards the newly minted reli-gion of Methodism.

The orderly ranks of the ordained were nothing if not scep-tical of this new way of thinking, and there was, among the great and the good, some disdain towards their tendency to suck up to the rabble. But the most curious thing about Methodism in this period was its utter conviction as to the reality of the super-natural, a character trait of its founder, John Wesley, and his childhood poltergeist experiences.[4]

Any clergyman who could prove beyond doubt that the dead were an active force surviving and observing the living, agitating for justice, would have become a star in the firmament of Meth-odism. Although there's no evidence in his actions that Moore was a vainglorious man, he must have been aware of the glorious prize which, potentially, awaited him. His decision, after one séance, to have faith in the truthfulness of the Parsons family, and to accept that the shade of Fanny Lynes really was accusing her husband of murdering her with a poisoned drink, was to be his ruin and lead to his early death. It was a monumental act of folly by an educated man. The Cock Lane ghost affair seems to have tainted everyone who touched it; it was a malignant creature.

Some accounts[5] maintain that Parsons approached Moore about the ghost, but the most recent and plausible analysis[6] puts the situation the other way round. It's a vital distinction; the Parsons family were involved in their own little psychodrama with their neighbours and friends and did not actively mean for their parish joke to go city-wide, let alone nationwide. Alarm bells should have started ringing when Moore found that Richard Parsons was, shortly after Christmas, already charging an entrance fee to the séances.

In the first of a series of miscalculations (quite rightly reasoning that an up-front viewing fee would throw immediate doubt on the veracity of events), Moore offered Parsons a stipend from both St Sepulchre and a separate Methodist bank account; he was later to offer him the possibility of a much better-paid position in the Methodist Tabernacle off Cambridge Circus. Moore was now in deep with the Parsonses. He was to regret it, later on. What did Moore find so persuasive? All the accounts of the séances paint a similar picture. Betty and her sister, Anne, were put together in a bed; a single tallow candle was lit at one end, and the room was dark and shadowy. Their parents sat nearby. Those who were invited as guests – usually up to twenty people – traipsed upstairs to sit around the bed, which was usually in the centre of the room. These séances began at about ten o'clock and would often last all night. To begin with, a family friend, Mary Frazer, a well-known local troublemaker, acted as master of ceremonies, behaving much as a prototype medium in this 'pantomime', as Walpole called it.

Various scratching noises were produced, on one occasion described as sounding like a cat fossicking a cane chair, as well as knocks, thuds and raps. Moore was much taken with what he thought was the sound of fluttering wings. At the séance which took place on 5 January 1762, Moore, with all the spiritual authority he could muster, introduced himself. A question and answer system was developed: one knock for yes, two for no. The details of this séance tend to be overlooked, but something very significant happened in it, and it happened with a silence. While Moore was interviewing the spirit, he asked, 'Are you returned for a purpose?' and there was one knock. 'In life,' continued Moore, 'were you harmed by someone?' There was another single knock. 'Were you murdered?' And there was silence.

When Betty was examined under controlled circumstances in a house in Covent Garden about six weeks later, the fraud was exposed. She had been creating noises both on the side of the bed and by beating her chest; her hands and fists were calloused. When she was restrained, the noises didn't come. Eventually, she was caught red-handed with a piece of wood which she had been using under the bedclothes to create the unearthly messages. Despite all this, it's generally thought that the whole family was involved in the production of the noises. Up to that point, all the scratches and knocks had been clearly localized around the bed where Betty and Anne lay.

Yes, knocks Betty, Fanny was harmed by someone. But when Moore asks Fanny whether she was murdered by William, Betty cannot bring herself to knock out either yes or no. Considering what comes later, the question goes mysteriously unanswered. Moore, flustered by the silence – as was Richard Parsons, one supposes – asks another question: 'Were you poisoned?' At this point, witnesses to the event notice that the knocking moves from the bed, and there are at least thirty-one knocks around the room.

Richard Parsons was really quite brazen in his aims, something that becomes clear at the séances in the following weeks. His new income allowed him to spend even more on drink. When William Kent attended one of these sessions, to see at first hand whether his dead wife really had returned, there is again a hesitation at the question 'Has any injury been done to any person that lived in this house?' and another pause before the single rapped reply to the question 'Is your murderer in this room?' At this point, Parsons, seated across at the other side of the room, violently interjects. 'Kent!' he bellows. 'Ask the ghost if you shall be hanged.'

After Moore published two pieces about his séance at Cock Lane in a new newspaper called the *Public Ledger* (an interesting choice – it was pitched towards the rising mercantile middle classes), Kent immediately went about recruiting allies – the apothecary and doctor who had treated Fanny on her deathbed, and the man who buried her in Clerkenwell, the Revd Stephen Aldrich. Aldrich was to prove Parsons' most implacable foe and the man who brought him down, mainly, at the will of the Lord Mayor of London, by creating a committee to examine the Cock Lane ghost (this committee consisted of a host of worthies, which included Dr Johnson). It was a measure of the seriousness of the charges that Kent even found himself opening Fanny's coffin and gazing on her decomposed remains as part of the process of proving his innocence.

It was Moore, not Parsons, who was the architect of the Cock Lane ghost. If he had not written about it or incentivized Parsons' dishonesty, the story would never have gone past the level of a joke designed to disturb a local publican. It's also very clear that doubts about the authenticity of the ghost were expressed very early on, and during the séances, and that it was Moore who dived in to defend the family on at least two occasions: he acted to stop a hostile witness leaving during a séance, and he reinterpreted the ghost's desires when it agreed to appear in Aldrich's house, on both occasions trying to limit the ghost's exposure as a fraud. It was Moore who asked the mayor to arrest Kent, and he who invited peers and celebrities to attend the séances. Parsons was mortified at the way the over-serious clergyman kept inviting famous people to Cock Lane; he must have known that the detection of the fraud would be accelerated.

The Cock Lane ghost appeared in a total of seven locations (only two in Cock Lane) and was witnessed by a great many people – conservatively, well over two hundred, if there were between twenty and fifty people at each of the almost nightly séances in January 1762. Hundreds more massed in the streets nearby – a boon, observes Walpole sweetly, for the publicans and pie-shops. Both Kent and Aldrich on several occasions had problems getting to the front door, wading through a morass of the gawping and the credulous; Betty was also whisked from location to location (including two houses in nearby Hosier Lane and one in Crown and Cushion Court), in a fashion familiar to many a modern-day celebrity with the world camped outside the front door.

But it was in the media that the story really played out, especially when the writer Richard James became involved. James was a wealthy tradesman from Hosier Lane, and one of the five who eventually went to jail for the defamation of William Kent. On Friday 15 January 1762, his sensational account of Kent's first séance three days earlier set the world alight; the next day, local newspapers *The London Chronicle* and *St James's Chronicle* also began to run the story. By Monday 18th *Lloyd's Evening Post* was on the case too, and during the week the *Daily Gazette*, deploying a cash incentive, had poached Richard James to write for them. By Wednesday 20th January there was a national circulation war in full swing, with both the *Public Ledger* and the *Daily Gazette* headlining with the Cock Lane ghost. People all over the country read agog of the séance on Thursday 21st, when Fanny's sister Anne attended and was told by the ghost that Fanny's coffin should be examined. That morning, the Lynes family had orchestrated an attack on Kent in the *St James's Chronicle*.

The battle via the daily press continued throughout the following week, with Moore putting out what constitutes a modern press release: 'The fatigue undergone by Mr Parsons and his family has been such that he desires his house might be free from company for one night.' In other words, the Monday-night séance was cancelled, after three weeks of almost continuous all-night sessions. Monday was a significant day in the parish; it was the day on which St Sepulchre's rang a tocsin for any condemned prisoner about to be transported across London for execution at Tyburn. That press release was a death knell in itself; the establishment was massing against the feckless Parsons.

By the time Walpole arrived with the Duke of York at the

penultimate public séance on Saturday 30 May, there were already arguments underway there as to the degree of the fraud, and indeed Betty had been discovered faking sleep during an especially rowdy séance on Friday 22nd.

Saturday 23rd had seen a visit by all the major parties to the mayor's offices in Guildhall, and the first decisive intervention by the forces of law and order, when the mayor decreed that Betty should be removed from Cock Lane and examined by an impartial panel of witnesses. That morning, Aldrich had published a damning attack on the 'veracity of the knocker' in the *London Chronicle*. Later in the day, the evening séance didn't go well; Revd Aldrich, now emboldened, ordered a maidservant to lie across Betty's body in bed, to forestall trickery and, in consequence, no ghost was heard. The next day, Parsons did his best to stop Aldrich from taking his daughter away, but he must have known the game was up.

On Monday there was a press release from Moore and an attack from Aldrich in the *St James's Ledger*. On Tuesday Parsons hit back in the *Public Ledger*, and on Wednesday Aldrich delivered a further riposte in *Lloyd's Evening Post*. Why these dialogues jumped from paper to paper is unclear, but it probably has something to do with print deadlines. By 2 February, this battle had reached a new pitch, with Dr Johnson's report of the examination of Betty at Revd Aldrich's house in Clerkenwell rushed into the late editions to counter Parsons' pre-emptive attack in the *Public Ledger* that very morning.

In an extraordinary escalation, Parsons had an explanation for the committee's experiences on Monday night. The committee, in a thrilling development, had decamped to the crypt of St John's, Clerkenwell, after the knocking ghost claimed that it would rap from the actual coffin of Fanny Lynes. Parsons boldly accused the eight-strong committee – which included the Earl of Dartmouth,[7] as well as Aldrich and Dr Johnson – of stealing Fanny's body from her coffin. There was no other option to dispel the rumours but to open the coffin, on 25 January. The *St James's*

13. 'English Credulity or the Invisible Ghost': A contemporary cartoon
ridiculed the great and the good who had rushed to experience the
Cock Lane haunting for themselves.

Chronicle reported that it was an 'awful and shocking sight' and
expressed sympathy for Kent and the 'putrid object before him'.

By now there were signs of exasperation from the powers that
be, and an acknowledgement that this was shaping up to be a
major public-order problem. The affair of Elizabeth Canning,
who ten years earlier had claimed to have been abducted for a
month, was still fresh in people's minds. She had been seen in
Dorset during this period, and it was proved that she had made
the whole thing up. The mob did not accept the judge's guilty
verdict, however, and rioting ensued. By the first week of February 1762, the Bow Street Magistrate John Fielding was already
warning a Broad Street resident that their tales of a knocking
ghost – a new one – would lead directly to knocking out 'hemp in
Bridewell prison'.

'The mob' in general was something that struck fear into the men who ran London. Twenty years later, the Gordon Riots caused havoc and destruction throughout the Capital.[8] One German visitor described the mob in Ludgate Hill in 1770, after radical politician John Wilkes had been released from prison. 'Half-naked men and women, children, chimney sweeps, tinkers, Moors and men of letters, fish wives and elegant ladies, each creature intoxicated by his own whims and wild with joy, shouting and laughing.' And that was just when they were in a good mood.

By mid-February, it was the endgame for the Cock Lane ghost and the Parsons family. Other media were now making money out of the affair. The West End play *Apollo and Daphne* lampooned the ghost. From 12 February, young Betty was moved to the house of one Daniel Missiter, of whom very little is known, except for the fact that he was extremely diligent in breaking down the fraud.

Once the girl was removed from the locality, the spell was broken. Relentlessly, over eight nights, in a house in Covent Garden, Missiter subjected the girl to intense scrutiny and surveillance, at one point tying her up with her legs splayed. The ghost, inevitably, did not manifest itself.

From that moment, the main pressure was psychological. Missiter told Betty her father would go to jail unless the noises returned. Observed through a hole in the door, she was seen casting about the room until she found a wooden board by the fireplace, on which sat a kettle. She secreted it under the bedclothes. Knowing full well what she had done, Missiter allowed her to start making the scratching noises of Fanny's ghost before lunging forward and tearing off the bedsheets. On the theatre of the Cock Lane ghost, the curtain fell at last. A day later, the mayor issued warrants for the arrest of Moore, Parsons and his wife, Richard James and Mary Frazer. Kent had given Moore the opportunity for a public retraction, but, equivocal and confused, in denial that his great project had turned to ashes, he declined. The year he spent in jail so undermined his health that he was dead a few years later.

That March, Oliver Goldsmith published *The Mystery Revealed*. Weeks later, the poet Charles Churchill published 'The Ghost', and Hogarth reissued a modified print entitled *Credulity, Superstition and Fanaticism: a Medley*. At the top-right-hand corner, a mixture of a razor-sharpener and a door-knocker, there's the Cock Lane ghost; in the pulpit, decorated by well-known theatrical ghosts, including Caesar's, a preacher is deploying the puppets of the devil and a witch on a broomstick. The Revd Moore is being depicted not just as a patsy but at the heart of the illusion, pulling the strings for the theatre tricks.

Neither did poor Dr Johnson come out of all this well; he was ridiculed onstage in a play by one Samuel Foote, *The Orators*. (From May, there was a slew of related plays, including the broad comedy *The Farmer's Return from London*, in which a yokel regales his family with the tale of his attendance at the séance of a knocking ghost. David Garrick, the greatest actor of his day, performed the lead.) No matter that Johnson had been part of a committee that exposed the fraud; he had been prepared to believe it. Years later, when asked by Boswell, he refused to discuss the subject of the Cock Lane ghost.

On Saturday 10 July, after fifteen minutes' deliberation, the jury passed a guilty verdict on all parties. All five were remanded until they came up with enough money to satisfy Kent in the question of damages. In reality, this meant that three of them remained in jail until 13 February 1763, when James and Moore jointly managed to scrape together £300 plus £188 costs. Mary Frazer remained in jail for a further six months, and Elizabeth Parsons joined her, with an extra sentence of hard labour. Richard Parsons received another two years plus three stints in the pillories. On 16 March he was pilloried in Cock Lane. The local residents, instead of throwing bricks and rotten fruit at him, sent round a hat and raised a collection for his family.

Punishment was well on the way to becoming a feature of the

14. Hogarth's 'Credulity, Superstition and Fanaticism: a Medley.'

locality. Twenty years later, the condemned no longer had to journey the several miles from Newgate to Tyburn, and the scaffold was raised for executions just by St Sepulchre's, within spitting distance of where Parsons had been locked into a pillory. Dickens visited one of these hangings, in 1807, and this experience of the mob of Snow Hill, a site just yards from Cock Lane, contributed to a lifetime horror of ravening, murderous throngs of people. Some in that Dickensian crowd were surely present for the Cock Lane ghost.

All the people directly involved in the Cock Lane ghost affair faded from view soon after the case concluded. There were many William Kents in London, but it's possible that he is the individual who later ran a publishing business in Holborn. It seems he didn't live long; his widow remarried in 1785 in St Anne's Church, Soho. The Parsons family stayed together and pretty much continued where they left off. Moore died, aged just thirty-five, in 1768.

Two years after the conclusion of the affair, Horace Walpole published *The Castle of Otranto*. All supernatural-themed modern fiction comes from it, and it's hard not to think his interest in the supernatural, for all his droll asides, was piqued by the Cock Lane hoax.

One hundred years later, street vendors were still selling lurid pamphlets detailing the story, and many local people continued to believe the haunting had been genuine and that the authorities had protected their own. Betty was married twice but died young in the parish of Chiswick. She was only too happy to demonstrate to anyone who asked, with a series of well-judged raps and scratching noises, how she had fooled a nation for a few wild weeks all those years ago.

Bloodletting and the Brain Mirror

To see a ghost is, *ipso facto*, to be a subject for a physician.

– Charles Ollier, 1848

The diagnosis was violent giddiness.

The Berlin bookseller Friedrich Nicolai had a habit, and that habit was to attend a physician twice a year to be bled. The treatment was completely normal for the time – an Aristotelian adjustment of the bodily humours, opening a vein and bleeding a set amount of blood into a bowl. For whatever reason, Nicolai failed to attend his regular appointment late in 1790, and that missed doctor's appointment was to have far-reaching consequences.

Some years later, in 1799, Nicolai stood before the Royal Society of Berlin and read out a paper called 'A Memoir on the Appearance of Spectres or Phantoms occasioned by Disease, with Psychological Remarks'. In it, he described a quite remarkable turn of events. One morning in 1791, at home in his new house in the Brüderstraße,[1] apparently during a period of stress and depression, Nicolai looked up to see a ghost standing near him in the room, clear as day. However, his wife, who was with him in the same room, did not see it. Far from being terrified, Nicolai coolly resolved to study the phenomenon as objectively as he was able.

This went on for a few weeks, until further apparitions began to speak to him, and this was apparently one experience too far. In April, he took himself to be bled by his usual physician, and leeches were applied to his anus. In the few minutes while this was happening in the surgical room, Nicolai's suspicion was proven correct: as the leeches did their work, the hallucinations began to fade, until, by evening, the ghosts had gone altogether.

After their translation into English in 1803, Nicolai's observations were very much taken to heart by the medical establishment. People who saw ghosts were not necessarily morally suspect, intellectually weak or mentally ill, as had previously been thought; they were simply suffering from a distemper that might affect anyone. His refusal to *believe* what was actually in front of him was universally praised. The next phase, certainly in the English-speaking world, took place in Manchester.

The Mancunian physician John Ferriar published 'An Essay towards a Theory of Apparitions' in 1813, making the perfectly reasonable observation that there was no point pretending that people didn't see ghosts because, clearly, they did. His sophisticated theory revolved around modes of perception, and the way in which the brain creates much of what we think we see objectively. He believed that ghosts could be explained by a 'renewal of external impressions', which essentially argued for a disorder in perception rather than in processing. The brain's continual cognitive overlay of visual perceptions could, Ferriar believed, place a memory into an active visual experience. You could *see* a malfunctioning memory.

Ferriar's theories were expanded on in 1824 by another doctor, Samuel Hibbert, in his book *Sketches of the Philosophy of Apparitions; or, an Attempt to Trace Such Illusions to their Physical Causes*, which put ghosts into the same category as waking dreams. Hibbert argued that ghosts usually appear to percipients in contemporary or ahistorical garb because they are created in the mind of the percipient. A spiritualist would counter that the living mind was simply clothing the dead spirit.

In fact, the question of clothes on ghosts – whether they wore clothes and, if so, what type of clothes – is a conundrum that dates back to at least the time of Thomas Hobbes, who raised it in 1651 in *The Leviathan*. In 1762, *Anti-Canidia*, an anonymously written rationalist attack on supernatural belief, was published, and stated that souls were surely naked; ghosts didn't need clothes to keep warm. One commentator writing in the *Saturday Review* in 1856 mused on the idea of clothes themselves having ghosts, scoffing, 'All the socks that never came home in the wash, all the boots and shoes which we left behind worn-out at watering-places, all the old hats which we gave to crossing-sweepers . . . what a notion of Heaven – an illimitable old clothes shop.'

For many years, a ghost was presumed to appear in the clothes in which it went to its grave – that is, the winding sheet – and, consequently, this is how ghosts in seventeenth- and eighteenth-century chapbooks and publications are generally represented. (In fact, bodies were buried in just this sheet; unless you were wealthy, there would be no coffin.)

One of the pioneers of the Society for Psychical Research, Eleanor Sidgwick, discovered that, when the subject of clothes was raised with people who claimed to have seen ghosts, they could not recall them especially well, as if the ghosts were wearing clothes with no specific tag to 'any particular period'. Neither did ghosts tend to be garbed in what they wore at the actual moment of death, in other words, bedclothes.

Dickens illustrator George Cruikshank was much exercised on the subject, publishing a broadside in 1863 bemoaning the 'gross absurdity' of ghosts 'wearing apparel'; Ambrose Bierce also wrote about it, drawing on similar notions, in a discussion on the armour worn by the ghost in *Hamlet*. The spiritualist Newton Crosland proposed a 'spiritual-photographic theory' to explain it, whereby every moment in reality has a screen-capture function and can be accessed in certain circumstances, but others argued, in essence, that inanimate objects did indeed have something that resembled a soul. The eccentric Victorian geologist William Denton went so far as to posit that Nicolai's own clothes had produced his ghostly experiences, and that Nicolai was a possessor of psychometric powers, that is, the ability to pick up vibrations and images from apparently lifeless objects. However, this notion that professional sceptics are in fact self-hating psychics is still heard abroad today[2] and, in the past, in stories about Harry Houdini, who Conan Doyle always insisted was unconsciously performing psychic acts even while pursuing an active line in scepticism.

In truth, Nicolai wasn't just any ordinary *Buchhändler* but was active in fairly elite philosophical circles of the time and was a member of the Illuminati (founded in 1776), as was, incidentally, Goethe. Nicolai was also a wealthy publisher, and militantly Low Church, which meant that he was never going to accept the existence of ghosts. Many of the new wave of German writers and thinkers, including Immanuel Kant, viewed him with great suspicion, as a haughty and conservative taste-maker, and he was no friend of the Romantics. So it is curious that he should be the wellspring of all modern scepticism about ghosts, and even more curious that the medical treatment he received which cured him of his hallucinations has no basis at all in science.

Many tracts and studies followed in his wake. Much of the cutting-edge work was done in France. Jean-Étienne-Dominique Esquirol worked on the distinctions between hallucinations and illusions in the 1830s. His *Des Malades Mentales* (1838) raised the issue of the lack of surprise in those individuals when confronted with their own, apparently sudden, hallucinations. He was fascinated that the blind could apparently have visual hallucinations, and by the ability of some to dream while still awake. The Scottish medical establishment took this to heart; Glasgow physician Robert MacNish, managing to avoid the obvious joke about spirits, considered that 'spectral illusions' were little more than a sign of 'delirium tremens'.

The Edinburgh doctor Robert Paterson told of one upper-middle-class patient who had hallucinated the image of her father for a whole thirty minutes; his diagnosis rested on the notion of poor digestion, or perhaps congestion of the 'cerebral membranes'.

Walter Scott, who like Dickens had a complex relationship with the supernatural, declared in the 1830s that most ghost-seeing involved 'shades of mental aberration'. Between 1830 and 1850, it really did seem that ghost-belief was dying out, and that science and good sense had finally seen ghosts off.

It was a doctor who inadvertently reinvigorated the business of spirits. Franz Mesmer was born in 1734, the son of a Swabian forester. He believed very strongly in the influence of planetary bodies on the human body. Though he was trained both in law and medicine, the medical establishment regarded him as a crank. Still, marriage to a wealthy widow ten years his senior in 1768 made him rich enough to become a patron of Mozart. In the 1770s, Mesmer became increasingly interested in the use of magnets to improve health, and the whole idea of hidden forces having a powerful influence on the human constitution began to preoccupy him. He believed that passes over the body by magnetized stones, or even the hands of the adept, could summon what he called 'animal magnetism'. He sourced these magnets from a Hungarian Jesuit priest and astronomer with the magnificent name of Maximilian Hell.

Mesmer was nearly destroyed at the peak of his success in Vienna. There was a celebrity pianist, blind and eighteen years old, the daughter of a court official. She had received part of her musical education from Salieri. Her name was Maria-Theresa von Paradis (1759–1824). She had already succumbed to the full horrifying gamut of eighteenth-century medicine when Mesmer moved her into his house and began to treat her eyes, but soon it was whispered that those mesmeric passes were passing rather too close to her décolletage.

It was too much for the parents to bear. Fearing, they said, for their daughter's virtue, but just as likely to be fearful of losing her pension from the empress – certain to be withdrawn should her sight be restored – the von Paradis stormed the house, the father brandishing a sword and the mother smashing her daughter 'head first against the wall' when she refused to leave. Falling into a deep depression, Mesmer quit Vienna, his large estate, his practice, and even his wife, for good. It wouldn't be the last time that the deployment of unseen forces would lead to accusations of sexual impropriety; indeed, the séances of Victorian London and America would be riven by them.

Armand-Marie-Jacques de Chastenet, otherwise known as the Marquis de Puységur (1751–1825), was a wealthy aristocrat and artillery officer who had begun, before Mesmer's fall, to experiment with magnetic healing. If anyone can justifiably be said to be the founder of modern psychotherapy, it is Puységur. Working with Victor Race, a 23-year-old peasant, on the family estate near Soissons, northern France, the marquis discovered the 'perfect crisis', a somnambulistic sleep state in which patients carried out the commands of the magnetizer and upon reawakening exhibited no memory of their actions. With Puységur's spin on it, Mesmerism spread rapidly, and by 1843 his technique was renamed hypnotism by the Edinburgh medic James Braid – who later tried to change the word yet again, to neurophrenology. In the United States, Mesmerism became allied with phrenology and then, more extensively, with spiritualism, exerting an influence on William James, generally regarded as the father of psychiatry and important to our story as the man who set up the American Society for Psychical Research.

Puységur was caught up in the French Revolution and jailed for several years, and is now considered a pioneer of early psychotherapeutic treatment. Under trance conditions, Race had admitted personal problems he would not, under usual circumstances, have admitted to his master, and Puységur told him how to resolve them before waking him. Acting on this subliminal suggestion, Race resolved an issue over which he had quarrelled with his sister. Furthermore, under hypnosis, Race diagnosed not only his own illness, which appeared to be of a respiratory nature, but commented on the medical conditions of others. This further step away from the conscious self became quite a feature of the Mesmerism and hypnotism of the period – that in a somnambulant state an individual would appear to adopt the manner, voice and even class of completely different people. The idea arose that, in this receptive and other-worldly state, acts of telepathy and clairvoyance were possible. Though Mesmer always denied any aspect of the supernatural was at work and insisted on a proper scientific model, by the end of his life he was seeing his work mostly used as a conduit to the uncanny, and possibly to the dead.

Edgar Allen Poe used this powerful idea in his story 'The Facts in the Case of Mr Valdemar' (1845), in which an individual dies in a mesmeric state and becomes caught between two worlds.

Mysterious to report, one of Puységur's methods of treatment involved group healing around an ancient elm tree in Buzancy, also in northern France. Peasants, it seems, were attached by some kind of (possibly metallic) rope to the 'spiritized' and magnetized elm like maypole dancers frozen into a syncope. The old tree stood, the object of much curiosity, until a storm in 1940, when it was blown over and a miraculous spring came forth. The tree was still reported to have healing powers right until the end. When it was uprooted, the locals fled to carve off pieces of the precious wood.

After his death, Puységur became forgotten outside Soissons, until a famous medical man became interested in, and wrote about, his pioneering work. Charles Richet (1850–1935) was a French national who discovered anaphylaxis (and indeed coined the word) and auto-immune and allergy response, and, if that wasn't enough, the presence of hydrochloric acid in the stomach. For these discoveries he was awarded the Nobel Prize for medicine in 1913.[3] He had a great interest in poetry and literature and, not unusually for the time, the occult. It was Richet who devised the word 'ectoplasm' – those pseudopods of etherial matter that exuded from the orifices of mediums, but always in darkness, to the great belief of many Victorians in these contexts – borrowing it, it seems, from standard cell biology. As a kind of sideline, Richet invented the helicopter.[4]

As a medical student, Richet had intended to become a surgeon, but witnessing a hypnotic experiment on a group of women in a hospital ward in 1872 changed the course of his life forever. A similar experiment had been tried in London at University College, when in 1837 Professor John Elliotson (1791–1868) publicly mesmerized the Irish O'Key sisters (teenaged girls) and seemed to contain their convulsive and epileptic symptoms. The results were widely covered in *The Lancet*, with Elliotson demonstrating the treatment in May 1838 to several titled noblemen and some members of Parliament.[5]

Over the next few years, Richet mastered and deployed the technique, formulating what we would now identify as parapsychology. He was applying statistical methods as early as 1884, doing the very first experiments using the prediction of playing cards as well as conducting live tests on mediums, including Eusapia Palladino in 1905, with Marie Curie and physicist Jean Perrin. You might have thought that the future recipients of four Nobel prizes would have solved the mystery of life after death and seen through fraudulent mediums, but it was not to be, and the canny Neapolitan peasant outfoxed them all.[6]

By 1905, Richet was president of the Society for Psychical Research in London. He was the first to explain the idea of 'monitions', which essentially became orthodoxy for scientists in this field – monition as veridical hallucinations, or knowing things by ways other than the orthodox senses. It became clear to the scientists working in this field of apparitions and trance experiences that most spirit and mediumship experiences involved a strong element of telepathy and mind-reading.

The late-Victorian scientist in general didn't have much truck with the idea of returning souls; as Richet put it, he simply didn't see the possibility of a mind surviving with its sustaining physiological apparatus gone. The late-Victorian scientist believed in hallucinations that were mediated, influenced and informed by an information-gathering sense that didn't seem to conform to known science. If several persons saw a ghost, there would be one seed person generating the apparition and then communicating the apparition telepathically. For many scientists, this was the least bad option.

At around this time – 1894, to be precise – George du Maurier (father of Daphne) wrote a wildly popular story second only to Bram Stoker's *Dracula* in terms of sales. *Trilby* became a sensation after it was first serialized in *Harper's Magazine*; it was branded on chocolate bars, toothpaste, soap, sausages and, most famously, the elegant gentleman's hat. A town in Florida was named after the book, and the face of the heroine appeared on fans and writing paper; ice-cream bars were made in the image of her feet. Soirees were held at which devotees dressed up as the characters and read aloud from the novel. Herbert Beerbohm Tree was the producer of a hit stage play version at the Haymarket Theatre, London.

Trilby O'Ferrell is a pretty but tone-deaf girl more used to working as an artist's model; she's of Irish descent and lives in the Latin Quarter of Paris. Rendered into a deep trance by a Jewish hypnotist named Svengali (the source of the word) who is attempting to cure her headaches, she becomes a singer of sweet and surpassing brilliance; 'while hypnotised she sang before the crown heads of Europe, passed her dearest friends on the street; while "awake" she could not sing a note.' Du Maurier does not stint on the *unheimlich* aspects of this condition: 'when Svengali's Trilby was singing – or seemed to you as if she was singing – our Trilby had ceased to exist . . . our Trilby was fast asleep . . . in fact, our Trilby was dead.'

Were those in a trance in some way dead? It was an interesting and unnerving thought, and stimulated a debate that still continues between 'state' (those who felt the trance was simply an aggregation of traits) and 'non-state' (those who thought the trance was something completely removed from the limits of human physiology) beliefs.

Though modified over the course of the nineteenth century, the basic prejudice that those who saw or believed in ghosts were, at best, of poor cognition and, at worst, clinically mad was never very far away. It didn't help that one of the authors most associated with popularizing ghost-belief just before the arrival of the séance in Victorian England was prone to psychotic episodes herself.

For Catherine Crowe, it wasn't just the Christmas tree that the Germans gave to Britain. It was a folkloric, woodland darkness with a common currency dating from Anglo-Saxon antiquity. 'Whilst the scientific men of Great Britain and several of our journalists have been denying and ridiculing the reports of this phenomena, the most eminent physicians of Germany have been quietly studying and investigating them.' Responding perhaps to the Prince Consort's influence on the court, Mrs Crowe included many German stories in *The Night Side of Nature*, an otherwise very English book of legends, which with its first-hand stories, *dîtes* and rumours, remains one of the strangest miscellanies ever written. The title of the book is a literal translation from the German – a translation of an astronomical term for the side of the earth furthest from the sun: *Nachtseite*.

Catherine Crowe had already made a name for herself by translating *The Seeress of Prevorst* into English in 1845. The book was written by a physician, Justinus Kerner, who was later credited by the historian of psychiatry Henri Ellenberger for the actual 'discovery' of the unconscious. In this book, Kerner had written of monitoring a young 'ghost seer', Friederike Hauffe, from 1827, when the girl had seemed to be in an anorexic suspension between life and death, to 1829, when the latter caught up with her. In her introduction, Mrs Crowe takes a moment to launch an attack on the sceptics, picking up especially on Ferriar's *An Essay towards a Theory of Apparitions* and Samuel Hibbert-Ware's *Sketches on the Philosophy of Apparitions* (1825), which took the line that ghosts were some form of projected mimetic memory. Ferriar was not above using a certain amount of mockery in addressing the subject, and this in particular seems to have enraged Mrs Crowe. She writes in the preface: 'If I could only induce a few capable persons, instead of laughing at these things, to look at them, my object would be attained, and I should consider my time well spent.'

Crowe's own book is a ragbag of apparitions, ghosts and wraiths in all manner of circumstances – some returning to confess murder, others to impart important information: all the traditional roles. One interesting prevalence, however, is a sentimental one – the return of ghostly parents to offer support, love and succour to their bereaved offspring, as if even death is not an end to their parenting.

Mrs Crowe sounds quite a character. She had been friends with delinquents, including Thomas de Quincey, and possibly had a drug habit, which drew the opprobrium of Hans Christian Andersen on a visit to Scotland. On 17 August 1847, he describes her inhaling ether[7] with another woman at a party, and with a frisson of misogynistic horror he describes 'the feeling of being with two mad creatures – they smiled with open dead eyes . . .'

Some years after the publication of her book in 1848, however, Catherine Crowe was not in a good place.

Dickens mentions the incident in several of his letters; he had taken a keen interest in the book and its author from the time he reviewed it in *The Examiner*.

In a letter to the Revd James White dated 7 March 1854, he wrote of an incident in Edinburgh, where Mrs Crowe was then living.

> Mrs Crowe has gone stark mad – and stark naked – on the spirit-rapping imposition. She was found t'other day in the street, clothed

only in her chastity, a pocket-handkerchief and a visiting card. She had been informed, it appeared, by the spirits, that if she went out in that trim she would be invisible. She is now in a mad-house and, I fear, hopelessly insane. One of the curious manifestations of her disorder is that she can bear nothing black. There is a terrific business to be done, even when they are obliged to put coals on her fire.

It is now generally thought that Mrs Crowe had some kind of psychotic episode. A mesmerist magazine called *The Zoist* reported with some relish at the time that the spirits had driven her to both public nudity and madness, a Victorian double relegation, and despite a damage limiting letter to the newspapers from the weary authoress, written from a spa at Great Malvern, the story stuck and was much retold in private.

She claimed that a 'gastric' condition had made her babble about spirits, but nobody really believed her version of events. Catherine Crowe vanished from the scene, and Dickens used the case to illustrate the dangers of spiritualist investigations, and their potential for psychological harm. This incident led a famous Parisian alienist Marcel Viollet to claim that those with hereditary nervous dispositions seemed drawn to the subject of ghosts like moths to a flame, exacerbating their weak wills and damaging their weak intellects. As the middle classes became more powerful, an interest in ghosts became less respectable.

In the same year, 1854, the US *Daily News* ran a report on twenty-six people who had found their way into an Ohio mad-house 'by means of table rapping'. The seeds of doubt about the American-style table séance had been sown, even as it was arriving from across the pond.

One of Charles Richet's fellow travellers was Baron Albert von Schrenck-Notzing. Notzing (1862–1929), also a medical man, trained in Munich. One of his greatest finds was a pair of mediums,

15. A photograph of the ghost baron investigating Eva Carrière in 1909.

brothers Rudi and Willi Schneider, who hailed from the same small Austrian town as Adolf Hitler. Notzing was the first known psychologist called for his professional opinion in a court case,[8] a murder trial in Munich in 1896. Like Richet, he had developed an interest in hypnotism while a medical student, and they had become friends in Paris in 1889. In 1891, Notzing published a translation of Richet's work on telepathy into German.

It was the ghost baron who pioneered much of the work on testing mediums in laboratory conditions, including the requirement that they eat brightly coloured food before a session (to stain any muslin cloth they might regurgitate under the guise of ectoplasm). After researching one medium, Eva Carrière, in Paris in 1909, Notzing became convinced that ectoplasm, a Victorian staple of spirit photography in particular, was composed of leukocytes – a colourless blood corpuscles. He developed tight-fitting body costumes to eliminate the possibility of fraud; psychics sometimes had to be sewn into them. However, his reputation never quite recovered from a scandal: a photograph taken during one of Carrière's trances for Notzing (though I cannot locate this exact image), was said to show a ghostly face emerging from her head. On the other side of this spirit balloon, photographed from another angle at the same time, the letters LE MIRO could be picked out. A quick shuffle through back issues of *Le Miroir* magazine showed that the face had been clipped out.

Perhaps the greatest testament to medical interest in the paranormal lies in a machine still in use today. The electroencephalograph, or EEG machine, was originally developed to detect telepathy.

The story of Hans Berger was a tragic one. Born in May 1871, young Hans was a dreamy boy much given to the mathematics of the heavens (his grandfather was a well-known German poet whose first love was astronomy). When he enrolled at the university in Jena, it was to read mathematics, but shortly afterwards he took a break and enlisted in the cavalry.

One day, he was nearly killed. Thrown by a restive horse during a training session, he fell into the path of some heavy ordinance coming his way. Against all the odds, the horses drawing the cannon managed to stop in time. At that exact moment, many miles away, Hans's elder sister was suddenly gripped by the hideous conviction that something terrible had happened to her brother. So alarmed was her father that he sent Hans a telegram, which he received when he was relaxing in the barracks later that evening.

Somehow, his intense fear had reached his sister. Many years later, Berger wrote, 'This is a case of spontaneous telepathy in which at a time of mortal danger, and as I contemplated certain death, I transmitted my thoughts while my sister, who was particularly close to me, acted as the receiver.' After he left the cavalry, Berger returned to the university and began to study medicine, with the sole aim of discovering what had happened, finding instances of telepathy, and finally explaining it.

His long and solitary quest led him to develop a device that could record brainwaves – for a while the brainwaves we now know as alpha waves were called Berger Waves. He was not popular among his colleagues, who found the idea of a psychiatrist with a minimal understanding of electronics perfecting such a device absurd. When Berger announced in 1929 that you could monitor brain activity simply through sensors attached to the scalp, his revelation was greeted with derision.

His *Hirnspiegel* (brain mirror) never did prove the existence of telepathy, but the science of brain electricity was eventually accepted, after the tests and equipment were replicated in Cambridge by Edgar Adrian in 1934 and the EEG was recognized. For reasons that are not entirely clear, Berger was forced out of his job in 1938, but much of his failure to be honoured in his own country is held to be evidence of his antipathy to the ruling Nazi party. That he was considered a crank goes against the few things we know of the official Nazi line on parapsychology, which was to be regarded as a new Nordic science from March 1937. Bonn University created a *Forschungsstelle für Psychologische Grenzwissenschaften* in that year to 'investigate the incidence of supernatural phenomena within Germany and amongst Germanic peoples'.

Under somewhat mysterious circumstances (some accounts say he was hounded by the Nazis, others that he was an SS officer and a eugenicist), Berger hanged himself in 1941, in the south wing of the clinic where he worked. We do not know whether his sister sensed his passing.

There is a neuroscientist in Ontario, Canada who has taken Berger's telepathy machine one step further. He has developed a machine to induce psychic experiences.

Dr Michael Persinger from the Laurentian University has studied the relationship between temporal-lobe microseizures and the experiences described by telepaths for years. In cases of full-blown telepathic experiences, subjects can feel a disembodied presence nearby, overwhelming hallucinations, sensations of religious bliss or sometimes a tickling sensation on the skin (very commonly reported by those on ghost hunts, and a staple experience in TV shows such as *Most Haunted* – the ghostly tickle on the neck).

In 1977, Persinger wrote about the theory that geological and tectonic effects might cause fields inducing hallucinations in the human brain – on this occasion, UFOs and Marian visions. In 1988, he made a more fully realized case for a link between hallucinations and electromagnetic disturbances, effects being produced within the brain as a result of subterranean seismic activity, solar flares[9] or man-made machines such as large electricity generators. It's not really clear what the science here is, and the effects of solar flares on human physiology are not yet really understood. But a paper in 1991 suggested that you are more likely to experience a hallucination in the solar-flare peak months of March and October.

Persinger is described by John Geiger in *The Third Man Factor* as 'a gaunt man' 'overdressed . . . in a three-piece suit', and by one of his colleagues as a precise and dandyish figure who dressed in such a suit 'even to mow the lawn'. He comes across as something like the William Burroughs of neurotheology (the science of brain activity in relation to faith).

The helmet Persinger devised for stimulating the temporal lobe, dubbed the 'god helmet', was built by the technician Stanley Koren and is more correctly called the 'Koren' helmet: it's a modified snowmobile helmet with a magnetic coil placed to sit over the right temporal lobe. The magnetic strength exerted, and its duration, are regulated by a computer program developed in the laboratory, and individuals are invited to sit in an acoustic chamber, cut off from the world.

Koren based his science on observations made in Lausanne Hospital. During open-brain surgery, doctors treating a 22-year-old woman with epilepsy noticed that every time they stimulated the 'temporo-parietal' region of the brain with a mild electrical current, the patient would sense someone standing nearby.

A pre-surgical epilepsy unit at the University Hospital, Geneva also managed to reproduce this 'illusory shadow person' using similar techniques of electrical stimulation, reporting on it in the 2006 September issue of *Nature*. Though the results have never been successfully replicated elsewhere (an attempt was made in Sweden in 2005), they seem impressive – 80 per cent of the subjects had an uncanny experience, often seeing or sensing a dead relative, or a religious figure such as Jesus Christ. When scientist and professional atheist Richard Dawkins was sent to the unit in Ontario by the BBC, he felt absolutely nothing, but when parapsychology sceptic Dr Susan Blackmore was rigged up to the same kit, she had a powerful experience, one whose reality she stands by today, with some passion.[10]

This experience is especially common among Arctic explorers – a friendly presence often appears to encourage them and lead them to safety while they are struggling on the very edge of survival. Curiously enough, a housemaster at Eton and friend of M. R. James, H. F. W. Tatham, wrote a little-known genre story on exactly this theme called *Footprints in the Snow* (1910). Of the many polar explorers and mountaineers who have had this experience, perhaps the most famous is Ernest Shackleton, who wrote:

> When I look back at those days I have no doubt that Providence guided us, not only across those snow-fields, but across the storm-white sea that separated Elephant Island from our landing-place on South Georgia. I know that during that long and racking march of thirty-six hours over the unnamed mountains and glaciers of South Georgia it seemed to me that we were four, not three.[11]

This 'angel switch', as Persinger calls it, also seems the likely cause of some dream and sleep experiences; awakening in bed,

often paralysed, and feeling a presence in the room, usually neutral but sometimes intensely malignant. Sleep paralysis, or a
sensed presence standing or sitting on the bed (but not seen),
could be the temporal lobe hot-plating consciousness while the
rest of the brain snoozes.

The temporal lobe, whose epileptic fugues seem related to
religious experience and ghost-seeing, whose connection to hyp-
nagogic and hypnopompic hallucinations also seems like part of
the puzzle, remains at the heart of the mystery of the way in
which we experience ghosts.

There's a specific interest in the dorsal lateral prefrontal cor-
tex, or DLPC, where working memory, planning, inhibition and
evaluation take place. One aspect of DLPC damage is a reversion
back to behaving and thinking like a child.

The doctors with their white coats and Gladstone bags haven't
stopped running across the fields after it, and the veridical hallucination, and the recent discovery of microsleeps,[12] seems to
bring them closer to an issue on the fringes of human biology.

On the Vulgarity of Ghosts

The lower classes, who have always had a taste for the marvellous, are fully persuaded that this is a supernatural visitation by some troubled spirit, and numberless tales of the most extravagant nature have been circulated.

– *West Briton* newspaper, 1821

They had seen the ghost of Mrs Maria Manning in the window, glimpsed her from the street. She was looking down on them with her dead, murderess eyes.

She was wearing the same black dress that had sheathed her for the gallows in November 1849,[1] the same long gloves that protected her manicured hands as she stepped to the hemp in Horsemonger Lane. Gloves were an article of clothing not usually seen in such circumstances, creating quite a frisson for certain Victorian gentlemen. Charles Dickens was horrified by the blood lust of the crowd at this execution, estimated to number between thirty and fifty thousand.[2] He was later to immortalize this haughty, deadly Swiss lady's maid as Hortense in *Bleak House*.[3]

The woman *The Times* dubbed the Lady Macbeth of the Bermondsey stage had now returned post-mortem to Bermondsey. It was a trigger for a phenomenon which, though little known these days, was very common a century ago: the ghost-hunting flashmob. The great show of the trial, followed by the spectacle of her execution, had not sated public desire; Maria Manning had to return for the third act. She had been judged and spat out from Hell, and was now performing as a demon in satin.

And the papers loved the story. There was the tenuous royal

16. The fixed stare of the waxwork of Mrs Manning at Madame Tussauds
that proved a magnet for the Victorian public.

connection.⁴ As an upper servant, Manning was a woman who
had risen above her station, taken on airs and graces, and then
been cast low. She was a foreigner, a native of Geneva. She was an
adulteress who had killed her lover.⁵ She had been caught by the
use of a modern invention, the telegraph.

Her trial had begun just before Halloween, on 29 October.

Manning said of the man she had murdered and buried under
the flagstones of her kitchen, 'I never liked him and I beat his
skull with a ripping chisel.' Her lover had been a river excise man
and petty criminal. To the crowds, he was little different to most
of the people of Bermondsey, struggling to make ends meet.

Now, after twenty years in the grave, she was back in a house
in Bermondsey, looking out on a mob very like the mob that had
so thirsted for her death.

Before long, nearly four hundred people were gathering outside the house every evening. It wasn't even the house she had lived in, but that didn't matter. At every flicker across the window, every perceived movement in the empty house, the cry went up: 'There's the ghost! There's the black ghost! There are the Mannings.'

There was a substantial police intervention. Violence and disorder flared as south London teetered on the brink of summer riots. (Seven years later, these summer madnesses were still taking place. In July 1876 there was the trial of a 13-year-old named Robert Withey who became so frightened and agitated by the shouts that he began to throw stones at the windows, while all around him a mob howled to tear the house down.)

There's the black ghost. Until Victorian times, ghosts never dressed in black, but changing fashions meant that ghosts changed too: many accounts of 'nuns' date from this period, including the one at Borley Rectory. Reports to the Society for Psychical Research show a great upsurge in sightings of female ghosts wearing black clothing in the latter part of the nineteenth century, perhaps in part due to the Manning case.[6]

In medieval Western Europe, ghosts were seen dressed in black at the very first stage of their journey through Purgatory, and by the time they were dressed in white, the purification process had nearly ended. So there was a deep-rooted connection between black-clothed ghosts and a sense of very fresh malaise, and possibly even evil. Susan Hill's novel[7] *The Woman in Black* echoes the Maria Manning trope and her glossy silk corset, which suggests a malignant, coarse evil. This female ghost is dynamically strong, dangerous and resentful in a way analogous to the *huli jing*, or 'fox spirits' of China.

There was nothing unusual about this substantial mob, growing in number outside a house in the expectation of seeing a ghost. In academia over the past ten years, one of the great rediscoveries has been the phenomenon of ghost flashmobs in Victorian London and in bigger cities such as Manchester, Hull or Norwich.

People have always wanted to see a good show. Crowds have always gathered outside haunted houses and churchyards in response to rumours. The fascination of the working classes with ghosts has a long history. Richard Baxter, in *Certainty of the World of Spirits*, wrote of the large crowds that gathered outside a house in Lutterworth which was plagued by a stone-throwing ghost in February 1646. And in the Georgian era, there was the Hammersmith Horror.

The Hammersmith ghost began plaguing west London at the beginning of December 1803. Hammersmith was then relatively rural, and one of its residents was the Swiss painter Philip de Loutherbourg, David Garrick's Drury Lane Theatre set designer, who had a deep interest in the occult – perhaps he took an interest in this case. The ghost was said to be the roving spirit of a man with a cut throat, according to the local newspaper *The Morning Chronicle*. He wore a shroud or, sometimes, an animal skin. Most of Hammersmith was then freshly built: it was where the city met the countryside. Beyond the new, white houses were the hedges and trees of the boundaries.

From around the time of the Hammersmith ghost, people's attitude towards ghosts was becoming confrontational. Young men sought to conquer their fears. Every evening, groups of them would be seen prowling the area, looking for the ghost, and anyone wearing light clothing could become a target.

A bricklayer, Thomas Milward, wore the apparel traditional to his trade – white linen trousers, a white flannel waistcoat and a white apron. One evening as he was walking home through the dusk, a gentleman and two ladies, alarmed in a passing carriage, shouted: 'There goes the ghost!' Milward's robust response to the shrieks was to swear at the carriage and threaten to punch the man's head.

His mother-in-law warned him it was not safe to continue wearing such clothes on his journey home but, stubborn as a mule, Milward went on doing so.

The Hammersmith Ghost.

17. A contemporary engraving of the Hammersmith Ghost, wearing a shroud.

As he walked down Black Lion Lane, he was shot dead with a fowling gun by a frightened excise officer named Francis Smith, egged on after a drinking session with local watchman William Girdler in the nearby White Hart pub. They had been exchanging tales about the ghost that had frightened the wife of a locksmith to death, and saying that two others were seriously ill after the shock of another encounter. Smith was imprisoned for murder, but pardoned just a few months later by the king, who seemed to take pity owing to the unusual circumstances – evidence again of a long-standing royal fascination with the subject of ghosts.[8]

It's difficult to overstate the hysteria that gripped Hammersmith; people roved in armed groups looking for the ghost, and others feared to leave their houses after dark. But a taste for the public ghost scare was growing. Mere days after the conclusion of the Hammersmith scare, on Friday 13 January 1804, *The Times* reported that a soldier in the Coldstream Guards stationed in St James's Park had seen the ghost of a headless woman between one and two o'clock in the morning near the Recruit House; the soldier was so shocked by his experience he had to be taken to hospital the next day and, subsequently, other soldiers signed depositions that they had seen the same apparition. One of them, George Jones, was summoned to the Bow Street Magistrate's Court to repeat his story, but *The Times*, after an investigation, claimed that it had solved the mystery – two Westminster schoolboys had deployed a magic-lantern projector in a nearby empty house near Birdcage Walk. The hardened war veterans had been spooked by teenagers with a toy.

In 1821, the military were once again at the heart of a supposed supernatural incident, at a depot in Truro, Cornwall. Stones, apparently thrown by a ghost and consequently smelling of 'brimstone', were hurled, and crowds dutifully turned up to gawp. These flashmobs became regular occurrences in many urban areas, and London, with its vast and sudden rise in population, was the backdrop to most of these popular dramas. At St Andrew's

Church in Holborn in August 1815, large crowds gathered to see the ghost that someone thought they had seen there; *The Times* noted with some displeasure that 'the light-fingered gentry had become so numerous and successful, that it required the utmost vigilance of the police to prevent these disgraceful proceedings.' In August 1834 in St Giles, a slum area off Holborn on the old tumbrel route for criminals off to be hanged at Tyburn, there was a similar ghost scare, again with large crowds; but when several men climbed over the fence and into the graveyard, it wasn't a ghost they found but a bereaved Irish mother guarding her son's grave against the resurrection men.

Ghost mobs were definitely most common in deprived areas There were at least three major instances in Bermondsey, then a grim area of south London marked by evil-smelling tanneries and dusty calico works. Records of the period show a huge amount of impoverished casual workers living there, mostly sleeping five to a room: ghost stories were the soap operas of the age.

In July 1830, an entire police division was tied up in Bermondsey when some two thousand people gathered every evening outside a house in Grange Road. It had belonged to a clergyman who had recently died; it was supposed to be haunted. The crowd was very unhappy about being moved on by the authorities, some complaining loudly that they had walked for miles to see the ghost.

But the view of the police and the magistrates was simple – ghost hunts were an infelicitous mix of public disorder and ignorant, craven superstition. As one Victorian magistrate from Dewsbury remarked on similar displays of infectious mob-led enthusiasms, 'All intelligent and thinking persons [have] nothing to do with the fifth of November celebrations.'

In Bermondsey again in August 1868, when a body was fished from the Thames and taken to the statutory dead-house beside St James's Church for an inquest to be convened, rumours spread like wildfire that the dead body was up and about and walking the churchyard at night. In consequence, an estimated two thousand people congregated nightly outside. Efforts by the vicar and parish officials to disperse the crowd were entirely in vain; as the police arrived, one James Jones, aged nineteen, climbed up onto the railings and shouted at the murmuring, agitated crowd, '*Don't go – there it is again – there's the ghost!*' He was promptly arrested.

It happened in the provinces too. In February 1843, news spread through Sunderland that a mariner aboard the *Myrtle* had received a visit from his dead sister, and that when the ship docked at midnight she would rise from her grave and walk down to the docks; a thousand people surrounded the churchyard and waited for it to happen. In Norwich in October 1845 four hundred people, mostly boys, searched for a ghost after it was seen vanishing into a tower, according to the *Norwich Mercury*. In late October 1852, between two and three thousand people gathered every night in Hull's Wellington Lane, hoping to hear the ghostly knockings that had been reported in a tenement there.

Yesterday night [reported *The Hull Packet*], although it was dull, drizzly and cold, crowd upon crowd besieged the spot, standing, in spite of the cold and wet, 100 yards from the haunted house, anxiously discussing the nature and object of the ghost's visit, and patiently waiting to learn from the police, or those who were fortunate enough to get near the house, when it had knocked last.

Back in London in May 1865, *The Times* reported on 'mobs' that had gathered at 9 p.m. in front of St George's Church in Southwark; they didn't disperse until 4 a.m. the following day. The short-tempered police brought in from outside to control the high street and keep it open to traffic arrested a man who kept shouting 'Here's the ghost!' Two years later, nine young men were charged with affray and resisting arrest after they were involved in scuffles in Woburn Square; again, the rumour of a ghost was to blame, and the men had been doing the rounds of every door in the square, kicking each one and roughly demanding that the ghost should appear.

This kind of disorder reached its apogee in July 1874 (notice the persistence of those midsummer and Christmas dates) when a rumour went round that a ghost had been seen in the churchyard at Christ Church, on Broadway in Westminster. (It's now a public garden after Mr Poynter's church was destroyed in the Blitz.) When some bright spark pinned a ghost made out of paper to a nearby tree, an estimated five to six thousand people a night turned up to see it.

Belief in ghosts has always been vulgar – as vulgar as illness, which it has always superficially resembled. What you think about ghosts and how you perceive them – indeed, how you process that perception – once depended on where you came from, your own profession and the profession of your parents. To some extent, it still does. Since the 1940s, studies have shown that professing a belief in the existence of ghosts has become more socially acceptable; but for most of the last few hundred years, only the upper and lower classes tended to believe in them.

The middle classes have always deplored the idea of ghosts. Professional sceptics are usually drawn from this strata of society. Your middle-class sceptic would say that toffs like ghosts because it is a symptom of their decadence, the plebeians because they are ill-educated.

The twin polarities of the haunted British landscape make it clear: the haunted pub and the haunted stately home; the poltergeist in the beer cellar and the white lady in the minstrel's gallery. If you were poor, it was because you hoped for the future; and if you were aristocratic and rich, it was because you trusted in the past. The king and queen of British ghosts were Dick Turpin and Anne Boleyn. Dick Turpin haunts as many pubs as Anne Boleyn does palaces and stately homes. There is a pub (now disused) that is haunted by Turpin not two hundred yards away from where I write this, in Shoreditch.

Not everyone thought ghosts were real, meaningful, or a suitable subject for study or discussion. From the late eighteenth century onwards, the middle classes have taken an increasingly straightforward and sceptical line when it comes to the supernatural, considering a belief in spectres and apparitions to be inherently unhealthy and unhelpful; credulity was a symptom of poor education, infantile, and possibly even something to do with mental illness.

Ghosts were, in a nutshell, embarrassing.

In 1934, Ernest Bennett noted, in *Apparitions*: 'In some middle-class circles it is generally not considered good form to mention ghosts except in a jocular way; and many devout Christians who anticipate, with some assurance, eternal happiness hereafter, regard any mention of disembodied spirits as an unpleasant and depressing topic.'

Research by the sociologist Geoffrey Gorer in the 1950s showed that there was more of a belief in ghosts among the poor and the upper-middle classes. Things have changed in the multi-media age of the last sixty years. Ghosts have become democratized and classless. But this ancient division of station is still interesting. Gorer noted that those most sceptical about ghosts were prosperous working-class men; it was, after all, common among socialist radicals to laugh about the superstitions of their youth, as if to say: *look how far I have come!* This was in spite of clear links between early socialism, Fabianism and the world of Victorian séances and spiritualist churches.

The now forgotten novelist and writer Elizabeth Bonhôte (1744–1818) depicted the working classes in a state of superstitious dread, frightened out of their wits and forever jumping at their own shadows. In *The Parental Monitor* (1788) she writes, 'After the sun has withdrawn his rays, though the bright beams of the moon illumine their paths, they see an imaginary ghost in every tree, gate or stile; and when they retire to their apartments by themselves, they are in a continual dread, lest the curtains should be undrawn by the hand of some visible or invisible spectre.'

A few years later, in 1791, a similarly well-meaning Mary Weightman in her *The Friendly Monitor; Or, Dialogues for Youth against the Fear of Ghosts* was preoccupied with banishing 'tales of the nursery' from good middle-class homes. Sarah Trimmer and Maria Edgeworth both added their voices to the reform of superstition; they tended to write books imploring parents to keep an eye on the female servants of the household filling their children's heads with nonsense. Bonhôte was a tribal enemy of the 'ignorant nurse' and was an unfortunate contributor to the notion that female servants and their brimstone tales of ghosts and spirits would render their charges effeminate; the Elizabethan writer Reginald Scott, in *Discoverie*, believed that some men were prone to imagining ghosts because of a parenting issue earlier in life, ghost-belief in an adult male simply demonstrating an 'effeminate and fond [i.e. foolish] bringing up'.

So it's all the more interesting that the founders of the Society for Psychical Research, set up in 1881, came from the upper middle classes. It's widely assumed that Victorian séances took place in large Kensington homes, among the titled and entitled of the day, and was largely a foolish habit of the monied.

The reality was that mediumship as we now understand it was first exported to England by the son of a Darlington weaver in 1853. His name was David Richmond, and as a result of his stewardship, for many years table-rapping and séances were popular among the working classes in Yorkshire. The women who invented table-rapping, the Fox sisters, were after all the daughters of a blacksmith, and this working-class aspect of early spiritualism, and its curious correspondence with early socialism, feminism and the emancipation of slaves, is one of the least-known aspects of the period.

Everything about Richmond, had the members of the SPR

committee met him, would probably have appalled them. He was an autodidact, self-trained, vegetarian, anti-authoritarian, an anti-establishment shoemaker and itinerant wool-comber all his life. His obituarist quoted him as saying, 'If all men were like me there would be no need of governments wanted.' Richmond remained 'a communitarian socialist' all his life.

The SPR – which, by the way, is still in existence – was hugely advanced in many ways and, in others, a complete mirror of its times. One of the principal reasons that Harry Price found himself unable to get very far with it was that Eleanor Sidgwick described him as 'not quite a gentleman'.

The SPR was always minded to suspect fraud, especially by the lower orders, who, 'like children', were always drawn to mischief. When the SPR was first set up and began gathering evidence of the supernatural, it would not take accounts of hauntings and paranormal events from servants; servants, it was thought, were credulous and, on occasion, capable of outright malice. One of the founding members of the SPR noted at a meeting in November 1889 that he preferred the evidence of educated to 'that of uneducated persons'. And in the SPR *Proceedings* of 1885 there's a discussion of how servants were widely perceived as susceptible to local tales of ghosts, murders and hauntings. The resultant disconnect between the folkloric reality of oral tradition and the hard-nosed investigation of psychic phenomena is with us to this day. You're either in one camp or the other.

Of the several committees set up by the SPR after its foundation, the one on mediums had the hardest time, since it was quickly established that out of the hundreds then in London and the major cities, there were no candidates worthy of consideration. Sex, class and gender were never far away when respectable upper-middle-class scientists tried to investigate working-class mediums, some of them rather saucy.

It was ever thus. In the eighteenth century, the Benedictine Abbot Calmet wrote that hauntings often turned out to be the work of a 'thievish or dissolute servant, who conceals his thefts and debaucheries by counterfeiting a ghost'. In 1818, the vicar of Great Gransden blamed a fear of ghosts on 'frauds by wicked servants'.

In Pimlico in 1823, a stone-throwing poltergeist on Queen Street was thought to be a servant girl, Maria Herbert, though a lack of hard evidence saw her acquitted. In 1825 a mischievous servant, Anne Page, was sent to jail for her role in smashing windows in Newington, at the time blamed on a ghost by the locals. In 1878, a young servant girl was prosecuted for a staged haunting on a farm in Somerset which involved crockery being moved around, straw ricks set on fire and a pig trough mysteriously moving to the front door of the Goathurst farmhouse.

A servant in Maidstone in 1859 shook doors and rang doorbells in her employer's house in order to cover up a secondary career as a prostitute. In Tottenham Court Road in 1839, a pawnbroker found himself the victim of a haunting hoax when a maid devised inventive ways of letting her flesh-and-blood lover into the house at night, and called it haunting.

The journalist Charles Mackay, who wrote one of the most magnificently titled books of the Victorian era, *Extraordinary Popular Delusions and the Madness of Crowds* (1841), tells of a similar scenario in Stockwell in 1772. It's a story usually referred to as 'The Stockwell poltergeist.'

Mrs Golding, an elderly lady, lived alone with her servant, Anne Robinson, near Vauxhall. Around Christmas time, the most amazing events began to take place: 'cups and saucers rattled down chimneys,' writes Mackay, 'pots and pans were whirled downstairs, or through the windows; and hams, cheese and loaves of bread disported themselves on the floor as if the devil were in them.' Mrs Golding fought the fiend with the help of her neighbours but, if anything, the haunting got worse, with chairs and tables moving, and the china dashed to smithereens. The devastation stopped only when Anne Robinson was dismissed from service; she later confessed to a local vicar that she had orchestrated the whole thing. As with the girl from Tottenham Court Road, Anne had engineered the haunting to facilitate her meetings with her boyfriend. She placed china on shelves so it would fall at the slightest vibration, and attached horse hair to objects, which she would then jerk to send them flying.

Such scenarios were not unusual, and within the middle classes it became a commonplace, as Calmet believed, that tales of ghosts and hauntings were used to cover up nefarious activities, including criminal, money-making and licentious behaviour, among the rowdy lower orders. The taint of fraud and criminality has always been in the foreground of the pointed middle-class distaste for the supernatural.

Some aristocrats warm to their ancestral ghosts, but the higher-minded will always disapprove of them as vulgar. Those close to executive power and the established Church have a duty to set an example, to be cool and hard-headed.

There's one story concerning James Boswell. He was having dinner with the Duke and Duchess of Argyll in 1773, and the subject of conversation was running to the 'middle state' between death and resurrection. Boswell discovered that not everyone, as he had supposed, believed in second sight and ghosts. He laid his cards on the table. Like his mentor, Dr Johnson, he did believe in them. 'I fancy you are a Methodist,' the duchess observed tartly. 'This was the only sentence her Grace deigned to utter to me,' Boswell records, a trifle miserably, in his diary. The powerful do not believe in ghosts: there is no need to.

As early as the fourth century, the Christian apologist Lactantius (d. 320) targeted upper-class pagans in a direct attack, saying that ghost and supernatural belief was fit only for the unwashed. He ridiculed ordinary folk who 'believed that the souls of the dead wander about their tombs,' and thought the belief, common at the time, that a soul 'disentangles itself from the body slowly, beginning with the feet and working upwards' was an absurdity. There's been little in the way of academic research into the class structure of ghost-belief. Neither has any correlation been proven between IQ and ghost-belief. In recent years, popular tabloid newspapers in the UK have gradually lost the tone of disapproval they were obliged to rehearse in more Reithian times, though many of the stories they run are pretty much identical to the ones known to the Victorians.

Ghosts remain reliable tabloid fodder, especially in times of economic unease. In January 2009, for example, the *Sun* put a ghost on its front page. 'Haunted Hospital Calls in Exorcist,' it claimed, revealing how shift workers had seen a black-cloaked ghost, thought to be a Roman soldier, in Derby's newly built City General Hospital. The online edition had the space to elaborate, and 'ghostbuster' Michael Hallowell gave advice on how 'unwanted spirits are said to be removed'. Derby, we were reliably informed, 'was Britain's most haunted city even before the hospital spook appeared!'

In earlier times, a paper like *The Mirror*, writing in both the case of the haunting of Borley Rectory and the Enfield poltergeist, would have put in a call to the Society for Psychical Research. They'd send along a photographer and, at some point, a reporter, but they would still defer to this essentially sceptical and science-based organization.

Nowadays, the primacy of programmes such as *Most Haunted* and *Most Haunted Live* can be seen as a return to the Victorian flashmob; the figure of the compromised working-class medium also returns with, for example, Derek Acorah.[9] Of course, now, you don't have to turn up outside a church or an empty, broken-windowed house – you can watch it live or monitor the locked-off cameras on the live web-feed. *Most Haunted*'s tendency to whip up a pleasurable sensation of fear while at the same time remaining fairly ambivalent about the reality of the phenomena is significant.[10] No explanations or analysis are ever offered – only stories, stories about people now dead, stories about their lives. Travelling mediums such as Psychic Sally (also on TV) attract a fairly solidly working-class crowd. Those in the audience seem pleased enough when a name known to them is mentioned. No information of any interest is revealed, no big secrets, least of all the secrets of the afterlife. Following a critical report from industry watchdog Ofcom in 2006, *Most Haunted* now begins with a disclaimer stating that it is for 'entertainment purposes only'. It has quietly dropped any attempt to present itself as genuinely investigative, instead focussing on sentiment, reducing its resident parapsychologist Ciarán O'Keeffe, a distinguished man in his field, to assessing the happenings from a cool sociological standpoint.

And since there are few more middle-class professions than that of the critic or the scientist, both of them by nature enforcers of sceptical positions, the voices raised against such shows in newspapers and other more self-consciously sensible TV shows always have the vinegar tang of those eighteenth-century tracts complaining about working-class superstition.

The gentry and aristocracy, however, seem only too happy to lend out their stately homes to groups of local enthusiasts for ghost-hunting, thrilled that people will actually pay hard cash to be haunted; in the faded bedroom where previously no one would sleep, the wicked earl murders an infant nightly and a long-dead aunt brushes her long hair, still growing in the grave. Some aristocrats, such as Count Emmanuel Swedenborg, as good as invented the modern spirit world, and there are those who investigated it: Baron Albert von Schrenck-Notzing in Germany; future prime minister of Great Britain Arthur Balfour, who had a special room and a chair with leather straps for testing mediums in Carleton Gardens; and the Marquis of Bute, who investigated the 'most haunted house in Scotland', Ballechin House, Perthshire, in 1896. But as Noël Coward pertly mentioned in his comedic song 'The Stately Homes of England', it is commerce that has been the great coming-together of the classes over the supernatural in modern times. Owners both of large, crumbling houses and of old pubs flag up their haunted rooms as something entirely desirable. Ghosts remain, however, in essence, vulgar.

The Thrilling of the Tables

I have reason to know that the power at work in these phenomena, like Love, 'laughs at locksmiths'.

– Sir William Crookes

From the 1840s, in the north of England, the newly emergent spiritualist church was a working-class, proto-socialist movement. The town of Keighley happened to be the place where this new faith of spiritualism took root, and its adepts routinely linked it with a ragbag of anti-establishment positions, including votes for women and anti-vivisection. Down in London, things were very different. In the salons of the wealthy, in the plush Piccadilly hotels where the air was as light as champagne, in the well-upholstered Hyde Park residences and East End domiciles banked with the bawdy efflorescence of the music halls, séances were very much about one thing: sex.

The darkened room, the mixing of classes, the whispers, the secrets and lies – all had the markings of an assignation. Physical intimacy was part of the process of the séance as skin brushed skin in the rooms in which they were held. Flirtation, states of heightened awareness and excitement were commonplace.

Séances weren't sexy when they first arrived from America. They were formal and functional. The Canadian sisters Maggie and Kate Fox, inventors of the séance, were in 1848 living with their father in a small farmhouse in Hydesville, New York. Within hours of moving in, they started to hear things: bumps and rattles that disturbed their sleep, the sound of footsteps walking down into the cellar, and then, finally, a horrifyingly ice-cold hand brushed against the face of one sister as she lay in bed. Kate named the ghost Mr Splitfoot, a folk name for the Devil. In one incident that was to have enormous ramifications, she began asking the ghost to copy her handclaps and then started asking questions and requesting a response in knocks, either to signify letters of the alphabet, or a simple yes or no.

This was a radical departure for modern Western culture. For centuries, the accepted practice had been not to talk to the dead, but to fear them and banish them from the home by any means necessary. They were an infestation. Roman Catholics conducted formal exorcism and cleansing ceremonies, but even the Protestant churches came up with ways of banishing ghosts, even if it was simply reading psalms aloud for many days. The ultimate banishment for the undead, or demons pretending to be the dead, was exile to the Red Sea.[1] It was Alcatraz for the worst offenders of the paranormal sphere.

Word got around. Soon the Fox sisters had been recruited by the great showman P. T. Barnum to appear as fortune tellers in his busy New York venue, the American Museum. They sat there in neat dark frocks and white collars and charged a dollar a time. The author of *The Last of the Mohicans*, James Fenimore Cooper, came to visit them there and was unnerved by their replies about his dead sister. Soon, the sisters were being investigated by committees who wanted to test their 'powers' under controlled circumstances. Women checked the undergarments of the sisters for any instrument that might be producing the raps. The bad grammar of the shade of Benjamin Franklin was roundly mocked by a hostile group of sceptics. Not for the first time in such cases, it was suggested that the sisters were cracking their joints to produce the phantom sounds.

In March 1851, men finally laid their hands on the bodies of the sisters. No fewer than three doctors from Buffalo held firmly to Maggie's legs and knees for an hour as she tried to produce phenomena, and it set a precedent. In the name of science, professional middle-class men would henceforth lose no opportunity to truss, strap, wire up, restrain and interfere with the flesh and clothing of lower-class female mediums in their purview. They checked their corsets, examined their hands, feet and shoes, poked, prodded and dominated them.

The doctors would, one assumes, have thought that what they did was for the greater good. But neither were they about to be gulled by two barely literate young girls. Yet despite all their efforts, and even a sceptics' travelling show organized by Dr Charles Alfred Lee and hosted by a man with especially voluble joints,[2] nothing failed to dampen the growing public enthusiasm for spirit rapping.

It was expected that the scandalous court case that began in Chancery on April Fool's Day in 1868 would put an end, once and for all, to the fashion for séances, since the man who had made the séance fashionable, Daniel Dunglas Home, was now on trial for fraud and deception. The *Spectator* had no doubt about it: spiritualism itself was on trial, not this effeminate medium, for whom the term 'psychic' was first coined, or the wealthy widow who was now suing him.

Séances had by this time been commonplace in England for over fifteen years, and as the public's desire for ever more extravagant spectacle continued, so did the throb of scandal. The roster of respectable scientists and doctors whose careers were damaged by an interest in psychic phenomena is a remarkable one. Spiritualism's precursor, Mesmerism, had already shortened the career of the distinguished doctor John Elliotson. It was he who, in August 1840 at Lady Blessington's home, Gore House (on the site of the Albert Hall), taught Charles Dickens how to cast individuals into a trance. This fascinated the writer as a therapeutic technique, though his early enthusiasm for it may also explain his later, almost extravagant, horror of physical and trance-mediums in general.

The ringmasters started arriving from the US in October 1852; the first was Mrs Maria Hayden, the wife of a Boston newspaper owner. Despite the almost universal derision of the press, séances secretly prospered in London and the home counties. Mrs Hayden, with her stripped-down demonstrations of disembodied raps (three for yes, not two) and table-turning during tea and cakes in Cavendish Square, was merely a cupbearer for the real deal, Daniel Dunglas Home, with his miracle effects. This man could speak to the dead, cause heavy pieces of furniture to float, fly and take burning coals from a fireplace.

Home had performed in the Hayden household as far back as 1851, and the support of W. R. Hayden's newspapers was very much part of his rise to fame. It was a summer séance the following year that clinched it. In a large house in South Manchester, Connecticut belonging to a wealthy silk manufacturer, the spirits Home had summoned caused a table to roll in the manner of a 'violent tempest' before being subjected to 'regular, sullen shocks', as if of waves breaking against a vessel tossed on the sea. The table capsized, Homes rose transcendent above the jetsam, and a volley of raps crashed and shook around the room like a drumroll misplaced. It later emerged that two sailor relatives of someone attending the séance had been lost at sea.

Home was born in Edinburgh, Scotland, in March 1833. It is said that the dead used to crowd around his cradle, which was seen rocking without help, as if by unseen hands. The Homes lived in a cottage behind the paper mill, where the father of the family worked. William Home, drunken, morose, was certain he was the illegitimate son of the 10th Earl Home. On his mother's side young Daniel was related to a seventeenth-century mystic, the Brahan Seer, Scotland's Nostradamus, who gave written prophecies, mostly concerning the locality north of Inverness. As an adult, Daniel customarily wore a silver badge in his tam o'shanter with the motto of his mother's clan engraved on it – *Vincere aut mori*; 'Conquer or Die.'[3]

For whatever reason, Daniel Home, a sickly child, was sent off to an aunt in the Scottish town of Portobello and then across the Atlantic to Greenville, Connecticut to another aunt, who threw chairs at him when the paranormal rapping started. When his family followed him to America, he remained with this aunt, who later blamed him for bringing the devil into her house and turned to a trio of Congregationalist, Baptist and Wesleyan ministers to perform cleansing rituals. When the ministers proved sympathetic to the foppish, red-haired boy, further enraging his Aunt Mary, who then threw him out of the house altogether. Thus Home began one of the strangest itinerant lives of any Victorian, never charging for his séances, but living off the charity and generosity of his admirers.

There was no one to touch him for his kaleidoscope of ghostly effects. There were knocks and raps, of course, but there were also ghostly lights and extraordinary disembodied hands which would float around the séance room, shake hands with the sitters, move chairs or play ghostly music. He would ask sitters to hold his own hands and feet as these manifestations were taking place. Home would use his body as part of the drama, elongating or shrinking it. In August 1852 he performed one of his most famous turns – floating bodily. A journalist, E. L. Burr, who was sent along to expose him, came away confounded.

> I had hold of his hand at the time and I felt his feet – they were lifted a foot from the floor. He palpitated from head to foot with the contending emotions of joy and fear which choked his utterances. Again and again he was taken from the floor, and the third time he was taken to the ceiling of the apartment, with which his hands and feet came into gentle contact.

Among the many who attended his séances as his fame grew was the New York University professor George Bush,[4] a relative of the subsequent father-and-son US presidents, who had, in

1845, translated the works of Emmanuel Swedenborg into English and thus, it could be said, single-handedly created the environment in which spiritualism would flourish. In that year, Home also converted to Swedenborgianism, or the 'New Church', as it was called at the time. Swedenborg was an eighteenth-century Swedish aristocrat who argued in his many works for the imminence of a busy world of spirit activity just outside human ken (though, in essence, he remained a Bible-reading Calvinist). His key vision took place in a London tavern in 1745, and perhaps this was one of the reasons Home wanted to travel to the city. Though he later claimed his visit was for health reasons and to escape the clamour of his East Coast fame, it seems just as likely that he wanted to enjoy the second part of his career back in his native land.

Mrs Hayden's months in London paved the way for Home; he sailed to England in 1855 and found his career to all intents and purposes laid out for him by interested and receptive parties. From the moment he stepped into his complimentary hotel rooms in Cox's Hotel[5] in Jermyn Street, the owner, William Cox, wasted no time in introducing him to one of his most famous guests, Robert Owen. Owen knew exactly who Home was and welcomed him as warmly, according to one account, as a father welcomes a son.

Robert Owen (1771–1858) was an exemplar of social utopianism, now mostly remembered for his invention of the co-operative movement. His radical ideas concerning the welfare of factory workers proved highly influential. His experiments in setting up socialist communities reached as far afield as Indiana in the US. His friends and admirers were puzzled and alarmed when, in his eighties, he announced his conversion to spiritualism.

Home was soon conducting séances in the hotel for Owen and his powerful friends, including a former Lord Chancellor, Lord Brougham, and the writer and society lion Sir Edward Bulwer-Lytton. Unlike the lumpen Fox sisters or the provincial Mrs

Hayden, Home had an easy assurance and grace; consequently, a section of the Victorian elite quite took to him. The rumour that he was the illegitimate grandson of an earl perhaps helped a little. With his shock of red hair, his poetic and fanciful manner and dandyish attire, he was the Algernon Swinburne of the spirit world, a type they could recognize.

But he also made some powerful enemies. In a celebrated séance held in Ealing, a spirit hand placed a wreath on Elizabeth Barrett Browning's head to honour her as a poet. Her husband, Robert Browning, later wrote how his wife's dress had also been 'slightly but distinctly uplifted in a manner I could not account for – as if by some object inside – which could hardly have been introduced without her becoming aware of it'.

The seeds of Home's downfall had been sown. When he rose from the dining table where the séance had taken place, Robert Browning went away with an almost implacable hatred of Home, most completely expressed after his wife's death in the poetic diatribe 'Mr Sludge the Medium'. When the couple got home, Browning hurled the wreath from a window.

Was it, as some have suggested, jealousy that the spirits had crowned his wife and not him? From his later comments on the subject, it seems that Browning's fierce objection to Home was over something sexual; that he was an immoral man. He may have thought the medium had been interfering with his wife's dress and that Home was using darkened séance rooms to lay his hands on women sitters. However, it is more likely that his visceral reaction to the medium was Browning's conviction that Home was gay.

Home married twice, under extravagant and improbable circumstances, and appeared to father a son, but at least one of these marriages happened shortly after it was rumoured he had been jailed in France in 1858 for an 'unnatural offence'.[6] Browning was given to highlighting the 'unmanliness' of his nemesis, and certainly Home's obsessive attention to his physical appearance,

18. Daniel Dunglas Home styled as Hamlet: an actor talking to the dead.

and the excessive amount of rings on his slender hands, to many suggested effeminacy.

In 1868, Home moved into the all-male household of Viscount Adare's third-floor apartment in Ashley House, quite near to where Westminster Cathedral now stands. Adare had attended séances at the home of Dr Gully, a homeopathic doctor whose patients at his Malvern Spa practice included Charles Darwin and Florence Nightingale. Adare, the only son of the 3rd Earl of Dunraven, was fascinated by spiritualism. He became very close to Home in a way that, to modern eyes, seems highly suggestive but which, in the world of the Victorian boarding school, was not peculiar at all.

These were grown men who shared the same bedroom and kissed each other goodnight. Home would give Adare massages after warming his hands at the fire, looking over his shoulder to take the advice of the spirits who were guiding him while doing so. On one occasion, Home became possessed by a dead actress, whom both men had known when she was alive. Adare described it thus: 'He walked slowly over to my bed, knelt down beside it, took both my hands in his, and began speaking. I shall never forget the awfully thrilling way in which she spoke.'

Lord Lindsay was the third occupant of the flat, an Old Etonian and only son of the 25th Earl of Crawford. He too was a spiritualist, although at the time, aged twenty-one, he had joined the Grenadier Guards then stationed at the Tower of London.[7] One evening in mid-December, all three men were in Ashley House with a fourth companion, Captain Charles Wynne, a cousin of Adare. What happened next gives the sense of a hothouse atmosphere, with four very highly strung and suggestible men in a kind of emotionally romantic haze.

Home was manifesting strongly that winter evening. His body was elongating in a paranormal way and he seemed to be floating off the ground, dipping up and down. He suddenly announced, 'Do not be afraid and on no account leave your places,' and went out into a corridor. Lindsay exclaimed, 'Oh good heavens, I know what he is going to do, it is too fearful!', then told the group that a spirit was talking to him and that Daniel was going to go out of the window of the other room and come back in through the window of the room where they were all sitting.

The three heard the window open next door and then saw Home standing upright outside the window of their room, like a vampire petitioning for admission. He opened the window and walked in, laughing. Why? asked Wynne. Home responded that, as he was levitating, he had wondered, what if a 'policeman had been passing, and had looked up and seen a man turning round and round along the wall in the air'. This detail of him not floating in the air but rolling along the wall is especially eerie. This story was not generally known for years (although it did appear in a small, privately printed book by the Earl of Dunraven the following year) and it remains one of Home's most startling feats.[8]

One of the scientists who risked his reputation by endorsing Home was Cromwell Fleetwood Varley. Varley is best remembered as a leading electrical engineer who was responsible for solving the huge technological challenges in laying a transatlantic cable between Britain and the US. He is also regarded as a key figure in the 'prehistory' of the electron, since a paper he published in the 1871 *Proceedings of the Royal Society* anticipated a vital aspect of the cathode ray.[9] Varley knew Lord Lindsay and later worked with him, exploring the possibility that large magnetic fields might produce a physiological effect on the human body, something still being examined to this day.

Varley was not alone in believing that the rapping and movement in the séance room was evidence of a new force of nature; he stands alongside the co-founder of the theory of evolution (a gentleman's agreement was reached with Charles Darwin, who was to publish first), Alfred Russel Wallace, in that regard. In the 1850s Varley had taught himself the practice of Mesmerism, and duly entranced his wife Ellen. While she was in this state, she was aware for the first time that she possessed mediumistic capabilities; as a result of her pursuit of this, Varley publicly stated, in 1869, that he had seen ghosts in the séance room and had received information from the spirits that not only predicted events but also told him things only he could know.

Varley had no qualms about giving a character reference for Home at his trial for fraud. He observed, on the witness stand, that he had 'examined and tested [the phenomena] with Home and others, under conditions of my own choice, under a bright light, and have made the most jealous and searching scrutiny'. It was one of Home's best cards to play, and probably saved him from ruin. Varley wasn't to know it – he was a technically-minded and decent man – but this trial, like the séances, was really about sex. Or, rather, the lack of sex.

*

The Spiritual Athenaeum was created first and foremost to give Home a salary. He accepted the position as Resident Secretary, and lodgings in the new premises at 22 Sloane Street. But for the unannounced arrival one day of a lady in her sixties, it's quite possible he would have lived out his days there.

On 22 October 1866, a short, plump woman in late middle age walked into the offices of the Athenaeum. She had written to Home, she said, but after receiving no response, had decided to turn up in person. Her name was Mrs Jane Lyon. The illegitimate daughter of a cheesemonger, she had landed on her feet by marrying the grandson of an earl; Charles Lyon had died in 1859, leaving her wealthy. He was a Bowes-Lyon, from Glamis Castle, where they had honeymooned, and, as such, a distant cousin of Queen Elizabeth II. Mrs Lyon was also aunt by marriage to Dr Liddell, dean of Christ Church, Oxford, and consequently great-aunt of Alice, who inspired the tale of *Alice in Wonderland*.

Home was sufficiently intrigued by Mrs Lyon's eccentricity to talk to her about her interest in spiritualism and her own skills in mediumship. She seemed interested in his connections to the aristocracy and was shown evidence of the high regard in which Home was held by members of it. According to Home, Mrs Lyon claimed she had expected him to be 'proud and stuck up from knowing so many great folks, but I like you very much and hope that you will like me'.

She returned two days later and, after a further conversation, out of the blue Mrs Lyon suggested that she adopt Home as her son, to save him from future financial embarrassment. It seemed she was a rather isolated figure, not fond of her immediate family and with few friends to speak of. Again according to Home, she then 'threw her arms about me and kissed me' in an excessively passionate way. By 7 October, it was fairly clear where all this was going; Home promised to love her, rather pointedly, as a mother. She replied, just as pointedly, 'the less of that kind of love, the better.'

By November, Home and Mrs Lyon were sharing a cab taken from Bayswater to a lawyer's office in the city to sign over property deeds and money, accompanied by a joyous cascade of ghostly and approving raps from the spirit world. Mrs Lyon put Home in her will and gave him a large financial gift,[10] and he agreed to change his name by deed poll to Daniel Home Lyon. She lost no opportunity to express her physical desire for him, embarrassing diners at a dinner party, and the lawyers who watched in consternation as she handed over nearly half of her fortune.

Her true goal soon became manifest. She took over the use of his jewellery box (he did love his precious stones) and had the clothes of his dead wife Sacha altered so she could wear them. We don't know what suddenly changed her opinion of him, but looking back on the case of *Lyon vs. Home* now, it seems clear that she at last realized that Home was never going to take her to bed. On 10 June, he finally and completely 'repulsed' her attentions, and when she suggested marriage, he shrieked, 'That can never be while God gives me reason!' It was not exactly what she wanted to hear.

The next day, she wrote to him and coldly asked for her money back. On 12 June, Home wrote to her cajolingly as 'my darling mother' and offered terms for an amicable resolution; he would return the jewels and the two rings, but keep the £30,000. This horse-trading rendered her implacable.

Browning took an almost unseemly pleasure in the news of Home's demise. He was given the latest gossip by Dean Liddell. Liddell had 'told me all of the rascality of Hume [sic], and how his own incredible stupidity as well as greediness wrought his downfall'. The sheriff's officer arrested Home at a 'snug evening party' and escorted him to Whitecross Street Prison, then the debtors' prison in the City of London.

In her affidavit, Mrs Lyon claimed that the sole reason she had given Home the money and favours that so shocked her own solicitor was that she believed she was getting messages from her dead husband instructing her to. These messages, it almost goes without saying, came through Home himself, in séances, often in her own home. It was only later that she realized she had been made a 'dupe of by the defendant'.

The Times reported huge public interest in front seats for the court case, and those lucky enough to get in were not to be disappointed. A revealing portrait of life at the home of Mrs Lyon, 18 Westbourne Place, emerged. She lived there with a Mrs Sims and a Mrs Pepper, who would crouch outside the dining-room door while Home performed his séances, straining to hear every word. Feral relatives, the two Mrs Fellowes, also had their bad opinion of Mr Home broadcast to the court. It was clear in their minds that a fraud had taken place. However, a servant girl, Eliza Clegnow, testified that her mistress had loudly declared that she would retrieve her money by pretending she had been influenced by the spirit of her late husband. Mrs Lyon promptly turned on her, calling her a 'saucy, dirty, dangerous, story-telling slut'.

There were claims and counter-claims, each of the protagonists insisting that the other had designs on marriage. Home recounted Mrs Lyon's incessant fondling of him. Mrs Lyon responded by mimicking his voice and his entreaties to her to kiss him, which, according to the *Police News*, 'seemed to cause great amusement'. She produced a diary where she had written that Home was a 'greedy, fawning, sneaking, lieing [sic] hypocrite'. At one especially crucial moment, Home was asked to produce a spirit rap by the prosecuting council, which resulted, according to one of the press reports, in a silence underlined by a noiseless, eager leaning forward, 'particularly on the part of the ladies'.

In his verdict, the judge was damning of Mrs Lyon's testimony, but he was even more damning of the whole idea of spiritualism, which he deemed 'mischievous nonsense, well-calculated, on the one hand, to delude the vain, weak and foolish; and on the other, to assist the projects of the needy and of the adventurer'. It was an echo of an opinion the *Lancet* had published some years earlier, in its description of those susceptible to the allure of Mesmerism – 'clever girls, philosophic Bohemians, weak women, weaker men'.

Home had to hand back £60,000, but Mrs Lyon had to pay the considerable court costs. Many believed this was the death-blow to spiritualism. However, they were wrong.

There's a seminal picture from a Victorian séance in which the ghost of a woman looks down on an elderly man (see page 195). The ghost is dressed in white and wearing a white headdress, or what looks like a sheet, tucked behind her ears. Her face is serene as she looks down, extending her left arm to hold that of what looks like a Victorian clergyman beneath her. He is rapt in the moment, his lips pursed, eyes closed, his balding head tilted down in a kind of syncope. You can tell that, in his mind, he is communing with the dead.

The clergyman was in fact a doctor and has been identified as Dr James Gully (1808–83), one of Home's character witnesses at the trial.[11] And the ghost is Katie King, as conjured forth by Florence Cook. Katie King was supposed to be the spirit daughter of buccaneer Sir Henry Owen Morgan. Morgan, aka John King, was the most famous of all the spirit guides in America, appearing to many a séance table in full pirate fig, including swarthy complexion and long beard.

Just as spiritualism and the drama of the séance room seemed to be on the wane after the disgrace of Daniel Dunglas Home, a teenager from Hackney re-established its appeal. In June 1871 the secretary to the Dalston spiritualist association, Thomas Blyton, published an article on his protégée Florence Cook.

Florence Cook was born in 1856, in London. Her father had moved there from Kent and was a compositor in the printing trade and so, in class terms, pretty much lower middle. The family kept at least one servant. By the time Florence Cook reached the age of fourteen, she was constantly falling into trance-like states that disturbed her parents and three siblings.

19. The ghostly Katie King looks down on a supplicant, identified as Dr Gully, whose patients included Charles Darwin.

In 1865, a new railway spur linking Hackney to the city had opened, and one of the railway employees who lived just south of Hackney, in Dalston, Thomas Blyton, found himself running the local spiritualist group. This was held weekly, mostly at 74 Navarino Road.

Cook later described her indroduction and immersion in the spiritualist world as 'like catching a fever'. After contact with more experienced mediums Frank Herne and Charles Williams, whose spirit guide was the wife of the buccaneer John King, Cook acquired her daughter as a spirit guide, and made faces appear out of the gloom. Soon she moved from the séance room to a cabinet, essentially a cupboard with the doors removed and a curtain hung, which allowed the medium more privacy in which to conduct his or her spiritual affairs.

Looking back on these spirit cabinets now, they seem a ridiculous imposture, inviting fraud. However, to a Victorian spiritualist, the calling forth of the dead into material form was a procedure of great delicacy, and it was felt that any deviations from procedure, any disturbance of the medium while in a trance, could be extremely damaging to their mind and body. If there was a sceptic or a scientist in the room trying to monitor the situation, usually the medium would be tied up in the cabinet, and the often elaborate knots and straps carefully sealed – with sealing wax and the like.

Attendees at a Victorian séance generally consisted of a group of like-minded people who knew each other and met regularly. Usually, a serious séance would begin with a prayer, or a cheerful modern hymn such as 'Hand in Hand with Angels' or Longfellow's 'Footsteps of Angels'. The sitters would then join hands and form a circle. The first indication of some form of paranormal activity could be a cold breeze blowing across the table, or an involuntary twitching of the arms and shoulders of the sitters. The table might, in one description, appear to 'throb'. It might begin to move. The fastidious would, at this point, ensure that they were exerting only the lightest of touches on the table, to make certain that they were not assisting with the entity's manifestations. It is no wonder that the spiritualists called this the 'thrilling' of the tables; it seemed an exultation.

In the summer of 1873, Florence did something quite new.

Usually, in séance rooms, there were any number of disembodied hands, arms or staring faces floating around. The *Daily Telegraph* was by this point sending a correspondent to attend her séances, and he was lucky enough to experience a 'full-form materialisation' of Katie King. 'Though we had left Miss B tied and sealed to her chair, and clad in an ordinary black dress somewhat voluminous as to the skirts, a tall figure draped classically in white, with bare arms and feet . . . stood statuelike before us.' This episode was referred to as 'Form no. 1'.

In the twinkling of an eye, a familiar pattern ensued. Soon the door of the little Hackney home was opening to some very grand people: Lord Arthur Russell and his wife, for example, and the Earl of Caithness, with his wife and son. Cook was offered holidays in Paris, cruises on private yachts. It helped of course that she was very young,[12] vivacious and pretty, and that she liked to make her séances light-hearted and fun. The wealthy Manchester businessman Charles Blackburn was sufficiently enamoured by this ghost-whispering Lolita to offer her a private income, and she was able to leave her teaching post at Miss Eliza Cliff's school near Richmond Road. He was to make her sister, Kate, rich in his will.[13]

By this action, Cook became a 'private medium', which was a highly desirable position for her to be in. With good reason, many respectable Victorians looked down on public mediums as women of very low morals, little better than prostitutes; if the medium was protected by a wealthy man, however, they were less inclined to state their opinion. Having said this, there is an aspect of this relationship in which Cook became indentured to Blackburn, became almost his property. He required absolute control over how, where and when she performed her séances. While he was in his country residence at Parkfield, he delegated this duty to his friend J. C. Luxmore, but he soon turned over control to another man. His name was William Crookes. His investigation into Cook's paranormality was to become an erotic obsession that has echoes down the years. George Cukor considered making a film about the relationship, but made *My Fair Lady* (1964) instead, with its rather similar theme.

During 1873 and 1874, Crookes, a scientist and future president of the Royal Society, studied the teenage psychic. For much of that time he worked with Cromwell Varley, using the latter's elaborate circuit-breakers as safeguards, which created an extra level of surveillance in séance-room conditions; if a fraudulent medium managed to free him- or herself from the ropes and chains in which he or she was customarily placed, in theory, his or her movement would be detected. A version of this set-up was still being used by the likes of Harry Price in his National Laboratory from the 1920s. The system involved a two-cell battery, two sets of resistance coils and a reflecting galvanometer, the latter rigged outside the cabinet and giving real-time readings on the health of the circuit.

By 1873, Crookes was already a world-famous scientist. In 1861 he had helped to discover a new element (thallium). He was a pioneer in the use of vacuum tubes and the development of the cathode-ray tube; in essence, he is the godfather of the television set. Though august and well-respected, Crookes was largely self-taught, which meant he was not familiar with the routines of clubbability as usually expected from men of his status in Victorian London. Thallium is a potent neurotoxin, and many believed that his interest in the dead was proof that his handling of this element had poisoned his brain. It is said that the death of his younger brother, aged only twenty-one, while laying a telegraph line from Cuba to Florida in 1867, created in him a hunger to contact those beyond the veil. (Another distinguished scientist, Sir Oliver Lodge, was similarly affected when his son Raymond died in the First World War.)

Despite her apparently passive persona, it seems that Cook herself took the initiative after a nasty incident which, by the by, exposed a whole subculture of backstabbing and intrigue among the female mediums of London. It was a small pool, and the older mediums, such as Mrs Guppy, did not want younger versions coming along and stealing their clients. On 9 December 1873, one of the guests at the regular Dalston séance was a Mr William Volckman. He had been trying all year to attend. During the séance, the ghost of Katie King took Volckman by the hand, as was her usual practice. However, Volckman – who turned out to be a stooge for Mrs Guppy (indeed, he later married her) – instead tried to grab the ghost around the waist while exclaiming loudly that this was none other than Cook.

There was a violent scuffle as the dim gaslight was fully extinguished and Cook's supporters flung themselves at the man; Volckman had part of his beard torn out at the roots. After an interval of five minutes, the door was opened to the cabinet, and there was Cook, in a distressed state, yet with the tape secure round her waist, as it had been at the beginning of the séance.

Though there was much sympathy for Cook, and she hadn't, after all, been exposed (that was to come later), Blackburn, who had been at the séance, took a dim view of it all. He sent her a note with four words written on it: 'I shall stop payment.' Her whole livelihood was now in serious jeopardy.

In an incredibly bold and decisive move, she took it on herself to go secretly to Crookes' house, at 20 Mornington Road.[14] Whatever it was that she said to him, whatever guile she deployed, he agreed to subject her to scientific scrutiny. Crookes had found her 'young, sensitive and innocent' and had decided after talking to her that her treatment by Volckman had been 'a disgraceful occurrence'.

Cook began six months of séances at Crookes' house under controlled conditions, sometimes staying there for an entire week, the trains to Euston station rattling by on the sidings outside. One séance was given with her new friend and fellow medium, another pretty and flirtatious teenager, Mary Showers. Crookes had these girls all to himself, both human and spirit forms equally warm to the touch as they pranced around the room arm in arm like schoolgirls. Cook was later open about their affair. It was here that Crookes photographed Katie King as a spirit form with Gully.[15] All but four of the forty-four images were later destroyed by executors anxious to guard Gully's scientific reputation, much as many the library of a Victorian gentleman was stripped of erotica. Crookes was knighted in the 1890s and awarded the Order of Merit in 1910. After his death, not even the SPR, in the guise of Lord Rayleigh, dared mention the name of Florence Cook in a speech paying tribute to his work on the paranormal.

Crookes' experiments with Varley, who, it is said, first convinced him to take spiritualism seriously, took place at the house of J. C. Luxmore, at 16 Gloucester Square near Hyde Park. Two gold sovereigns were stuck to Cook's arms with rubber bands, and the coins were attached by platinum wires to complete the circuit. Katie King duly appeared and, despite a few dips in voltage, the circuit seemed to be maintained, and the legerdemain maintained. Crookes then moved the equipment to his own house to test Cook. The writer Trevor Hall believes that, by this point, she had completely entranced the scientist in a sexual snare. Incredibly, Crookes wrote a letter endorsing her genuine ability long before he'd finished testing her formally. It seems clear that Cook persuaded him to write this highly compromising interim report. So on 3 February 1874, he wrote: 'Let those who inclined to judge Miss Cook harshly suspend their judgement until I bring forward positive evidence which I think will be sufficient to settle the question.' Crookes had already made up his mind that Cook was not a fraud.

By January 1873, Mrs Guppy had reached the end of her tether. She had up to that point been the most celebrated female medium in London. Her great speciality was apports: tables would suddenly be strewn with dew-bedecked flowers, for example, and in 1869, she got the spirits to sort sugar plums by colour. At séances with Mr and Mrs Adolphus Trollope, Mrs Trollope's hands and

20. A book cover showing a comic depiction of a plump Mrs Guppy flying
through the air supported by spirits as 'the transit of Venus'.

arms were bedecked in jonquils. Dr Alfred Russel Wallace asked
for and received a six-foot-tall sunflower, complete with earth
around its roots. Prickly cacti appeared for Princess Marguerite
of Naples. Blocks of ice came, liquid tar, live lobsters, a host of
butterflies and starfish.

In January 1873 Mrs Guppy happened to call on some visiting
American mediums, Mr and Mrs Nelson Holmes, then living on
Old Quebec Street. Mrs Guppy wanted them to join her in a
scheme to neutralize Florence Cook; her matronly rage against the
girl she called a 'doll face' was very real. Three of her creatures, she
said, were to attend a séance and throw acid in the face of Katie
King, in the earnest hope that the ghost was indeed Cook and that
her greatest asset would be destroyed for ever. Mr Holmes ordered
Mrs Guppy out of the house and then wrote a letter of complaint.

Mr and Mrs Holmes were now Mrs Guppy's enemies. One of her men, James Clark, smuggled himself into one of their séances and lit a match. At the time, musical instruments, floating above the heads of the sitters, were being played; they fell to the floor with a mighty crash, but no imposture was found. It all got very ugly.

Holmes was enraged. He wrote that he could give 'the details of the infamous transactions of Mrs Guppy with Miss Emily Berry, 1 Hyde Park', and that she used her 'pretend mediumship for base purposes, and gave séances solely for assignation meetings to better certain disreputable parties to further carry out their lewd propensities'. Later, in 1876, Daniel Home stated that Mrs Guppy's séances took place solely for sexual dalliances, and claimed that most of his fellow mediums, female, smuggled in supposed apports to the room in their skirts. They knew that no one was going to search their underwear. By the turn of the century, several female mediums were specializing in pseudopods, as ectoplasm was called, that emerged from the vagina.[16]

The overt sexual aspect of mediumship was established quite early under Mesmerism. One of the female patients in the women's ward in the hospital on whom Elliotson conducted experiments in 1837 was a 20-year-old epileptic blessed, to the pleasure of the male observers, with a profusion of flaxen ringlets. When under a trance, she was pinched, prodded and interfered with. The doctor forced objects into her nostrils and shouted in her ear. Sometimes, her face took the rictus of a corpse. 'O Why Should Blushes dye my Cheek,' she would sing sleepily, seductively, as she awoke from her trance; she was described by those attending as a pythoness for this gnomic and suggestive utterance. Victorian gentlemen found the spectacle irresistible. The medium Emma Hardinge Britten was 'hounded by a variety of men, each of whom was convinced that she was their long[17] sought-after spiritual affinity';[18] they would send her passionate love letters and she was forced to take legal action against them.

Some female mediums took the chance to cross-dress; the

environment of the séance appealed to gay men and women. Annie Fairlamb would don a black beard and become 'George', and George did like to kiss the ladies, inviting the objects of his affection to dally in the cabinet with him. When Fairlamb was taken over by the spirit Minnie, she liked kissing men. Pocka, the Indian spirit girl materialized by Fairlamb's fellow Newcastle medium and friend Miss Wood, embraced one of the sitters, a corn-merchant; and repeatedly kissed the handsome Edmund Gurney[18] two or three times through the drapery, then with uncovered lips.

Later women mediums would also find deployment of their sexuality a useful tactic. Eusapia Palladino, a medium twice investigated by the SPR, was an earthy Neapolitan woman who would customarily wake from her séances hot, sweaty and aroused, and climb into the laps of her male sitters. Her dress would bulge. Pseudopodia would extend from her hips like a prosthetic penis, bumping the ribs of, amongst others, Frederic Myers.[19] She would sometimes shudder with pleasure as a phantom lover drew her to orgasm, to the awkwardness and embarrassment of the Cambridge academics who were studying her. Despite all these shenanigans, she kept producing phenomena no one could explain.

Houdini would have the same issues when investigating the 1920s Boston medium Mina Crandon, a flapper who would greet her sitters wearing nothing but a thin dressing gown, slippers and silk stockings, apparel that left nothing to the imagination. She was rumoured to hold some séances completely in the nude. Houdini, who conducted a lifelong war on fraudulent mediums, specifically warned researchers to avoid 'falling in love' with her.

The reason there were so many female mediums has been much written about; it proved a transition from a domestic space to a public one for many women in a way that had never happened before. It was linked, in its more serious form, to the drive for votes and equal rights for women. Mediums were frequently quite anti-establishment in tone, and some séance groups were specifically anti-Christian and anti-religious. At the same time, what came over from the US was the idea of a female hierophant; it had happened in England with the likes of Joanna Southcott, but it was in the New World that the idea took root.

The early Quakers had ambivalent views about the supernatural, but the eighteenth-century breakaway Quaker group, the Shakers, best known these days for their elegant furniture,[20] had been essentially matriarchal, founded by a woman called Ann Lee. The idea of an androgynous godhead also emerged from the Swedenborgians and the Saint-Simonian[21] doctrine, and Shaker beliefs certainly influenced David Richmond, the early socialist who essentially brought spiritualism to working-class 1850s England.

Almost without exception, most mediums were exposed as frauds or, rather, as people capable of committing fraudulent acts, which is not the same thing. Spiritualists are well aware that mediums can fake manifestations of the uncanny, and would say that those under pressure to put food on the table would know that, every now and again, the real deal wouldn't be available to them. They are forgiven by the faithful in a way that appalls sceptics. The august Cambridge academics of the SPR knew perfectly well that Palladino would fake things at every possible opportunity, and yet this barely lettered Italian woman produced situations in controlled conditions which no one could explain.

Houdini himself was sometimes hard pressed to offer the solution to perceived trickery, even when he witnessed it first hand. Throughout his entire career – or ministry, if you will – Home supposedly never took money for séances, and they often produced no results at all. Though rumours about dodgy séances in Biarritz circulated, Home was never exposed as a fraud. He seemed tortured by his public persona and kept trying to take up another profession. Try as they might, the great exposure never came for the SPR. Frank Podmore, the SPR's attack dog and arch-sceptic, wrote: 'Home was never publicly exposed as an imposter, there is no evidence of any weight that he was even privately detected in trickery.' Home died in 1886, a long, lingering death from chronic tuberculosis, and was buried in France. He remains a uniquely unexplained figure.

The lives of the Fox sisters, on the other hand, disintegrated into farce. The women who had launched the spirit communication business ended up living in squalor, after Kate had been arrested for drunkenness in New York, her children taken away from her. In 1888, Maggie announced on stage that their entire story was a fraud, and that they had indeed produced the spirit raps by cracking their joints. She demonstrated to a hushed auditorium of the New York State Academy of Music, as sister Kate looked on. But then in 1891, Maggie retracted her retraction, claiming she had been offered so much money it had been in her interest to claim she had faked everything. She died two years later, penniless.

Other confessions proved more beneficial. The medium Annie Eva Fay, who was also investigated by Crookes and pronounced genuine, went back to her stage career after proclaiming she was not psychic and had always only ever done tricks. She was rewarded in due time by becoming the first Lady Honorary Associate of the Magic Circle. She later told Harry Houdini how she had managed to outfox the Varley–Crookes circuit test.[22]

Like Kate Fox, many mediums became alcoholics, including Mary Showers, Florence Cook's friend, who had ended up conducting séances half drunk. Mary's own mother had put it about that she too was sexually involved with Crookes, but he claimed these notes to her were forgeries. Such was the estimation he was held in that he survived his spiritualist period unscathed.

On 9 January 1880, Florence Cook was giving a séance attended by the 20-year-old Sir George Sitwell, later the father of Sacheverell and Edith Sitwell. It was the third séance he had been to where Cook was performing full materializations. She had pensioned Katie King off six years earlier and now manifested a merry little girl called Marie. In an earlier séance, Sitwell had detected a corset on the ghost of Marie, who was supposed to be only twelve years old. He decided to bide his time and, on this occasion, Sitwell grabbed at the spirit and found he was holding Cook, dressed only in her underwear. He tore down the curtain of the cabinet and found her stockings, boots and other clothes around the empty Windsor chair.

There was a revival of séances between the two world wars, but during this time they lacked the glamour, intrigue and, most of all, the sexual frisson of the Victorian version. The most impressive séance ever conducted was one by Irish medium Eileen Garrett with Harry Price, in October 1930. It had been planned to get hold of Arthur Conan Doyle, but Flight-Lieutenant H. Carmichael Owen came through. He was the captain of the airship R101 which had crashed on a hillside just days earlier, killing forty-eight people. A wealth of technical detail came through, which impressed Major Oliver Villiers of the Civil Aviation Authority so much he asked for a special second séance to be laid on. Garrett, who had no bells and whistles in her act, proved one of the most impressive of her breed, long after the heyday of the séance salon.

The last of the famous séances took place on 19 January 1944, under the auspices of Scottish medium Helen Duncan. She had been holding a session in Portsmouth when it was raided by the police, and she was prosecuted under the Witchcraft Act of 1735 in a trial that lasted seven days, and infuriated Winston Churchill for its lack of moral seriousness and squandering of precious wartime resources. 'Hellish Nell' was thus the last of the witches and pretty much the last of the materialization mediums, and it is her image, a Margaret Rutherford image, that informs most people's idea of a medium today, rather than the flirtatious teenage sylphs of Victorian London.

Angels in the Skies and Demons in the Deep

I seemed to see a furnace of torment and death and agony and terror seven times heated, and in the midst of the burning was the British Army. In the midst of the flame, consumed by it and yet aureoled in it, scattered like ashes and yet triumphant, martyred and forever glorious. So I saw our men with a shining about them . . .

– Arthur Machen

She was a German Type UB III submarine, launched in Hamburg on 26 June 1917 and commissioned for service three weeks later after summer sea trials in the Baltic. The U65 was a small boat by modern standards: 510 tons, powered by a six-cylinder diesel engine and Siemens-Schuckert electric motors and with a top speed of just under 14 knots. There were four torpedo tubes forward, one aft, and a complement of ten torpedoes in total, at least some of them fitted with magnetic exploders. Living conditions were rudimentary and sanitation, with a curtained-off chemical lavatory, disgusting. Bolted to the deck was a 110-mm machine gun to be used when the vessel was coasting on the surface, larger than the standard 88-mm. And there's one other thing about the U65. It was haunted. Badly haunted.

In July 1962, the best-known version of this particular wartime ghost story was first published in the magazine *Blackwood's*. 'The Ghost of U65' was much anthologized in the sixties and seventies, even appearing in illustrated comic books for children. Its author was G. A. Minto. Little is known about this author, and he seems to have turned his hand to writing in retirement, after a lifetime of public service.[1] In 1955, he pops up in the international press as the can-do Burmese consul who hands over ransom money in Rangoon for retired army officer Colonel Perrott, kidnapped by pirates while out duck shooting.

Minto was part of the establishment, a sensible authority figure, with a taste for atlases and *Jane's Fighting Ships*. There's a touch of world-weariness, almost disgust in his tone. 'I have been a servant of the State for most of my working life and, up till very recently, believed that no Governmental activity, however exotic, could surprise me.' He had been astonished, he says, when he 'learned from clear, cold print that the German admiralty had, within living memory, officially laid a ghost on board, of all things, a brand-new submarine'.

Minto tells it something like this. In 1915, the naval policy of the Imperial Government of Germany changed its emphasis towards the use of submarines to take on Great Britain's enormously powerful navy. At first, this tactic was highly successful. One of these new submarines was the U65. But from the moment its keel was laid, something about this vessel seemed to attract death.[2] At the boatyard one day, a heavy steel girder slipped from its chains and fell downwards, killing one man outright and mortally injuring another. In another construction incident, three men were overcome by poisonous fumes in the engine room as they were installing the batteries.

'Her trial trip was equally marked by tragedy,' observes Minto. Heavy weather in Heligoland Bight saw one seaman fall overboard. While the vessel was submerged a ballast tank sprang a leak, making it unable to surface for over half a day, during which time yet another toxic gas leached from the batteries. It surfaced only just in time to save the entire crew from asphyxiation. Two did die from damaged lungs, bringing the total number of deaths on the submarine to eight.

Despite this succession of ill luck, the needs of the German

21. The hoodoo submarine from WWI: a later depiction from a comic book.

war effort prevailed, and the ship was finally commissioned with one Oberleutnant Karl Honig in charge. But while the submarine was being victualled and loaded with supplies, a single torpedo exploded, killing the second-in-command and injuring nine other men. Then, after lunch one day, while the U65 was still berthed in dock, several seamen saw the dead man walk down the gangplank, go on board and vanish.

The ship launched, destroyed enemy vessels. But the story was growing in the cramped submariner mind that the U65 was haunted. A man was seen to go into the torpedo room, and three times the torpedo room was found to be empty. In January 1918, while at sea, as darkness fell and the weather whipped up the wind and waves into more darkness, two lookouts crouched behind the canvas of the crude, small conning tower saw an officer standing in full fig on the open deck of the submarine, without oilskins and impervious to the conditions. It was the second-in-command, on secondment again from the cemetery in Wilhelmshaven, setting his eyes on the horizon.

To the stink of the latrines and the low-oxygen atmosphere was added a kind of unshakeable dysphoria. Men were seeing the ghost all over, even being talked to by it. By the time the submarine slunk into Bruges, the oberleutnant was ready to quit altogether, but an air-raid stopped all that. As Honig ran to the shelter in the city, he was killed by a bomb. The headless body was carried on to the U65, and his ghost was added to the roster. The night crew was slowly gaining control of the ship.

The German admiralty called in a Lutheran pastor, Franz Weber, and had the U65 exorcized. Far from reassuring the crew, the whole business seemed to upset them more. A new commander was drafted, Lieutenant-Commander Schelle. He took a no-nonsense attitude to the whole business of a haunted vessel, cracking down on discipline. By June, however, the ghost was seen again; two sailors deserted and were court-martialled and sent off to a penal battalion on the Western Front.

Early in the morning of 10 July, only months before the Armistice, the US submarine L2 was patrolling an area off Cape Clear and the southern Irish Coast. Cruising at periscope level, a German U-boat was spotted on the surface. Just as the American captain gave orders to commence an attack, a most unexpected event took place: a huge explosion ripped the German boat apart, leaving behind nothing but an oil slick reflecting the summer sky. It was the U65, and it had sunk with all hands.

Minto tells us that, in 1921, a Dr Hecht had access to German official documents during an investigation into the whole story of the U65. He could provide no satisfactory explanation for what took place 'as a man of science', but he ended his report with a slightly off-key reference to *Hamlet*. Minto himself signs off: 'There are also more things in our sea than our philosophy can yet compass.'

★

In 2003, Channel 4 in the UK commissioned a diving show called *Wreck Detectives* for a second series. Innes McCartney had discovered the remains of an unidentified submarine some sixty miles off Padstow, and since its identity had the relish of a mystery, this location was selected for an episode. It was a deep dive at the limits of the scuba gear, but the waters where the boat lay were crystal clear.

Below the warm Cornish waters, the submarine wreck showed no obvious clues to its demise. It was German. It was First World War. There was no sign of an explosion, or damage from an attack. The aft hatches were open, as if the crew had tried to escape. A propeller was retrieved and its serial numbers checked. There could be no doubt: it was the U65. Far from solving the mystery, the lack of explosive damage to the submarine had deepened it. Now designated a war grave, it immediately became off limits to divers. The producers of the programme and the divers who floated around the submarine had no idea that this was in fact the most cursed and haunted warship there has ever been.[3]

The origins of this story lie in a 1932 book by Hector C. Bywater. Bywater is an intriguing figure among naval experts of the interwar period, with deep connections to the British intelligence services and an almost unrivalled understanding of the navies of the larger powers. He writes about a surprise attack on US naval assets by Japan in a book written as far back as 1925, and these 'predictions' of Pearl Harbor and the rise of a Japanese hegemony in the Pacific have given him a special place in the heart of conspiracy theorists. His opinion was often sought by the *Telegraph* and the *New York Herald*. His mysterious death in London in August 1940 was rumoured to have been caused by a drop of oriental poison at the behest of the Japanese imperium. Not everyone in the US had ignored his 1925 prediction, and it may just have made the difference between an immediate capitulation and eventual victory. In 1926, he had been awarded a gold medal by the US Naval Institute.

Bywater's book was called *Their Secret Purpose: Dramas and Mysteries of the Naval War* and was partly culled from many reports he had filed for the *Daily Telegraph*. In the second chapter, 'The Queer Side of Things', we get what appears to be the first ever account of the U65. It is curious it was included at all, since this was a serious book from a well-respected naval correspondent. He tried to fend off raised eyebrows in the last paragraph of his introduction, dated April 1932: 'To forestall possible criticism of the chapter of the haunted German submarine, I may state that the data which reached me on this subject were carefully scrutinised, and, as far as possible, checked before being used.'

So what is his version of what he calls the 'hoodoo' submarine?

He writes that the U65 story was still spoken of 'with bated breath by veterans of the German U-Boat corps'. He mentions that he has read a pamphlet 'published after the war' by Professor Dr Hecht, and calls the U65 case 'one of the best documented ghost stories of the sea'. The reality is however a folkloric one – much retold, but very little documented.

The U65 was one of a group of twenty-four medium-sized submarines designed to operate off the coast of Flanders. Her complement was three officers and thirty-one ratings. Bywater mentions the ill luck of its construction, the girder that killed two men and the sea-trials gas-leak that killed three others before the boat was even commissioned. After the maiden voyage, in which one bluejacket was washed overboard, a torpedo kills the second officer, whose name we are not given. Some weeks later, a 'panic-stricken seaman dashed into the wardroom' with the cry 'Herr Ober-Leutnant, the dead officer is on board!' A bluejacket named Peterson was found cowering in the lee of the conning tower, having witnessed the apparition. The incident had a bad effect on the morale of the crew.

Bywater gives many more crew names in his account than

Minto, who curiously conflates the Lutheran pastor who exorcized the boat with the 'distinguished psychologist' Professor Dr
Hecht who wrote an account of it after the war. This suggests
that Minto is trying to disguise his source material, perhaps to
make his own account seem more first-hand, fresher.

On the evening of 21 January 1918, after an uneventful voyage
to Zeebrugge, a man in officer's uniform was seen standing on
the deck in the full raw face of the elements. The captain himself
also witnessed it.

The psychological effect on the entire crew was already becoming evident. On one attack on a steamer, with the ship damaged
and beginning to lower her lifeboats, the captain held back from
finishing the ship off as per usual practice since he became suddenly convinced that this was a 'Q' ship – a lure ship for submarines.
Convinced a curse was hanging over the vessel, the captain preferred not to take the risk and tempt providence.

Soon after this loss of nerve, the U65 was in Bruges to be resup-
plied, in a bomb-proof shelter, when an air-raid siren sounded.
The commanding officer had left the ship and was en route to the
officer's mess or casino, but retraced his steps when he heard the
alarm. This was a bad idea. A shell or a bomb splinter took off his
head. They 'carried the body on board'.

Rumours about the happenings going on around this submarine had now reached the commodore of submarines, who ordered
a Lutheran pastor, Professor Hecht, to go on board for 'a special
service to exorcize evil spirits'. There is of course no exorcism
ritual in the Lutheran Church, so if it did happen, we can only
assume that some prayers were said.

A new commanding officer didn't stay long, but he seemed
successful in calming the situation down. He promised dire punishment for anyone propagating 'that damned nonsense', and two
cruises passed off successfully. Perhaps it really was all just a case
of hysteria. In May 1918 Lieutenant-Commander Schelle took
over and, unfortunately, the ghosts returned with him. The next

few weeks were later described by a petty officer, who confirmed that the U65 had never been a 'happy ship'. 'Several of the Blue-jackets saw the ghost quite often, but others were unable to see it, even when it was pointed out to them standing only a few feet away.' When the captain was asked to look, he professed to see nothing, despite having told the officer's casino that the ship was 'haunted by devils'.

May was the worst month, cruising in the English Channel. A torpedo gunner named Eberhardt went 'raving mad and had to be tied up'. He screamed that the ghost was after him until the captain gave him morphia. When he awoke he seemed better, but when untied he promptly jumped into the sea and was lost. Off Ushant, the chief engineer slipped and broke his leg. On another occasion, on sight of a tramp steamer, the surfaced sub-marine opened fire with its deck gun before being swamped by waves that washed one Richard Meyer overboard and drowned him. 'Three times on that trip I saw the ghost, and so did several of my messmates,' the petty officer reported to Bywater, who quotes him extensively, never giving his name. 'The men were so depressed they went about like sleep-walkers, performing their duties automatically and starting at every unusual sound. I do not think any of us expected to get back alive.'

Everyone was expecting the worst. Their twinned ship the U55 had been destroyed, as had the U33 and U79 in the same area. The British Navy seemed to be on to them, off Dover. Shortly, they were being depth-charged; shattered bulbs plunged areas into darkness and the boat heeled at an angle of twenty-five degrees. The coxswain Lohmann lost his foothold and was dashed against the switchboard, dying three weeks later of internal injuries.

At that juncture Bywater's unnamed German source admitted that he had a stroke of luck, having been sent to hospital as they berthed once more in Bruges, and thus avoiding the destruction of the submarine. By now everyone on the boat had a death-wish. 'My messmate Wernicke came to see me the day before the U65 sailed. He had come to say goodbye as he knew he would never return. I knew it too. He left me most of his personal effects and asked me to forward it to his wife when "the news comes in".'

On 31 July the U65 was posted as missing.

The vessel found by the wreck detectives doesn't match the account of the fatal damage to the U65 given by the men on the L2, a key witness statement which has been written about by Commander Richard Compton-Hall, a former director of the Royal Navy Submarine Museum in Gosport, but which I have been unable to source. Seeming to quote from the US Navy account, he has the boats the other way round – in fact, the American sub was on the surface and the German U65 submerged. Seeing something like a buoy in the distance, the L2 altered course to investigate, when a tremendous explosion rocked the American boat and a plume of seawater was sent eighty feet into the air nearby. Seeing a periscope, Lieutenant Foster immediately gave the order to dive, intending to ram the enemy. They could hear propellers running at high speed close by. The C-tube sonar seemed to indicate two submarines; then there was silence. A Morse code oscillator contact kept resending a Morse message – dash-dash-dash dot (OE) which 'represented no known message'. By this time, the U65 was on the bottom, subject to 135 pounds per square inch of pressure.

Perhaps someone else had gone mad, and damaged crucial equipment. Perhaps the ballast tanks had ruptured again. Perhaps the batteries had once more begun leaking fumes.

Or perhaps the *spuck* captain, *spuck* second-in-command and *spuck* coxswain simply took the boat to the bottom of the sea. And there the men still lie, in their metal coffin, off Padstow, in the deeps.

There were ghosts, too, on land.

It's true, Sister. We all saw it. First there was a sort of a yellow mist like, sort of risin' before the Germans as they came to the top of the hill, come on like a solid wall they did – springing out of the earth just solid, no end to 'em. I just gave up. No use fighting the whole German race, thinks I; it's all up with us. The next minute comes this funny cloud of light, and when it clears off there's a tall man with yellow hair in golden armour, on a white horse, holding his sword up, and his mouth open as if he was saying, 'Come on boys! I'll put the kybosh on the devils.' . . . The minute I saw it, I knew we were going to win. It fair bucked me up – yes, sister, thank you. I'm as comfortable as can be.

Lancashire fusilier to nurse Phyllis Campbell, *London Evening News*, 31 July 1915

On 22 August 1914, the British Army set up defensive positions along a salient formed by the Mons–Condé canal with orders to hold back the German advance. Early the following morning, Germany attacked the British line but were swiftly cut down by rapid fire from the men of the Middlesex Regiment and the Royal Fusiliers. German field officers reported that the British were using machine guns, such was the expert fire of the Lee Enfields. The Brits also carried an entrenching tool that allowed the swift creation of dugouts, a piece of kit not yet available to the Germans. Despite these advantages, the British Expeditionary Force, slowly and inexorably, was being overwhelmed.

On 30 August 1914, *The Times* observed grimly that the war had started badly for the British. It wasn't looking good. It was looking very bad indeed. 'The battle is joined and has so far gone ill for the Allies . . . yesterday was a day of bad news, and we fear that more must follow.' The article went on to describe 'very great losses' for the British, with the German troops so numerous 'that they could no more be stopped than the waves'.

Despite its precarious position, the 2nd Corps of the BEF had managed an orderly withdrawal to Le Cateau, between 23 and 26 August. The British public were left under no illusions that the British had survived by the skin of their teeth, and that reinforcements were desperately needed. It was certainly not the glorious first blow against the beastly Hun everyone had expected.

One writer for the *London Evening News* took a keen interest in the events in France. His name was Arthur Machen. The son of a Gwent vicar, Machen (1863–1947) was an occultist with a deep interest in Celtic and Welsh mysticism, and an accomplished writer of fiction. The issue of 29 September 1914 carried a story he had written called 'The Bowmen'. Appearing on page three and covering seventeen column inches, it purported to be a first-hand account of how the BEF had been rescued by supernatural bowmen who had served in Agincourt under Henry V. It was almost certainly a nod to Rudyard Kipling's story 'The Lost Legions',[4] which features dead English soldiers attacking some hill men, thereby rescuing their live colleagues from being over-whelmed during an ambush.

In his darkest moment, the British Tommy of the narrative recalls, of all things, a vegetarian restaurant at 37 St Martin's Lane, London. This restaurant, the Orange Grove (a favourite of George Bernard Shaw, as it turns out), had dinner plates with Latin on the rim and a patriotic motif. The establishment was later to be renamed St George's House. The Tommy murmurs the words on the dinner plates: '*Adsit Anglis Sanctus Georgius*' (St George help the English). He feels 'something between a shudder and an electric shock pass through his body' and perceives a kind of silence. There's a multitude of voices invoking St George and, before the British lines, beyond the trench, appear armed men 'with a shining about them' who then mow down ten thousand German soldiers with volley upon volley of spectral arrows still sharp from the Hundred Years War. Not a wound is found upon them, and German High Command can explain the fatalities only as a gas attack.

There was a brief flurry of interest in this extraordinary story, and the *Evening Standard* received two requests to reprint it, one from the spiritualist magazine *Light* and the other from *Occult*

Review. But in the psyche of the British public, a glorious dream was fomenting in the shires. And it began, very appropriately, in parish magazines.

Father Edward Russell was a Roman Catholic deacon at the church of St Alban the Martyr in Holborn, chaplain to the nursing guild of St Barnabas and a 'conductor of parish magazines'. The issue containing 'The Bowmen' had sold out, and Russell was asking for permission to publish the story in pamphlet form. He also expressed an interest in knowing the original sources of the report. Machen replied patiently that the story was a fiction invented solely by himself. The petitioning priest refused to believe him. Machen was appalled, and wrote that he felt he had failed as a writer to make the process of his fiction clear, even though it was in truth the *Evening News* who had framed it with such calculated ambiguity, and the newspaper was now garnering all the royalties. For the first time, he appreciated that a 'snowball of rumour' had now swollen to 'a monstrous size'.

Historian Granville Oldroyd interviewed a recruit who had joined the army in October 1914, after the retreat from Mons. 'He heard nothing about angels either at home or on the Western Front but the story was going round before Christmas 1914. There were no actual eye-witnesses but a man from another regiment had seen something.' Two powerful forces were at work here – the tradition of the English Christmas ghost story and the beginning of a huge revival in spiritualism, just as it seemed about to die out. England had nearly lost the war within its first eight weeks and this was the national equivalent of a crisis apparition; these were not the conscripts of popular legend, the stableboys, footmen and swains, but battle-hardened professional soldiers outfoxed by Germans who were discovered, on capture, to have '*Gott mit uns*' stamped on their belt-buckles. It needed to be cleared up, the matter of whose side God was on.

Another parish magazine that established a leading role in

the development of the story was that of All Saints Church at Clifton, Bristol, in which the vicar Revd M. P. Gilson wrote that one of his parishioners, Miss Marrable, had met two army officers who told her that they 'had seen angels which had saved their left wing from the Germans when they came right upon them during our retreat from Mons'. One officer had been a 'changed man ever since'.

The vision is no longer St George and the hosts of archers but an angelic miasma. This change can be traced back to the occult magazine, *Light*, which ran a story on St George's Day (23 April), 1915, under the headline 'The Invisible Allies: Strange Story from the Front'. The author of the piece claimed recently to have had a visit from a military officer who explained that 'whether Mr Machen's story was pure invention or not, it was certainly stated in some quarters that a curious phenomenon had been witnessed by several officers and men in connection with the retreat from Mons. It took the form of a strange cloud interposed between the Germans and the British . . .'

The story caused a kind of euphoria, and it was true what these pieces of local and national journalism were saying, that by spring 1915 it was becoming unpatriotic not to believe in the Angels of Mons. Letters arrived at Clifton from all over the world begging for copies of the pamphlet in which the story appeared. The influential non-conformist minister Revd R. F. Horton, speaking in Manchester in a sermon in June, claimed that 'no thoroughly modern man is foolish enough to disbelieve . . . or pooh-pooh the experience as hallucination'.

There was quickly a confusion as to whether it was angels who had appeared or the spirits of dead archers from Agincourt. In Miss Marrable's case, the angels appear and simply protect the soldiers from harm, as opposed to the Machen model, where the bowmen actively kill the enemy. Sources could not be revealed, it was said; to do so was to endanger national security during a time of war. But Machen believed it was an article written by Alfred

Sinnett in the *Occult Review* in May 1915 that was the tipping-point, since it referred to a 'row of shining beings'.

The truth of the matter was that arrows really had killed a great number of Germans as they advanced on the River Marne. In the first month of hostilities, steel darts known as *fléchettes* were dropped on German troops. Canisters containing around 250 were loaded under the wings of Allied aircraft. The London *Daily News and Leader* described it on 21 September 1914, a week before Machen published his story:

> Two airmen flew over a German regiment at the frontier at a height of 500ft and dropped a shower of arrows as the soldiers were in camp. It is estimated that the two airmen shot 50 arrows, killing and injuring 13 soldiers. The arrows were made of steel and were not poisoned.

I have in front of me the one-penny edition of *The Angel Warriors at Mons*, written by Ralph Shirley, editor of the *Occult Review*. It is a slender pamphlet with a reddish-orange cover, published in 1915. On the back there are advertisements for publications on similar themes, including *Prophecies and Omens of the Great War* ('Twenty thousand sold since 31 October'), at sixpence. Another is called *The End of the Kaiser* and tells how his fate had been prophesied three hundred years earlier.

Shirley acknowledges the possibility of hallucinations. The weather was hot at the time, and there were long marches. He cites one letter from a young officer who writes: 'I have the most amazing hallucinations marching at night, so I was fast asleep, I think. Everyone was reeling about the road and seeing things.' The following night: 'I saw all sorts of things, enormous men walking towards me and lights and chairs and things on the road.'

Interestingly, he does not sweep aside the tricky subject of Machen's fiction but deals with it head on. Far from Machen inventing the tale, claims Shirley, 'such stories had been widely

22. A highly romanticised depiction of the Angels of Mons by Arthur Forrestier that appeared in the *Illustrated London News*.

current in France at the time of the retreat from Mons – nearly a month before the appearance of Machen's story'. He tells of a lance-corporal who, that hot and clear evening at nine o'clock, saw 'three shapes, one in the centre having what looked like large outspread wings . . . they appeared to have a long loose-hanging garment of a golden tint, and they were above the German line facing us.'

The vision lasted three quarters of an hour. The mood seems to have been one of tranquillity, with no actual fighting going on.

A soldier with the Dublin Fusiliers described the angelic vision as more of a cloud that seemed to conceal them from harm and enemy snipers; a Weymouth clergyman read a letter from a soldier describing a whole choir of angels standing at the top of a quarry where they had taken refuge from the German advance. The Roman Catholic paper *Universe* also quoted a Catholic British officer who had seen the men with bows, and been asked by a

German soldier who the man atop the white charger was. The implication was that it had been St George. The French troops seem to have seen both St Michael and Joan of Arc.[5] (One French soldier from Joan's hometown of Domrémy saw her on a hill, brandishing her sword and shouting, 'Turn! Turn! Advance!') There are also stories that the Russians saw their own supernatural helpers.

Also mentioned is the nurse Phyllis Campbell, who gave to Shirley the record of her experience as a front-line nurse that appeared in the June 1915 issue of the *Occult Review*. Shirley neglects to mention that both young Phyllis and her aunt Lady Archibald Campbell were regular contributors to the magazine; in 1913, Phyllis Campbell had two articles on French ghost stories published by him. So this was no fresh-faced ingénue reporting on unforeseen marvels, she was the well-bred daughter of a novelist with an established interest in the paranormal.

That said, Campbell was genuinely a nurse tending the wounded at a hospital at St-Germain-en-Laye, some nine miles from the westerly point reached by the German army at that time. Campbell was a beguiling witness. One person described her as 'extremely pretty – child-like and sensitive', adding that despite her youth she had witnessed scenes 'that would drive many people mad'. She assured anyone who would listen that the French press was full of accounts of the angels. She impressed a journalist from the *Evening News* for resisting the temptation to 'varnish her story in the slightest degree'. The extraordinary thing is that no one wanted to notice that she was not even talking about Mons but about Vitry-le-François. The events she describes happened three weeks after the retreat from Mons, around 8 September, when she was working at a temporary railway dressing station at one of the railway halts in the Forest of Marley.

So, picture the scene: Phyllis is in a cattle truck in a siding, holding a lamp, seeing the wounded and hearing the sounds of the wounded soldiers lying on the straw. It is 4.30 a.m. when she hears that there is a British soldier who requires 'a holy picture'. He was propped up in a corner of the cattle truck, his left arm tied up with a peasant woman's handkerchief, his head newly bandaged. No, he says. He is not a Catholic. He is a Wesleyan Methodist, and he wants a picture of St George. He had seen St George on a white charger caparisoned in brightly shining golden armour, rallying the troops. 'Come on, boys!' he had cried. 'I'll put the kybosh on the devils.'

It suited, it little needs saying, the French and English war effort to encourage such stories. One English reporter from the *Sheffield Telegraph* described an open-air commemoration of Joan of Arc at Harfleur in Normandy in May 1915. Many wore medallions or were dressed in her light-blue and white colours. Catholic chaplains addressed the crowds, and mass was held, with an air of rapture and devotion. A French *curé* claimed that the turning-back of the Germans from Paris was a miracle, that the military password for the day had been 'Jeanne d'Arc'. It was said over and over again, like an invocation, until she appeared.

Also on that side of the Channel, Brigadier-General John Charteris was on the case. In his memoir, *At GHQ*, published in 1931, the true story seemed to emerge for the first time: evidence that Machen was not the author of the story, as he had supposed. Charteris refers to rumours of the Angels of Mons among the BEF in a letter home dated 5 September 1914, three weeks before the Machen story was published and round about the time Phyllis was hearing first-hand accounts from the troops she was treating. While researching his book *The Angels of Mons*, David Clarke for the first time tracked down the original letters. It seemed Charteris had still been pushing the official line in public as late as 1931. There was no letter of 5 September, only a postcard, and a letter dated 7 September did not mention the angels. The letter he quotes in his own book was in fact imagined by him many years after the war had ended.

Between 1915 and 1917, Charteris was Chief Intelligence Officer at GHQ in France and was behind one of the grimmest pieces of British propaganda of the era – that the Germans were running a 'corpse factory' which dismembered dead bodies to extract nutrients for animal feed and human fat for candles and ordinance. This story sank so deeply into the British psyche that it was still being retold during the Second World War by a Somerset labourer, who insisted he had worked there.

In a report of an after-dinner speech by Charteris during a visit to the US in 1925, by which time he had retired from the army and become an MP, the *New York Times* stated that he had personally claimed credit for inventing the *Kadaververwertungsanstalt* (corpse factory) story – a nice little anecdote for the cigars and brandy stage of the evening. His cunning plan involved forging the diary of a German soldier. All the same, he went on maintaining the reality of the angels to the end. Or so it seems. As a propaganda coup, it went viral. Perhaps he just didn't have the heart to admit it wasn't true later in life, or perhaps, by the end, he actually convinced himself it really happened. Such is the power of stories.

Clarke concludes that 'the absence of an original letter referring to the Angels of Mons among the Charteris collection leads me to conclude that the testimony provided him dates not from 1914, but from 1931.'

In his pamphlet, Shirley recalls a similar incident in which the imperial integrity of England was blessed by angelic intervention.

It is curious to note that similar phenomena to those which have occurred in the present war were narrated of the siege of the British Legation by the Boxers at Pekin [sic]. The occupants of the Legation found the house they occupied untenable, and were obliged to move to another position, and while the removal took place the British were in full view of the Chinese insurgents, who they took for granted would fire upon them. To their great surprise they failed to do so. An Englishman who was present on the occasion and who knew Chinese as well as his own native language took the opportunity afterwards of asking one of the Chinese soldiers why they missed such a fine chance. The Chinaman gave as a reason the fact that 'there were so many people in white between them and the British that they did not like to fire'.

In fact, many people tried quite hard to establish the truth of the Mons story at the time, and the Society for Psychical Research established its own official investigation.

Of first-hand testimony, there was none to be found . . . after the rumours had been discounted, we are left with a small residue of evidence, which seems to indicate that a certain number of men who took part in the retreat from Mons honestly believe themselves to have had at that time supernormal experiences of a remarkable character.[6]

Strangely enough, Conan Doyle's brother-in-law Malcolm Leckie was one of the first to fall at Mons. Doyle was to become an almost obsessive spiritualist after his experiences of loss in the First World War. One of the bridesmaids from his second wedding, Lily Loder-Symonds, was able to channel Leckie some years later, and it was this experience that removed all remnants of scepticism from the creator of Sherlock Holmes. If anyone was going to mention the Angels of Mons, it would have to be the shade of his soldier brother-in-law who was there at Mons, to the greatest supernatural evangelist of the age, but mention came there none.

What is the truth behind the whole incident? No single first-hand account has ever been found. Historians including Alan S. Coulson, Michael E. Hanlon and Lyn MacDonald have been through thousands of transcripts and 1,500 hours of oral record-ings and uncovered nothing on this subject. But a perfect storm took place in which early French reports of help from Joan of Arc and St Michael became incorporated in Arthur Machen's fiction in people's heads. Add to the mix a government keen to gloss over the initial reverse of Britain's forces and putting out a call for more men to join the army, and it was the perfect inspiring story. Catholic priests and officers feeling the role of Catholicism grow-ing in British society after centuries of abeyance, theosophists keen on a new dawn and spiritualists sure of a way to prop up their flagging position – all these people had a vested interest in the story. And then there was the common role of the folkloric, how stories change in the telling, and how stories want to be told. Even today, people want to believe in angels and even now, people think they spread their wings that day.

The Imperial War Museum concluded of the matter that 'to pursue the supporting stories to source is to make a journey into the fog,'[7] and the most recent attempt to collate source material, by Kevin McClure, concludes: 'I still don't know what happened during the Retreat from Mons: I doubt that I ever will.'[8]

In 2001, an article in the *Sunday Times* claimed that a diary and some film footage that seemed to prove the existence of the Angels of Mons, and an angel that appeared many years later at Woodchester Mansion, a famous haunted house in the Cots-wolds, had been found in Monmouth.[9] They had been the property of a First World War soldier named William Doidge. Even *Variety* picked the story up, when it was rumoured that Marlon Brando had expressed an interest and had even bought the old black and white footage for a reported £350,000. A man named Danny Sullivan claimed he had found the old canisters and box of papers while browsing in a shop in Agincourt Square, Monmouth, paying a mere £15 for them. There was a photograph of what appeared to be one of the angels from Mons, which had begun to appear in the Cotswolds after the death of twenty US servicemen in the grounds of Woodchester. The *Sun* published it in a two-page spread.

Sullivan later confessed the whole story was a fraud, cooked up by him to sell a book he was writing on the occult history of Woodchester. Yet, curiously, the owner of the junk shop Bonita's in Monmouth, John Read Smith, remembered the objects and Sullivan buying them. Sullivan, however, was puzzled: he had never bought anything there, though he did know the shop. As with the original story, this one has outgrown its initiator and carries on quite independently in the minds and perceptions of others.

In classical literature there were haunted battlefields, and fiends who haunted the battlefields.

The mutilated dead, or *biaiothanatoi*,[10] were one of four kinds of ghosts you might encounter. 'I would rather be a paid servant in a poor man's house,' wails the ghost of Achilles to Ulysses, 'and be above ground, than king of kings among the dead.' Living, Achilles too had experience of the ghostly; the ghost of his lover Patroclus appeared to him. When Achilles tried to grab him, Patroclus disappeared, 'gibbering and whining into the earth'.

Lucan's *Pharsalia*, which takes place in the civil wars between Caesar and Pompey in 49–48BC, tells of a Greek witch named Erictho who was sought out to predict the eventual winner of the wars. She has her pick of the fresh corpses, which are rapidly decaying in the heat. She is careful in her selection; she wants a corpse whose face, lips, lungs and throat are undamaged. She selects the body of one soldier, who, though his entrails have been torn from him by from a 'deadly wound', has intact lungs.

She stuffs his body cavities with magical substances, invokes his spirit 'just descending'. The ghost of the man appears; he is as alarmed as a child who has just woken from a nightmare and extremely reluctant to re-enter his damaged body. He is forced; she whips him with live snakes, screaming oaths, bullying him to life. Frightened, he slips into his wrecked body, prophesying, sadly, with tears streaming down his face. She then rewards him by burning his remains so he cannot be disturbed again.

The motif of the ghostly armies still clashing in the night has been a lively one since antiquity. The most famous of them all are Pausania's reports concerning the blood-soaked plain at Marathon, and how at night people could still hear the sounds of horses[11] and of men fighting, as if the battle was still being fought. According to Plutarch, ghosts appeared at the battle itself. 'Many of the Greeks who fought the Persians at Marathon thought they saw the apparition of Theseus in armour fighting on their side against the barbarians.'

There was a painted *stoa* at Athens with a depiction of the battle showing Theseus rising from the underworld. Herodotus reports that the supernatural assistance did not end there. When the Persians returned under the command of Xerxes, miraculous apparitions appeared again – on this occasion, the ghosts of Phylacus and Autonous – 'two hoplites of larger than human stature who pursued the Persians and cut them down'.

In 1643, a curious tract was published entitled 'A Great Wonder in Heaven, showing the late Apparitions and Prodigious Noyses of War and Battels, seen on Edge Hill, neere Keinton in Northamptonshire. Certified under the Hands of William Wood, Esquire, and Justice of the Peace for said Countie, Samuel Marshall, Preacher of Gods Word in Keinton, and other Persons of

Qualitie'. It had been rushed off the presses exactly one month to the day since the events described in it had been witnessed, and exactly four months since the actual battle took place, on 23 October 1642.

It was midnight on one of the few days between St Lucy's Day and Christmas Eve when the noises were first heard by shepherds and others: the sound of drums beating martial tunes and the 'noyse of souldiers, giving out their last groanes'. After first hearing the wall of sound there came figures up high in the sky – cannons, horses, muskets firing, the whole battle re-enacted, and the whole thing so real the countrymen dared not move a muscle, not wanting to engage the attention of the crazed and angry soldiers in one of the nastiest battles of the English civil war. They had to wait until the battle was at an end, with Cromwell triumphant, the king routed. The shepherds ran to Keinton, hammering on the door of the Justice of the Peace, telling their story of the tumults of war acting out in the sky. It's said he got out of bed to hear their story and summoned a next-door neighbour also, and so, on Christmas Eve, many local people walked to the site of the battle, where they saw the whole thing all over again, like a film projected on to the clouds. The author especially draws attention to the 'spite and spleen' of the ghostly combatants.

The king heard of it, in Oxford. He sent some of his gentlemen to witness – Colonel Lewis Kirke, Captain Dudley, Captain Wainman, and three others. The spectral show vanished between Christmas and New Year but then started up again, and the king's men could even make out the faces of the combatants, including Edmund Varney, who died during the battle. Later writers were outraged, particularly Lord Nugent in his *Memorials of John Hampden* (1832), by the 'pure, inexplicable working of fancy' upon the officers who confirmed the story. In Nugent's view, they should have known better when dealing with the 'weakness of a peasantry'. Class is ever present in such stories.

The author of the tract concluded that it was God's judgement that both sides should sue for peace, rather than endlessly replay the Parliamentary triumph; as a piece of government propaganda, it doesn't entirely make sense, since most devout Protestants of the period did not believe in ghosts. And, in truth, the outcome of the Battle of Edgehill is generally judged a Royalist advantage, so the ghostly Parliamentary win was a fiction. One of the cavalry captains on Parliament's side on the day of the battle was Oliver Cromwell, and it was the king's dithering around this battle that lost him the war when he failed to grasp the initiative and march on London.

Most of the landscape of the battlefield still remains off-limits as Ministry of Defence land, used in training soldiers for battle.

The author of that little orange one-penny book about the Angels of Mons, now deposited in the British Library, concludes that 'in some peculiar way great wars open up fresh channels for the psychic senses, and the physical struggle of great armies appears ever to have its counterpart on the spiritual plane.'

The Angels of Mons and the ghost of U65 begin and end the chapter of the First World War during which the landscape of Europe and of the European mind was changed for good. Both stories, as we see them today, are the work of professional journalists, though one had a mind for fiction and the occult and the other was a military analyst with no publishing history of spooks. With the Angels of Mons, we have a scenario straight out of late-Victorian England, a mix of parish piety and imperial flag-waving. By the end of the war, gone was the folkloric innocence of the Mons story, where ordinary men summoned up first of all the spirits of other ordinary men and then the patron saint of England himself. By the end of the war, it is the story of the U65, a tale which is recognizably one of modern warfare, a tale partly about technology.

The boat itself was not a ghost but a mobile haunted house, with the extra twist that its occupants could not escape. By this stage, after years of carnage, no one was talking about God and angels any more but about the malignity of manmade objects; all the ghosts of U65 seem melancholy and lost, officers on deck looking out to sea, a sense of dread and doom permeating their situation. The war began with a blessing and ended with a curse. And by the end of the Great War, a relationship between the supernatural and technology, which previously had been seen only in theatre and stage shows, had entered the mainstream.

During the First World War, Sir Oliver Lodge wrote a bestseller about trying to contact his dead son Raymond via various mediums after he had been killed in action during a mortar attack. *Raymond, or Life and Death* was onto its ninth edition by the time the war ended. Along with Marconi, Lodge was one of the pioneers of radio, and the inventor of the radio 'coherer'. For two prisoners-of-war, Lodge's book was their ticket to freedom. Imprisoned in the camp at Yozgad, Anatolia, Lieutenants E. H. Jones of the Indian Army and C. W. Hill of the Royal Flying Corps managed to get a copy of the book while still confined. They considered it nonsense, but hit upon a plan for using it as a virtual blueprint. Hill and Jones artfully convinced the camp commandant and his aide, Moise, that they were in communication with spirits, leading them on a wild-goose chase to find the Armenian treasure that the Turkish army were convinced was buried nearby. In fact, their plan had simply been to be considered mad. Eventually, the Turks stopped looking for gold and concluded that the men were indeed mad. Hill and Jones managed to fool every Turkish doctor who examined them, including an authority on mental illness, and were duly released to the British authorities in Egypt.

Two years later, in October 1920, Thomas Edison, perhaps mindful of Lodge, told the *American Magazine*, 'I have been at work for some time building an apparatus to see if it is possible for personalities which have left this earth to communicate with us.'

He told *Scientific American* in the same month:

I don't claim that our personalities pass on to another existence or sphere. I don't claim anything because I don't know anything about the subject. For that matter, no human being knows. But I do claim that it is possible to construct an apparatus which will be so delicate that if there are personalities in another existence or sphere who wish to get in touch with us in this existence or sphere, the apparatus will at least give them a better opportunity to express themselves than the tilting tables and raps and ouija boards and mediums and the other crude methods now purported to be the only means of communication.

The war had left a legacy of grief which technology, far from easing, seemed to cultivate with false hopes.

The Brown Lady of Raynham Hall

Even if I saw a ghost, I wouldn't believe it.

– Albert Einstein

One morning in the late summer of 1936, Gwladys, Lady Townsend, was opening her letters. One was from a man whom history knows as Indre Shira. He was, he said, a 'court photographer' with a business in Dover Street, Piccadilly, and, as the marchioness recalled it later, when the case became famous, he was most interested in coming to her stately home to photograph her ghost.

She turned down his request to stay overnight at Raynham Hall, but she did give him permission to visit. So early on 19 September – slipping in with the formal visit of the Archaeological Society of Norfolk, who were that day visiting the grounds hoping to uncover signs of the distant past – Indre Shira, his wife and his friend Captain Provand made themselves known at the front door of Raynham Hall. By the end of the day, they had snapped probably the most famous ghost photograph ever taken.

Indre Shira already knew all the stories about the Brown Lady. The marchioness herself had written about it in *True Ghost Stories*, co-edited with her friend Maude Ffoulkes. The book opens with her take on her family ghost. The Brown Lady was the unhappy sister, Dorothy, of Sir Robert Walpole, the first prime minister of the United Kingdom. She married Charles, 2nd Viscount Townsend, at the age of twenty-six. She was pampered, privileged. In the family papers, there is a reference to her having bought a great deal of chiffon. Lady Townsend daintily insisted that 'no breath of scandal was associated with her name'.

Tradition has it, however, that her husband was a jealous and unpleasant man, and the discovery that his new wife was the mistress of Lord Wharton[1] proved disastrous. It was said she was confined to an apartment in the house, under lock and key; another, even stranger story claimed that it was Lady Wharton who held her hostage. She died in March 1729, it is said either of smallpox, as a result of a fall down the stairs, or of syphilis contracted from Lord Wharton.

Lady Townsend repeats a family legend that Dorothy was not allowed to bring up her own children,[2] who were raised, instead, by their grandmother, and that she starved to death. Legends grow very quickly in rural localities such as Norfolk, and even within families over just one or two generations, but somewhere in them there is generally a kernel of truth. What accounts seem to agree on is that Dorothy died young and was unhappy.

Her portrait shows her dressed in brown brocade and with large, black eyes, which, when night falls, are said to take on a glittering watchfulness.[3] In 1904 the portrait was known to be hanging in the hall, and before that it had been, unwisely, in a bedroom.

It's said that the future George IV woke one night and saw the Brown Lady, probably in the other house with which she is associated, Houghton Hall, and refused to stay another hour. In 1849, she was in visitation on one Major Loftus,[4] a Townsend relative, over Christmas. On the first occasion he was going to bed very late after a long game of chess and, as he went up the stairs, a friend named Hawkins drew his attention to a lady standing on the landing. When he hailed her, she vanished. The next night he sat up to watch for the ghost and, when he saw her glide into view, being sufficiently well versed in the geography of the house, he managed a short-cut and cut the ghost off from its retreat.

Loftus then came upon her in a side-passage and to his horror, face to face, as he held up a lamp, he saw that there were only sockets where there should have been eyes. He later managed a sketch, which he showed people the next day. When the story reached the servants' hall the entire staff gave notice, and although Lord Townsend had seen the ghost himself, he became convinced the whole thing was a practical joke and hired a 'capable staff of detectives', who remained at Raynham for months without ever finding anything amiss.

Then there was the Captain Maryatt incident in 1836. Maryatt[5] had come to live nearby in Norfolk, on his own estate at Langham. The young Townsend baronet had just taken possession and, having redecorated, the household was busy throwing parties. 'To their annoyance,' wrote Maryatt's daughter Florence many years later, 'soon after their arrival rumours arose that the house was haunted, and their guests, one and all (like those in the parable), began to make excuses and go home.'

In an echo of the Hinton Ampner case, the naval captain, believing there was an imposture taking place connected to smugglers or criminal elements, determined to stake out the haunted room.

Maryatt took possession of the haunted room where the portrait then hung, and slept with a loaded pistol beneath his pillow. For two nights, nothing happened. On the third night, two nephews of the baronet knocked on his door as he was undressing. Rather improbably, they said they had had a new gun just delivered from London, and would the captain like to see it. Maryatt joked that he must take his pistol with him in case they met the Brown Lady and, when he took his leave of the nephews, they in turn joked that they must follow him back, armed, for the same reason.

The corridor was long and dark, and all the lights in the house were extinguished. As the three men reached the midpoint of the corridor, they saw the glimmer of a lamp coming towards them. It was decided that this must be one of the nursemaids, and so Maryatt, not being properly dressed, hid with the nephews behind a bedroom door to let her pass.

Through a chink in the door, he watched as the figure

approached, until she was close enough for him to see what she was wearing. She was dressed in brown. He recognized her face from the painting. As the figure passed by, it stopped and looked straight at him – grinning. The men jumped forth and Maryatt discharged his pistol, the bullet passing through the figure and lodging in the panel of the inner door of the bedroom opposite.

This grinning ghost is said to have been seen in 1903. In 1918, the vicar of West Raynham wrote to the vicar of Weston, Otley, 'I have heard that children of people in the Hall – years ago – asked who the Brown Lady was who came into their room frequently.' Writing in 1936, Lady Townsend observed:

> She was seen quite recently by my brother-in-law's (Mr James Durham) sister Mrs Cyril Fitzroy, and her daughter . . . her last but one appearance was to no less a person than my son George, when, as a small boy, he and Walter Rothermell, a little American Friend, met a lady on the staircase who not only frightened, but puzzled them, because, as George said, they could see the stairs *through* her.

It wasn't just Lady Townsend, there were various other, widely published sources telling tales of the ghosts of Raynham. The Monmouth Room, for example, which was haunted by the ghost of the duke, who appeared as a 'Red Cavalier'. There was the ghost of a child in the Stone Parlour, seen by Lady Townsend's German governess Miss Baumer; one afternoon, a visit by Lady Norah Bentinck and her two little children brought forth the enquiry, who was the third child who was standing there as they got out of the car, a little girl wearing a 'picture frock'? There was no third child.

In October 1935, Maude Ffoulkes heard the patter of a ghostly spaniel. In the 'Royal Bedroom', the heavy chairs would be found arranged around the table when morning broke, as if an overnight gambling session had taken place.

And, yes, the staircase – oaken, old, panelled. When the 5th Marquis died and Raynham Hall was let out, the tenants were 'awakened by hearing footsteps of many people passing up and down the staircase, and when they proceeded to investigate, waves of blackness alone flowed past them, and there was not a sign or a sound of anything or anyone'. The same thing happened the following night, and the next morning came the news that the marquis had died in Paris.

We do not know whether Lady Townsend spent much time with her curious visitors, but after a long day taking photographs around the house and, it seems, the grounds, at about 4 p.m., as the late-summer evening began to fall, Shira and Provand found themselves at the main staircase.

> Captain Provand took one photograph while I flashed the light. He was focusing for another exposure; I was standing by his side just behind the camera with the flashlight pistol in my hand, looking directly up the staircase. All at once I detected an ethereal veiled form coming slowly down the stairs. Rather excitedly, I called out sharply: 'Quick, quick, there's something.' I pressed the trigger of the flashlight pistol. After the flash and on closing the shutter, Captain Provand removed the focusing cloth from his head and turning to me said: 'What's all the excitement about?'
>
> I directed his attention to the staircase and explained that I had distinctly seen a figure there – transparent so the steps were visible through the ethereal form, but nevertheless very definite and to me perfectly real. He laughed and said I must have imagined seeing a ghost – there was nothing now to be seen.

Provand was mystified by Shira's behaviour, and claimed later he was sceptical when he heard the explanation. They continued to argue about it on the drive back to London, with Provand increasingly worried by the threat to his reputation Shira's claim would unleash.

Back in Piccadilly, at 49 Dover Street, they were in the dark-room together when the negatives were being developed. To

23. The famous photograph of the Brown Lady of Raynham Hall from 1936.

Provand's surprise, as he told it, there was indeed an inexplicable shape on the negative. Shira took one glance and decided to call in a third party, Benjamin Jones, manager of Blake, Sandford and Blake, chemists, whose premises were downstairs.

The photograph subsequently appeared in the Boxing Day issue of *Country Life*, and the December issue of *Life* magazine in the US, and almost overnight became a sensation. 'Mr Jones, Captain Provand, and I vouch for the fact that the negative has not been retouched in any way. It has been examined critically by a number of experts. No one can account for the appearance of the ghostly figure,' Shira wrote in the accompanying article.[6]

Within weeks, the SPR had launched its own investigation into the case, and the file collated by one C. V. C. Herbert remains in its archives in Cambridge. Among other things, he examined the old-fashioned camera used, looked at the lens (rapid rectilinear), established the type of film used, which was SS Ortho (or orthochromatic). Herbert's final conclusion was that the 'bellows' on the old camera might be letting in a chink of light. He nevertheless remained puzzled by the odd visual effects, since the banisters did not seem to line up just where the ghost appeared, which was suggestive of some kind of double exposure.

This was still being held up as an issue as recently as 2006, when a simple examination of maps of the house and clear uncropped versions of the print by writer Tom Ruffles resolved it:[7] there was a small landing on the staircase just above the thirteenth step, and this was the reason the banisters did not seem to line up optically; the apparent doubling of a portrait on the stairs was in fact a piece of panelling where the landing was.

On 8–9 January 1937, the much-venerated psychic investigator Dr Nandor Fodor paid a visit to Raynham Hall and took along with him someone who knew about cameras, a Mr Arthur Kingston, camera-maker. Fodor was then the research officer for the International Institute for Psychical Research. His wife and daughter also accompanied him, obviously determined to make a day of it.

Having found the staircase in question, they set about trying to reproduce the famous image; among the puzzles was why the ghost wasn't blurred, since during the six-second exposure, it had moved from stair three to stair thirteen. Fodor stood on stair thirteen for one shot, and then his wife did so. One can imagine the family stopping to look at the portrait and wondering.

On 14 January, Herbert typed up his report. The sheaf of documents remained largely forgotten until 1989, when it was rediscovered in the SPR's Cambridge archive. There are about forty documents within the folder, but the two crucial ghost photographs had been filched long ago. Fatefully, Herbert decided not to identify Indre Shira, other than to mention that he was a Scotsman. This peculiar decision means that the truth of Shira's identity and the truthfulness of his photograph may never be established; curious for a man reporting to an organization keen on verifiable facts. Herbert had examined both the camera and the negatives of both photographs taken on the staircase that day. 'Both Shira and Provand seem to me honest,' a view echoed by others involved in investigating the case, including Harry Price.

Historically, it remains one of the most flawed investigations ever undertaken by the SPR. There was never any chance that Fodor would deliver an objective assessment of the Raynham case, for the straightforward reason that he was friends with Lady Townsend. It's startling to open her *True Ghost Stories* and find his gushing introduction. 'In no case have I seen the sinister touch which the persistent calling of Little Alfred and William on cruel John Craven shows,' he notes, referring to one of the accounts by the various titled and wealthy individuals drafted in for the job. 'Fresh thrills even to the most inured creep addicts will be found in Grave No —, Kensal Green,' he goes on. The date of his introduction is 1 August 1936, six weeks before the photograph was taken.

Lady Townsend confided in Fodor that she had been surprised to hear of the ghost photograph, since Shira had said nothing to her at the time, despite his claim to have seen the figure as Provand had his head buried beneath the cloak of the antiquated camera.[8]

And yet she initially believed it was a vision of the Virgin Mary, something suggested, perhaps, by the fact that she had her own Catholic shrine beneath the staircase, where she would burn incense (the smell of incense also on occasion haunting the house, according to her book). However, she declared it a 'beautiful apparition' to Fodor, adding that she felt Shira would not risk his reputation by faking a ghost.

It's hard to know what this reputation was. In the accounts, the court photographer Indre Shira was above the chemist's in Dover Street but, looking at the London directory for 1936, the business there is William Marshall, solicitor. It also lists the chemists as Blake, Marshall and Blake, which could point to a further process of anonymizing the name Marshall. Could Shira have in fact been this solicitor? Was this why Lady Townsend was unwilling to think of him as 'risking his reputation' on a 'fake'?

As with so many ghost cases, *look to the woman*. There are two key women here whose roles are rather overlooked – Lady Townsend and the wife of Indre Shira. Lady Townsend mentions her arrival that morning with the two men – and how she 'described to me exquisite influences all over the house . . . she behaved as a psychic.' Now where was she at four that afternoon, when the famous photograph was taken? Was she, by any chance, and for whatever reason, coming down the stairs?

Even though sales of Lady Townsend's book undoubtedly benefited from the publicity, the photograph was published only on 26 December, when the biggest book-buying season of the year was already over; if it had been a calculated tie-in, it is more likely it would have been published a month earlier. However, it does seem that Indre Shira placed a framed copy of the *Country Life* article outside his premises, causing Fodor to say to Lady Townsend, 'Indre Shira is out to make capital of your ghost.' He also had a very brisk trade in selling 8x10 prints to the public for a guinea a pop.

If the photograph was faked, it was, in my opinion, a collusion by Shira and Provand. That they were court photographers with thirty years' experience seems doubtful; there seems to be little evidence of their work in existence. It was decided by the SPR investigators that Shira himself had no obvious knowledge of photography, and the work done by Provand seems amateurish. It is far more likely that it was the solicitor Marshall (that is, Shira) in collusion with the chemist beneath his offices (that is, Provand) who might well have been a relative. We do know that the *Country Life* article was framed on the railings outside the chemist, so the address at least has not been disguised.

And if it was faked, it was either done with Mrs Shira posing on the staircase for a double exposure or, as has been suggested, the duo photographed some Madonna-like statue and used the image of that to create a new negative. The scale of the figure against the stairs would seem to suggest that it was about four feet tall – another anomaly. But with the SPR report scandalously disguising critical details, it's a mystery that may never be solved. It could, after all, really be a ghost.

The history of the ghost photograph starts with a beautiful mistake and ends with imposture on an almost industrial level. Early photography involved glass plates treated with gelatin silver bromide which were reusable and, when not properly cleaned, often resulted in ghost images where previous photographs began to leak through. The earliest ghost pictures are lost to us. Sir Arthur Conan Doyle in *History of Spiritualism* puts the date for the first one ever as 1851. The Russian spiritualist Alexander Aksakov puts it closer to the mid-1850s.

At around this period, when the physicist Sir David Brewster was examining a calotype (the name of the Fox Talbot patented process) of the front of York Minster taken in 1844, he could not help his eye being drawn to a boy sitting on the steps who appeared to be translucent, a ghost indeed, simply because he had moved away during the long exposure time it took to make an image.

That ghost boy in front of a regal ecclesiastical structure, that phantom child against a gothic backdrop gave him the idea for his book *The Stereoscope*, which was published in 1856. 'For the purpose of amusement the photographer might carry us even into the realms of the supernatural,' he wrote. 'His art enables him to give a spiritual appearance to one or more of his figures, and to exhibit them as "thin air".' *The Stereoscope*, with its interest in optical trickery, remains one of the very first manuals to talk about the use of 3-D effects for entertainment and pleasure purposes.

The idea developed by Brewster was instantly commercialized by the London Stereoscopic Company in Cheapside in 1857, and their shows were so popular, with their colour-tinted spooks, that

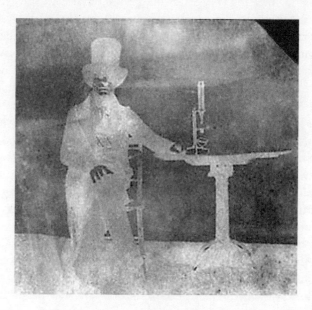

24. Calotype negative of Sir David Brewster, seated at Lacock Abbey, taken in 1842.

they were obliged to take out an advert in the winter of 1857 warning people not to buy pirated versions of their product – one of the earliest entertainment piracy panics on record.

There was no attempt to make them naturalistic – these ghosts were all theatrical, shrouded like medieval cadavers, hands in the air to induce a feeling of dread and visitation. As with Brewster's dictum, there was no attempt to deceive the audience with these cartoon-like and folkloric spectres; indeed, they rather got on their high horse that they were proving the 'folly' of ghost belief, insisting on the educational nature of the show. In this brief period between the waning of the magic-lantern show and the arrival of cinema, ghosts were a good way to get the public in. In the US, similar shows were put on in the mid-1860s by Underwood and Underwood, a publisher of stereoscopic prints, their name a pleasing pre-echo of the veteran British psychic investigator.

This period saw a parallel development of something darker, which did have the intent to deceive. Spiritualism was one of the great landscapes of the Victorian world, and spiritualists were quite happy to use new technology as a means of communicating with departed spirits. Most famous of all the impostures were those of the Boston engraver William Mumler (1832–84), who in 1861 announced that he had inadvertently photographed the ghost of a dead cousin while using some photographic equipment belonging to a friend.

Within a very short time, he was so inundated with requests from the public that he actually left his day job as an engraver to set up a full-time spirit-photography practice in Boston. It was a riotous success. His most famous client was the widow of Abraham Lincoln, who duly visited when Mumler took the photograph, to the satisfaction of everyone involved.

But the lights came on in the darkroom in 1869 when Mumler was prosecuted for fraud, and amazingly was acquitted, despite it being established that one of his ghostly visitants wasn't even dead.[9] His lawyers, not for the first or last time in a modern trial, quoted the witch of Endor, and speculated that had he had a chance, the prophet Samuel would have jumped at the chance of using a camera. In 1875, a photographer, Edouard Buguet, with studios in Baker Street, London and at 5 Boulevard Montmartre, Paris, was prosecuted in Paris for fraud, and his confession was widely reported both in England and France at the time. His way of simulating the spirits had been to make a preliminary photographic exposure of a wooden doll wrapped in gauze, on to which he would attach photographs of faces fairly crudely stuck on cardboard. When they raided his studio, the police found 240 examples. The doll-like aspect to the Raynham Hall ghost may point to this method being used, though without the obvious fakery of the faces.

Before too long, the practice of spirit photography was something done by spiritualists for other spiritualists, a closed world of rapt belief in visitations. The October 1871 issue of a French spiritualist publication, *Revue Spirite,* asked for 'photographer mediums' to come forth, and many medium-photographers did make a name for themselves. In 1895, the journalist William Stead sat for one of these photographers, Richard Boursnell, and while he was being photographed was ever mindful of Boursnell's spirit-guide, Julia. An image of a beautiful woman duly appeared, though Stead, while communicating with her later via his usual channel of automatic writing, was informed that this image wasn't really her – just a 'thought form'. Thought-form photography, or thoughtography,[10] as it is sometimes called, became of interest in the mid-twentieth century, and for many there was a belief that images could be directly laid on vchemical film by thought alone and without the use of a camera. The term 'thoughtography' was coined by Tomokichi Fukurai, Professor of Psychology at the Imperial University in

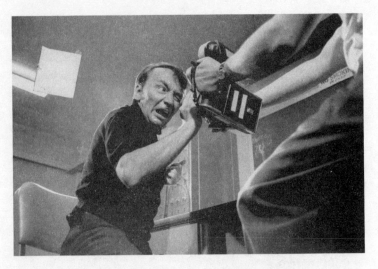

25. Ted Serios: mental images thrown into cameras.

Tokyo at the beginning of the twentieth century. This is yet another possible explanation for the Raynham photograph – that it was a mental image generated somehow by the people in the vicinity.

The best known of all the mind-imagists was a bellhop named Ted Serios. He worked in a Chicago hotel in the early 1960s. Later, sceptics pointed to his alcoholism and incipient sociopathy as discrediting factors. He discovered he could imprint images onto box cameras and, later, instant polaroid film, and was investigated by the Denver psychiatrist and parapsychologist Jule Eisenbud, enduring thousands of trials and producing hundreds of mysterious photographs. Not only did Serios produce images – the Hilton Hotel in Denver, crosses, people standing – in controlled environments, including placement in a Faraday cage, he produced hundreds of what were known as 'blackies' and 'whities' – photographs which were either hugely over- or under-exposed.

One of the most intriguing is of Eisenbud's ranch outside Denver, which, when 'photographed' by Serios, depicted the house without the white shutters Eisenbud had added a few years earlier. There were differences to the barn too, with the Dutch doors missing. It was perhaps a paranormal snapshot of the past, but it also reminded Eisenbud of the dream distortions of his psychiatric patients. In 1845, the physician Alexandre Brierre de Boismont published a study of hallucinations in which he described ghosts simply as 'the material embodiment, the daguerreotype of an idea'. Here then were the daguerreotypes.

In pictures, Serios looks scrawny, neurasthenic, with a lick of dark hair across small and weary features. It ended for him with a sudden dissipation of his powers in June 1967; the last image he produced was of a curtain. Though it was widely reported that the professional sceptic James Randi had duplicated the Serios thoughtographs, his only known attempt to do so, on the *Today* show on 4 October 1967, ended in failure.[11]

In September 2005, the Museum of Modern Art in New York held an exhibition entitled 'The Perfect Medium: Photography and the Occult', in collaboration with, among others, La Maison Européenne de la Photographie, Paris. In many ways it was a tombstone to the double exposure, mainly because, since that year, the use of chemical film has almost entirely died out. Photographs still pop up, and indeed are actively collected on websites; and they still make it into the news, especially in times of financial crisis and public anxiety. They are digital now, and people trust them even less.

Gone are the ectoplasm, the cavity-smuggled scissored animal parts and regurgitated cotton smeared in goose fat of the fake mediums, and here instead are the orbs floating around, with increasingly sophisticated graphics programs for the amateur interested in the manipulation of images. The Brown Lady these days would be captured on a mobile phone and posted within minutes on the internet.

Murder at the Parsonage

Every ghost story begins with a love story.

– Stacy Horn

Late one evening in the dying days of February 1958, a private eye sat in the lobby of a North Dakota hotel. He was waiting for Marianne Foyster, sometimes known as the Widow of Borley. The detective had been hired partly for his rugged good looks, since it was known that she had an eye for male beauty. Foyster was a mysterious and slightly sinister figure: a femme fatale, bigamist, possible murderess and the nexus of one of the most famous hauntings of the twentieth century. She had pulled off a spectacular vanishing act at the end of the war, skilfully avoiding the enquiries of the Suffolk police, who were then searching for her. But here she was, coming in from the snowy winter streets, a collision of worlds, a Raymond Chandler gumshoe straight from central casting interviewing a vicar's wife straight out of an Agatha Christie novel.

When she realized her cover had been blown, her immediate panicked reaction had been to threaten suicide. This was understandable: she had much to hide. She had broken the law on countless occasions, and was terrified that she might be deported to England and sent to prison. But after some gentle negotiation and reassurance, including the promise to set up an education fund for her adopted son, she agreed to be interviewed about her experiences at Borley Rectory, the most haunted house in England.

*

One morning in June 1929, a junior editor at the *Daily Mirror* opened a letter from a vicar in Essex addressed to the 'Notes and Queries' section of the paper. The vicar hadn't intended it for publication and in fact had simply wanted advice on how to contact the Society for Psychical Research. The Revd Guy Smith was an Indian national, a genial, well-fed former civil servant who had been granted the living at Borley in October 1928.

This new life, partly taken up to aid the health of his neurasthenic wife, was turning into a disaster. British rural culture was alien to him and he simply couldn't face another rainy British winter. And there was a second and much stranger problem: the house was haunted. The *Mirror* promptly sent a journalist and a photographer to check out the story. They stayed a week and, convinced that the phenomenon was real, started filing front-page features.

Over nine months, Smith and his wife had been assailed by all sorts of phenomena. Mabel Smith had found a skull wrapped up in brown paper in the library when they first moved in, which hadn't helped. Staff had left after seeing ghosts. There was the figure of a woman who walked the gardens, and a spectral coach which drew up to the door. The Cracknell & Mercury servants' bells rang and rang of their own accord in the kitchen corridor. Other unwelcome noises included sinister 'sibilant whisperings' and the voice of a woman, apparently being attacked.

It seems strange that Smith would have contacted a newspaper rather than, say, his superior, the Bishop of Chelmsford. But Smith had few friends in England. He had accepted his Borley appointment without having seen the house. Built in 1863 by the Revd Henry Bull, Borley was only remotely functional with a large amount of servants to run it. Smith had no idea that twelve other clergymen had already rejected it or that the sprawling 23-room mansion had no mains water or electricity.

In short, Smith wanted to move out as soon as possible. But he had to give his bishop good cause, and so he needed a report from a reputable organization to back up his claims. Though in slow decline from its mighty Victorian origins, the SPR was still very well regarded as an essentially sceptical organization run by reputable scientists and a scattering of well-connected peers. It wouldn't happen these days, but back then a bishop just might have taken it seriously – if only because its membership still included powerful members of the establishment.

Smith was bewildered to open the door to a reporter, pencil poised as the camera of his trusty side-kick photographer flashed. And when the Smiths complained about the unwelcome publicity, the newspaper sent in someone even less suited to dealing with delicate situations.

A cadaverous figure with the demeanour of a secular exorcist, Harry Price arrived at Borley Rectory little imagining that this ugly building in an insignificant part of England would come to dominate his life for the next twenty years. He assured Smith that he would get his report on the ghostly activity, which he could in turn show to the bishop.[1]

Price discovered that, although the building itself was relatively new, there was a tradition of its locality being haunted. The house had originally been constructed from an urban template entirely unsuitable for its location, with another wing added not long after.

Its builder Henry Bull had found slipping on his Sunday vestments something of a chore. Lands around Sudbury gave him income enough to be able to afford his (at least) twelve children, and the house was gradually added on to as they arrived. He would career around the countryside, whip flying, in a fast chaise, or take pot-shots through the open French windows of the library at rabbits lolloping on the lawn. On that lawn he also raised a summerhouse to watch, or so he said, the ghost of a nun who liked to walk the grounds at dusk, beneath a cedar of Lebanon that seemed to date from an earlier house. It was said that talk of the ghost was a family joke he shared especially with his seven daughters.

His son, another Henry who is for convenience usually referred to as Harry, took over the living when his father died. Harry Foyster Bull (1862–1927) was a sensitive and rather ineffectual man, who found it very hard to fill his father's shoes.

Sporting a thick moustache of the Kitchener school, Harry paid local lads to come over to the rectory and box with him. He liked to take his cat to church with him and could on occasion be found in the East End of London, no doubt on the business of the Lord, where he was quite able to defend himself when set upon by youths intending to rob him. He married suddenly when he was forty-nine and his sisters, none of whom had ever married and who had fully expected to end their days at Borley Rectory, were told to move out. His new wife, Ivy, and stepdaughter, Constance, found living in rural Essex tiresome. When Harry died, the sisters began to whisper that his wife had murdered him. Their main purpose was to discredit his will. Harry's ghost, in a plum-coloured dressing gown, often carrying a small wallet for papers, no doubt the will itself, was duly added to the spectral population of the rectory.

Whilst living, Harry had assured his sisters that he had made provision for them in his will, but on his demise it appeared he had not. The hated wife and loathed stepdaughter packed their bags and flounced out of Borley, taking Harry's income with them.

In consequence, when Ethel Bull heard that Price was coming over, she insisted on staging a séance in the Blue Room above the library, the master bedroom of the house, where both Henry and Harry Bull had died. The Bull sisters maintained that Ivy had in fact murdered their brother for his money, and so it was no surprise when the séance in the Blue Room confirmed that yes, Ivy was indeed a murderess. Price did not publish this detail at the time, since it was libellous, mentioning only that for an hour the sisters conversed with the spirit of their brother on 'private matters'.

As an experienced (and highly cynical) ghost-hunter, Harry Price would have known that almost everything to do with this haunt was folkloric. The dining-room window bricked up by Revd Henry to stop the ghostly nun peering in, the discovery of a human skull in the house, the tale of a nun walled up after running away with a monk and losing her virtue, a phantom coach, sometimes with a headless man driving it, the headless man in the garden, rumours of subterranean tunnels, the sound of footsteps – always the sound of footsteps: all these were off-the-shelf ghosts of the period.

The Bull sisters had first encountered the ghosts of Borley as children. On 28 June 1900, returning home from an afternoon party in Sudbury, as Ethel, Freda and Mabel entered the rectory grounds via the eastern gate, they distinctly saw a figure standing on the lawn. It appeared to be a nun, 'telling' the beads of a rosary. The sisters initially mistook the figure for their mother. Then they realized it was the figure their father used to see. It was a ghost. And in broad daylight. They called another sister, Elsie: Come and see the ghost, Elsie. 'What nonsense! I'll go and speak to it.' As she approached, the nun looked up and vanished into thin air.

The Victorian high summer of their childhood at Borley never quite left the Bull sisters. Brothers Alfred and Walter always said there were no ghosts at the house, and neither Harry's wife nor his stepdaughter experienced anything in ten years. But, like his sisters, Harry felt comfortable with the notion of the ghosts. A neighbour observed that 'he could hail a spectre as easily as I can hail a friend.' He spent hours in the summer house late on summer evenings, hoping to see the ghost and 'commune' with her.

From his student days, Harry had been well known for suddenly falling asleep; he may have been suffering from narcolepsy. But since we also know that he had bad breathing problems, a more likely explanation of his sleepiness was that he suffered from sleep apnoea and that he was, in consequence, living much of the time in a waking dream.

The nun was first seen in 1843. This was only two years after the Georgian rectory originally on the site burned to the ground. It was not rebuilt for over twenty years, and stood a ruin by the church all that time. It's hardly surprising then that local ghost stories started to be told about it. The nun never seemed to enter the house, though footsteps, doors opening and locks locking were sometimes ascribed to her influence; 'the nun was very active last night,' Harry would tell people, with a solemn look.

If you look at photographs of the old house as it was furnished in the time of the Bulls, there's a fireplace that Henry Bull supposedly bought at the Great Exhibition. Whenever the children ate in the dining room, there it was. On either side of the hearth was a stone-carved figure in ecclesiastical garb, praying, one a tonsured friar and one cowled and monk-like under a hood, like ghosts coming through a wall.

In a household full of children with a father quite capable of making up stories about these mysterious figures, it is easy to understand how legends of this kind were created and passed on. Henry Bull announced he had bricked up the window of this same room, not because it overlooked the road, from which passers-by could see the family eating their eggs and bacon, but because the nun peeped in through it.[2]

Price was intrigued by his June visit to Borley; his interest was piqued. A maid, Mary Pearson, at first seemed a credible witness. On 12 June Price witnessed, in the evening, objects thrown down the main staircase and the disconnected bells ringing of their own accord. But any hope he had for greater access was to be dashed; when the bishop, sulphurously enraged by the publicity, the six features in the *Mirror* and the coach parties that were now turning up to gawp at the house, decided this was bringing the Church of England into disrepute. On 20 April 1930 Smith preached his last sermon at Borley Church, and the rectory was subsequently left uninhabited.

Seizing her chance, Ethel Bull managed to renew her family's influence over the parish and rectory by finessing the appointment of a vicar, the Revd Lionel Foyster, related to her on her mother's side. He arrived from Canada with his much younger wife, Marianne. Few people go on to marry a girl they had baptized as a seven-year-old, but Foyster was one of those people. This was the girl whom our private detective was to meet, many years later, as a fugitive at the North Dakota hotel.

In hauntings that appear to last over a long period, it is always worth looking for repeated patterns in domestic arrangements. So once again we find a weak Anglican clergyman of ambiguous sexuality with a self-possessed, Catholic younger wife. And, like Harry Bull, Foyster was a sick man, whose illness may well have had an effect on his mental state.

With the Smiths gone and the casebook closed, Price no doubt thought that was the end of the Borley business. But phase two of the haunting was about to begin.

From October 1930 there were workmen in Borley Rectory, though they could do little to make the house more comfortable. After the workmen left, the events came thick and fast. Marianne, who was recovering from a major operation, imagined she heard her name called. There were footsteps. Unfamiliar hymn books appeared. Irons, stones, cotton reels, walking-sticks and coal were thrown. In one of the most sinister episodes, on 28 March 1931, Marianne was touched on the shoulder by what she described as a 'monstrosity'. An attempt to exorcize the house ended with a vicious hail of stones. Objects such as wedding rings (unclaimed) appeared and disappeared. A kitchen table was found upside down and a bedroom window was somehow closed against its hinges.

A piece of brick dropped on the supper table beside the Revd Foyster's plate, and another tripped Marianne as she exited the bathroom. Objects would be found burning on the floors of unused rooms. Husband and wife often woke to find piles of stones arranged around their pillow; logs rolled through the kitchen and stones down the stairs. Pieces of paper with the word 'Marianne' appeared all over the house, and there was even writing on the walls, asking her to say prayers.

Like the Smiths, the Foysters weren't happy. Lionel's health was deteriorating. The local gentry was suspicious of their familiarity with the locals, who in turn didn't like their kindness towards vagrants. In May, the ghostly events became so vehement that the Foysters fled the rectory, rushing to their neighbours, Sir George and Lady Whitehouse. Lady Whitehouse was a spiritualist and her nephew Edwin, shell-shocked from the war and en route to becoming a monk, became obsessed with the poltergeists of the house and started to linger at the rectory, to an unhealthy degree.

On Michaelmas Day, 29 September, Price was working in his ghost laboratory in Mayfair when Ethel Bull and one of her sisters came to call, and a few days later, at their insistence, Revd Foyster sent Price a letter inviting him to see the fresh hauntings for himself.

When Harry Price made it up to Borley in October 1931, he didn't endear himself. Marianne was taken aback by the full fig of his arrival, with company and carrying a hamper of sandwiches, with the intention of doing a full-scale overnight vigil. Price could also barely disguise his fury on discovering that experts from the rival SPR had been there a few days earlier. And, even worse, Foyster had taken the SPR's advice to get Price to sign a document restricting his ability to make public statements about themselves and their house.

Price was unimpressed by what he found at Borley and felt he was being made a fool of. He made his feelings quite clear to the Revd Foyster: as far as he was concerned, Marianne was faking all the phenomena. After this episode, and after parting on bad terms with the Foysters, Price no longer had access to the house.[3]

In Marianne, Price had met his match. She made up as many fantastical stories about herself as he did. Among her other pathological achievements, she had neglected to divorce her first husband when she married Foyster, who was nearly twice her age; after they came to Borley, it wasn't long before Marianne brazenly moved her boyfriend Frank Peerless in as a lodger. Peerless was a cockney con-man who sold flowers outside Stoke Newington cemetery; he casually described Marianne to her own son as a 'sex maniac'. Some of the footsteps heard in the corridor had more to do with its human inhabitants prowling bedrooms than with the visitations of the dead.

Crippled by arthritis, Revd Foyster was wheelchair-bound by the end of his tenure at Borley. Husband and wife became more and more dependent on Catholic techniques to help them cope; a relic of Jean-Baptiste Vianney, the Curé d'Ars (a French priest canonized in 1925), which was carried everywhere by Foyster, was used to release doors locked by ghosts. He found that the only way to stop the spirits moving his sermon was to tuck it into a Bible, or so he told Mr Salter from the SPR.

In the typescript of his book *Fifteen Months in a Haunted House*, Foyster also mentions Edwin's gift of a scapula for both Foyster and his wife, a small medal they each pinned to their underwear, 'changing them when we undressed to our night clothes'. Considering the bedroom-hopping going on, it's a delicious detail that they put so much trust in their underwear.

Lady Whitehouse later described Marianne as mad and said that her ministrations did Edwin 'no good at all'. Indeed, Borley tipped him over the edge, and for a while he was in a mental hospital in St John's Wood.

In early 1932, Marianne fainted after seeing the ghost of Harry Bull, but the bigger ghost at the feast was the Foysters' increasingly parlous financial situation. Increasingly desperate, increasingly crazy, they began concocting money-making schemes of a quite bizarre nature.

In a coldly calculated move, Marianne became a double bigamist during their last year at the rectory. On 23 February 1935, she married a commercial traveller called Henry Fisher in Ipswich, giving her maiden name as Voyster. It was, essentially, a scam, but Foyster was in on it.[4] At one point, Marianne even moved Fisher into Borley and Foyster passed himself off as her father, and her adopted daughter and son as her siblings. After Foyster collapsed while reading one of his sermons at the church, he was forced to resign his living and move in with his wife and her new husband in Ipswich. Marianne described her husband at this time as 'off his rocker'. He would shout and rave about sin.

But it was Fisher who ended up in an asylum, and soon Revd Foyster was dead too. Marianne's list of victims was growing.[5] Foyster's death certificate reveals that he was covered in bedsores when he breathed his last. She had adopted a baby girl and passed it off as her own to get Fisher to marry her, and she did the same thing again, months later, adopting yet another baby boy,[6] when she met and married a US serviceman called Robert O'Neil only four months after the death of Lionel. It appears that she was still married to Fisher at the time, as if she couldn't bear the escape from bigamy for more than a few weeks.[7]

By a very strange coincidence, at least to those interested in famous ghost stories, her last hours in England were spent in a military base in Hampshire. It was a transit camp for GIs and their brides. That camp's name was Tidworth (a later spelling of Tedworth), and it was on the former estate of Zouch Manor, better known as Tedworth Manor,[8] which was being used as an officers' mess at the time. Where once a demon drummer had terrorized a seventeenth-century family, now the 'Widow of Borley' took her leave of England.

Back in Essex, meanwhile, Borley was about to be rented out by the Church Commission – to Harry Price.

Haunted House. Responsible persons of leisure and intelligence, intrepid, critical and unbiased, are invited to join a rota of observers in a year's night and day investigation of alleged haunted house in Home Counties. Printed instructions supplied. Scientific training or ability to operate simple instruments an advantage. House situated in lonely hamlet, so own car essential. Write Box H989, *The Times*, EC4.

Price's 1937 advertisement was placed between a notice for Chelsea Flower Show and an advertisement for terrier kennels. It was 1937.

Price received about two hundred responses in all. Some were from bored society ladies craving a thrill, others from journalists and superannuated army officers wanting to be paid for their efforts. One friendly occultist sent in a sew-on pentagram to afford 'protection' from any evil spirits that might be lurking in the many decaying rooms of the rectory. Yet Price kept going back to the first letter that arrived, from Sidney Glanville.

Though Glanville was not especially qualified, as a consulting engineer, he was, Price assures us, a 'collateral descendant' of the remarkable man who investigated the Tedworth Drummer in 1661.[9] He was to become one of Price's most trusted investigators of 'The Most Haunted House in England'.

To the puzzlement of many, Price made it clear from the very beginning that he didn't want to be much involved in the Borley project. He simply intended to manage and oversee some kind of orderly surveillance of the property, lasting from six months to a year. Nothing of this sort had been attempted before. He prepared a 'Blue Book of Instructions' for his new recruits, and each was required to sign a declaration which restricted their ability to use anything uncovered from the experience for their own gain. They were also required not to disclose the location and identity of the house, which was, however, already famous after the

26. A photograph of Borley's hall at the time of Price's residency. Many objects were thrown into the hall from above.

front-page features in the *Mirror*. Participants could not photograph anything on the property without permission, or even sketch it. Most importantly, they were to pay for their own expenses and furnish Price with a comprehensive account of their stay.

Controversially, Price also gave a potted history of the haunting and mentioned the variety of its known phenomena, including the bell-ringing and the phantom nun. In later years, this was held against him as being too obviously suggestive.

On 2 June 1937, Price had driven up to Borley from his home in Sussex accompanied by one of his new discoveries, Ellic Howe[10] who was to go on to forge German stamps for the British Special Operations Executive during the war. Price concentrated his mind by setting up a 'base room' in the library on the ground floor, below the haunted Blue Room; this was the same library from which Henry Bull had taken pot-shots at rabbits on the lawn, and where his son Harry used to conduct household prayers as the gardener made faces in the French windows behind him. These windows had huge reinforced shutters built across them, which lent the room a fortified air.

After a trip to nearby Sudbury for supplies, Price made his 'base room' at least tolerably comfortable. He set up a metal camp-bed with a mattress, a paraffin table lamp, a methylated spirits kettle and a supply of tea, condensed milk and sugar. There were also twenty 'readable' books, on neutral subjects, to stave off boredom.

Price and Howe arranged a number of trigger objects around the house – a now familiar practice in ghost-hunting expeditions – objects they hoped might be of interest to ghosts and encourage them to move them. Price records these as a 'match-box' and a 'cigarette carton' – they were clearly hoping to attract a smoker – and various 'odds and ends'.

As they were carefully ringing every single object in the house, including the trigger or 'control' objects, and every single bit of

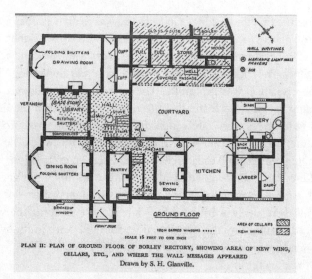

PLAN II: PLAN OF GROUND FLOOR OF BORLEY RECTORY, SHOWING AREA OF NEW WING,
CELLARS, ETC., AND WHERE THE WALL MESSAGES APPEARED
Drawn by S. H. Glanville.

27. A plan of the ground floor of Borley drawn up by Sidney Glanville
showing where Marianne's messages appeared.

writing on the wall, with coloured chalk, they came across a tatty
serge coat[11] hanging on the door of the Blue Room upstairs. It
had not been there two weeks earlier, when Price had last been in
the house. Inexplicable items of clothing appearing as if from
nowhere were a feature of this period, but are evidence of locals
trysting in the abandoned house rather than random apports of
poltergeist activity.

After examining the house and checking the grounds, the two
decided to make a night of it. After nine o'clock they began to
hear taps emanating from the passage just outside, and then,
shortly afterwards, after they had checked the passage, there
were two loud thumps from upstairs, as if someone had thrown
one heavy boot to the floor, and then another, and the sound of
a door being slammed.

★

Almost the first thing Sidney Glanville did was to draw proper architectural plans of the ground and first floor of the house. Sidney and his son Roger then set about securing the doors with , wax and adhesive tape. They found the silence oppressive and unnerving. The house's isolation was profound. 'The only sounds heard were the scuttling of a few mice and the intermittent and mournful calls of owls in the trees; very rarely a belated vehicle would pass through the lane.' At regular intervals, they would tour the whole house, including the attic and cellars, checking the seal on every door.

Sidney later complained of 'the continual strain on our ears to catch sounds, especially during the first few nights'. Some of the sounds were easily accounted for – a briar rose scraping the window, a dripping tap, the occasional scrabble of mice in the walls and floors.

Others were not.

In September, there was what appeared to be a perfectly human and criminal break-in through the drawing-room window. It really wasn't working out as a controlled environment. Still, Glanville and his son Roger came and went. One day, two RAF officer friends came to visit.[12] That afternoon, Glanville drove to a nearby town to get oil for the lamps.

On their return, the RAF officers they had left to guard the house reported that, while sitting in the base room with the doors open, they distinctly heard 'light tripping footsteps' coming down the stairs, then stopping. They had been listening to gramophone records and singing along just shortly before. The bottom step was only eight feet from where they were sitting. But there was no one there, no one at all.

By 19 September, Glanville wrote to Price that the 'phenomena has definitely waned of late'. He added, 'Perhaps the fact that I personally am not at all psychic has a bad effect.'

It was exactly because Glanville wasn't psychic that Price wanted him at Borley Rectory. The truth was that Price's mind was elsewhere. He was finishing a book and he appeared to be in the critical final phase of getting his National Laboratory for Psychical Research sold off to Bonn University. He'd put this 'laboratory' together over many years and had a considerable amount of showy equipment in it. The Bonn sale would mean a large amount of ready cash and, furthermore, the possibility of some kind of academic post. His life then was about to be transformed, and he was about to achieve everything he most desired; a shabby little rectory haunt in Essex which he had already decided was a fake was really not high in his list of priorities.

Glanville, rather surprisingly, given his methodological nature and scientific bent, decided to escalate matters by inaugurating seven table-tilting and planchette[13] séances. These revealed that a nun was buried beneath the house, and that the spirits in the house were planning to burn the rectory to the ground.

In the end, Borley didn't burn down – or, at least, not on the evening predicted by the planchette. The Price incumbency (as it is called in the literature, almost as if he is one of the vicars) was drawing to a close. In April 1938, some of the control objects were moved and rapping sounds heard, but time was running out. After being examined by the Church commission, Borley was deemed unsuitable for the purposes of the modern clergy, and the rectory was bought by one Captain William Hart Gregson in October of that year. Price and Glanville moved their equipment out.

By December, Price knew that his most cherished dream had failed. His Nazi friends had gone cold on him and it became obvious his lab wouldn't go to Germany; the equipment was out of date now, and in the US the work of J. B. Rhine at Duke University was making almost everything Price had achieved look amateurish and old-fashioned. His laboratory was packed into eighty-seven tea-chests and stowed away, its large X-ray machine sold off to Guy's Hospital. It's said that among the treasures in the laboratory are a bottle of teleplasm snipped from the pseudopods of medium Helen Duncan and a portable ghost-hunting kit;

it includes soft felt slippers, headache pills, and cigarettes. Hitler's British ghost lab sits there still, waiting to be sent.

On 27 February 1939, Borley Rectory burned to the ground. The spirits, it seemed, with their shaky sense of the passing of days, had simply got the day wrong.

On the summer solstice of 1939, a 'psychic fête' was held beside the ruins in the rectory grounds to raise money for the Borley Church fund.

Putting a brave face on it, Price held court with Captain Gregson – and what a pair they made: Price, who had written personally to Hitler asking for a seat at a Nuremberg rally, and Gregson, who had been an area organizer for Mosley's Blackshirts and the British Union of Fascists in Maldon before he moved to Borley.

Many years later, Gregson's son claimed that his father had burned down the house as an insurance scam. Certainly, his insurer was intensely suspicious of the £10,000 claim for a house for which he paid £500. The story Gregson stuck to was the upset of an oil lamp while he was sorting piles of books, which had then been set out on the floor to dry out. New ghosts had been seen at Borley – a man in a bowler hat against the flames of the burning house, and a woman in the ruined building, where no floor existed, silhouetted in the haunted Blue Room, or where the Blue Room used to be.

Borley was and is a vortex of unnerving pathologies. In the 1990s, Marianne's son Vincent ran the definitive internet site on the Borley haunting before unexpectedly withdrawing from the whole business, claiming he no longer wanted to encourage tourists to go to Borley, as they were disturbing the lives of the locals. He now refuses to make any public comment, or to engage in correspondence on the matter.

In 2002, a book, *We Faked the Ghosts of Borley*, caused a stir among literary editors with its provocative title, but it turned out to be a fake itself, the work of yet another narcissist, who called himself Louis Mayerling (born George Carter, in Wood Green, London).

Claiming to have been a child-prodigy violinist who knew Marilyn Monroe and George Bernard Shaw, as well as being charged with the maintenance of T. E. Lawrence's motorcycle and working as a driver–companion to the Prince of Wales and Mrs Simpson, Mayerling seems in fact never to have even been to Borley, let alone stayed with the Foysters, Smiths and Bulls at the rectory itself.

Deception is the ghost that haunts Borley. Even Harry Price invented evidence.

In April 1944, he made his final visit to Borley Rectory, just as it was being demolished. Price later recalled the incident in his book *The End of Borley Rectory*.

As Mr Scherman pressed the trigger which operated the shutter mechanism of his camera lens a brick, or part of a brick, suddenly shot up about four feet into the air of what remained of the kitchen passage . . . we walked over to the passage where there were many bricks lying about . . . no strings or wire was attached to any of them, and we saw no workmen at all on that side of the rectory.

The now famous photograph of the brick in flight was published with the caption: 'If indeed this was a genuine paranormal phenomenon, then we have the first photograph ever taken of a poltergeist projectile in flight.'

You'll note the clever, almost legalistic balance of that sentence. Price was later challenged about the photograph, and he wrote, in response, with a characteristically short-tempered swipe positively bellowing with outrage.

I will give £1000 to any charity you care to name if you can prove it was faked . . . the only possible explanation is that the brick was thrown from a long distance . . . or that Miss Ledsham [writing an article on Borley for *Life* magazine], Dave Scherman and myself were in collusion. They are still available and would swear in any court of law that there was no trickery.

Price was again choosing his words most carefully, and in mentioning a court of law there was an implicit threat. After he died in 1947, it took less than ten years for Price's enemies to take him out, and their most convincing piece of evidence was the Borley brick. In 1956, they published a report called 'The Haunting of Borley Rectory' and, taking up Price on his challenge, indeed contacted Miss Ledsham about her recollection of that April day. She was still angry about it.

28. The uncropped version of the famous version of the flying brick (circled) from 5 April 1944, that Price strongly implied was 'a poltergeist projectile in flight' – but see the workman (also circled) who was throwing them – who was cut out of the version Price published.

I had first-hand experience of the most bare-faced hocus-pocus on the part of the late Harry Price . . . he refers to a mysterious flying brick photographed by Mr Scherman. As Mr Price pointed out, there were no strings, no wire attached, but what he failed to mention was that there was a brawny workman still at work behind the wall. All three of us saw him as we passed the house towards the spot where the photograph was taken. There is no doubt at all that the flying bricks, several of which came out at regular intervals, were propelled by this workman as part of his demolition work.

The photographer confirmed the story: the whole episode was supposed to be tongue-in-cheek, for the magazine feature. Scherman was more amused than annoyed. 'We later discovered that Mr Price, who was in on the joke, had the effrontery to pass off the incident as gospel evidence of poltergeists.'

Other evidence published in the last twenty years has also been damning – the original uncropped version of the Borley brick photograph on the previous page shows the workman in the corner of the demolition site as the 'flying brick'[14] photograph was taken. Examples of Marianne's handwriting on official US documents show that her signature almost exactly resembles the 'Marianne please get help' pleas that appeared on the walls of Borley, which, like the Borley brick, were constantly reproduced in books about the supernatural in the sixties and seventies. It is now widely accepted that this writing was produced either consciously or unconsciously by Marianne.

Even if she did write the messages on the wall, they seemed to keep on coming, even when she wasn't there. Yet there was no doubt that locals were breaking into the house. Price and Glanville failed to notice the trapdoor that led into the cellar until quite late in the day. The house was left empty for many long periods over its lifetime, and it was used by courting couples, children on dares and the adult indigent creeping in from the roads.

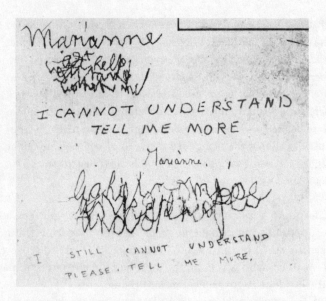

29. 'Marianne' graffiti at Borley Rectory: it later turned out that her handwriting was almost exactly the same.

There were a total of four outside doors, on top of the cellar trapdoor entrance. Marianne later maintained that many of the spontaneous fires were in fact caused by tramps lighting them in bedrooms. But it's curious that no one was ever caught, given the amount of people observing the house over a relatively long period, listening, looking and charging towards the sound of footsteps.

The haunting didn't stop with the destruction of the house: Gregson was to make even more money charging people to set up camp in the rectory grounds. On 27 June 1947, the BBC broadcast a programme on the Borley haunt; it included the sound of tapping which the producers, Peter Eton and Alan Burgess, had recorded coming from the cellars of the rectory. Many people began to think that the ghosts had moved to the church – there were raps, taps, things moving, and an organ was heard playing when no one was inside the church. And the nun continued to be seen by people driving a car past the rectory – in 1965, by a Canon Leslie Pennal, for example – and the sighting was often coupled with mechanical problems with the cars being driven.

Harry Price, who noted that in the period 1885–1943 a total of seventeen people had seen the apparition, also tampered with some of the stories about the ghost to make the stories more compelling. Ethel Bull's famous account of seeing her on the summer lawn with her sisters was switched from a dusk setting to a bright afternoon, and Price also adjusted the description of her having a sad face. The face was not seen, and nor were the prayer beads she was supposed to be counting.

Borley is notable for its unreliable witnesses. Many of the most important, including Ethel Bull, Marianne Foyster, Mabel Smith and the maid Mary Pearson either reneged on early statements or implied they hadn't told the whole truth. Harry Price listed more than two thousand events at Borley during the Foyster period alone which he considered paranormal, and lists in *The Most Haunted House in England* a huge array of sightings and experiences – they include apparitions of the nun, the apparition of Harry Bull, of a tall, dark man, a girl in white or blue, a black hand, a headless man, an old man, a figure wearing a bowler hat, a coach, and a column of smoke on the lawn. Aural phenomena were even more numerous – footsteps, bell-ringing, taps and closing doors. But the house was never secure. It was impossible to make it so.

Of the fifty or so professional parapsychologists at work now, only a couple of them are out of the lab and regularly involved in staking out haunted houses. Borley proved it was not possible to make an ordinary environment secure, and that it was not possible to rely on anyone to make accurate observations.

Borley might be called a viral haunting. People 'caught' it. One of the facts used to discredit Revd Foyster's account of the haunting, as first uncovered by the SPR, was in his manuscript *Fifteen Months in a Haunted House*, which Price used to write much of his books and, according to Marianne Foyster, simply stole from them and claimed he had 'lost' when asked for it back. In it, Foyster fictionalizes the visit of a spiritualist group to Borley, and gives one of them the unusual surname of Teed. This name also happens to belong to the sister and brother-in-law of Esther Cox, the woman at the centre of the Great Amherst Mystery of 1878.[15] The Foysters lived near to Amherst when they lived in Canada, and it seems likely they knew the story. This one word alone, 'Teed', is held up as evidence that Foyster was peddling a fiction.

Revd Henning also wrote a book about the Borley ghosts, with an introduction by Elizabeth Goudge. It was self-published and, incidentally, remains one of the best, and most atmospheric, of the lot.

In SPR researcher Eric Dingwall's[16] own copy of Henning's *Haunted Borley*,[17] which he bought from the cottage opposite the pond on a day-trip there, one of his least waspish observations can be found in chapter ten, where the author elaborates on his belief that 'the phenomena at Borley are due either to the performance of the Black Mass or to witchcraft or possibly both . . . an old parishioner told me that when she came to Borley over 40 years ago there was said to be a witch – not a woman, but a man.' Not recorded before in the Borley literature, as far as I am aware, Dingwall writes cryptically in his tight, fluid hand, in blue ink, 'if Black Mass was performed it was by Harry Bull.'

As part of his investigation, Price had been looking for a hidden vault in the church. On 17 August 1943, before the house's cellars were dug up, Price went to the church for a brief search of the Waldegrave vault.

The seventeenth-century Waldegrave tomb is a notable presence in the church, reportedly still the focus of supernatural activity, and not altogether different from the tomb imagined by M. R. James in his story 'Count Magnus', whose climax takes place only three miles from Borley, in Belchamp St Paul.[18]

A large flat stone beneath the chancel step was raised, but

nothing was found beneath it except sand. However, the mason involved suggested that this slab might have been the original altar of the church, hidden during the Reformation.

After the war ended, in 1947, Henning began a project to get the altar restored. It was the least he could do, and Price volunteered to give a talk to raise funds. The day of the lecture, Henning recalled later, was oppressively hot. Price wanted to see the restored altar, and so Henning took him to the church at five-thirty that evening. No one was about and, as they went into the church, they left the west door open.

> While we stood there talking about the altar, we were interrupted by an insistent and prolonged screeching of birds near the west end. I should almost describe it as a panic screaming of the rooks, which inhabit the elms overhanging the tower. I have often heard the birds making the usual noise when coming on and off their nests, but nothing approaching the din which was going on behind us.
>
> Mr Price asked 'Do they always go on like that?' and I had to say that, as far as I knew, the noise was unusual. I think what I really meant was that I had grown so used to the birds and the noise that generally I did not notice them. The very fact that I was now noticing them pointed to the noise being out of the ordinary.
>
> But the noise died down, and in the stillness after the birds were at rest again, came the sound of footsteps in the porch. I thought to myself 'What a pity. Visitors are coming in just when we wanted to be undisturbed to talk.' We waited for people to appear but no-one came. I hurried down the church thinking someone had heard our voices and did not like to enter. I was astonished to find no one in the porch and, going quickly through the churchyard, I looked up and down the road. There was not a soul to be seen.

It really is a scene from M. R. James. An artefact has been disturbed in the church. The Waldegraves were stirring in their vault. There is now a countdown to Harry Price's death, and perhaps those footsteps, which so alarmed the rooks, followed him back to Pulborough, where he was found dead, sitting bolt upright, only six months later, on 19 March 1948.

One thing you can say for sure about Borley is that it may or may not have attracted ghosts, but it certainly attracted writers looking for a good subject. When Dennis Wheatley's library was being sold off in the early eighties, his copy of *Harry Price – The Biography of a Ghost Hunter* was found to be annotated with the following observation: 'Used by me when writing my stories with occult background.' Upton Sinclair wrote a script about Borley after signing an agreement with Price in 1947 for £10.[19]

There was something mythomaniacal about most of the players on the Borley stage, and so it should come as no surprise that they too wanted to write up the story of the rectory.

Price's secretary, Lucy Kay – with whom he was having an affair – wrote an unpublished play about Borley.[20] Mabel Smith later fell out with Price when he failed to help her sell her novel to a publisher – the manuscript novel was called *Murder at the Parsonage*, and it was based on the scurrilous tales told to her by the Bull sisters. Marianne Foyster, who seems to have been fond of books and writing herself, was forever planning an autobiography, as well as wanting to write the 'great American novel'.

Trevor Hall, the nemesis of both Price and Marianne Foyster, published an execrable novel called *The Last Case of Sherlock Holmes*, in which the detective becomes involved in the Borley case, investigating the death of Revd Harry Bull and pointing a finger to a poisoning by his wife, Ivy. It is a great lump of undigested research upholstered as fiction. Hall was later instrumental in tracking down Marianne Foyster, though she had the last laugh. He was, essentially, waiting for her to die before publishing his deeply libellous book. But she managed to outlive him, dying at ninety-three in 1992, four decades after coming out of the shadows on that snowy February evening in a North Dakota hotel.

The King of Terrors and
Other Tales of Technology

These disturbing phenomena seem to deny all our usual scientific
ideas. How we would like to discredit them! Unfortunately, the
statistical evidence, at least for telepathy, is overwhelming.

– Alan Turing

The sighting of ghosts has long been such an emotional and hysterical affair that the best way to prove the existence of ghosts is
by means of science and technology and, indeed, a whole branch
of laboratory-based practice has been devoted to this very task for
many years. But technology has not always been the servant of
the truth in such matters: it has more usually been the master.

There was most optimism about the possibility of science being
able to uncover the truth about the paranormal in three decades in
particular: the 1890s in Great Britain and France and then the
1930s and the 1960s in the US and the Soviet Union. Take the
1890s. In the opening months of 1896, two spooky new forms of
technology arrived in London within weeks of each other. Both
seemed to offer windows into another world, a spirit world, just
as the fashion for séances was beginning to fade.

The first of these new technologies was the 'invisible photography' pioneered by Wilhelm Röntgen. Medical use was not at the
forefront in those early days of the X-ray, and its initial presence
was not in hospitals but at funfairs, shows and pop-up commercial events. People would pay and step in front of the machinery.
They would move about and laugh at their own bones and the

bones of others. It was fun and, of course, extraordinarily toxic.[1] For the first time ever, people could see dancing skeletons in broad daylight.

Thirty years earlier, in 1866, Lionel Beale had produced an optical toy in which a simple hand-crank would produce a dancing skeleton,[2] and indeed the idea of such a creature, popping its head on and off like a bonnet, has a long folkloric history. There was no ambiguity in these ghostly encounters in which a headless subject was self-evidently and gratuitously dead.

So the X-ray machines proved a massive draw in the lowest, darkest weeks of the new year. Even the prime minister Lord Salisbury arrived to have his hand skeletized by what was then called the 'skiagraph' or 'shadow picture'. It was shortly to find a rival. On 21 February 1896, the Royal Polytechnic Institution in Regent Street showed the first ever public projection of a film in the United Kingdom, by the Lumière brothers,[3] and soon the public were also flocking to see this second novelty.

For a while, shadow pictures and movies were seen as rival forms of entertainment; for a few months, the two technologies existed side by side in some of the better penny gaffs.

Maxim Gorky was one of the first to write about the inherent ghostliness of cinema when he reviewed the same Lumière programme at the Nizhny-Novgorod Fair in July 1896. 'It is terrifying to see, but it is the movement of shadows, only of shadows. Curses and ghosts, the evil spirits that have cast entire cities into sleep,' he observed, with a shudder. Of a clip of men playing a round of cards, he says, 'It seems as if these people have died and their shadows have been condemned to play cards in silence into eternity.' He referred to cinema as 'the Kingdom of Shadows', which somehow evokes some of the earliest Babylonian descriptions of the afterlife, where shadowy forms shuffle in the dust.[4]

X-ray was for a year the main threat to cinema as a form of entertainment, which is why in 1897 George Méliès was making a movie called *The Vanishing Lady*,[5] in which a woman becomes a skeleton and, by 1900, Thomas Edison was issuing films such as *Uncle Josh in a Spooky Hotel*,[6] featuring an actor, Charles Manley, of sepulchral association,[7] afflicted by a skull-faced mischief-maker. Many of the early films of Edison and Méliès revolve around jokes about skeletons and decapitation, and indeed the first ever special effect in any movie was the decapitation of Mary Queen of Scots in a film by Alfred Clark in 1895.

There has been a convergence between technology and ghost-belief for many centuries. As early as the 1530s, the occultist Cornelius Agrippa wrote about how mirrors could be used to create onstage illusions, and expressed an enjoyment, further-more, of being in control of such a process when the mind of man is so easy to fool. When 'ignorant men' see what they believe to be 'the appearances of spirits or souls', they have no idea that these images are 'without life'.

The camera obscura, a box with a convex lens that pro-jected onto a white surface in a darkened room, was used in the Renaissance to observe the sun and its eclipse. But it took the Neapolitan nobleman and polymath Giambattista della Porta (1540–1615) to fix the technology so the image wasn't upside down, and to create a substitute for the sun in the form of actors and scenery.[8]

A strong contender as the inventor of the magic lantern is the polymath and mathematician Christiaan Huygens, the discoverer of the rings of Saturn. The man who made the magic lantern widely known, however, was Jesuit priest and inventor Athana-sius Kircher (1602–80).

Former Capuchin monk turned Lutheran divine Johann Grien-del was also famous for his magic-lantern shows in Nuremberg. Our first record of its projection in England is on 19 August 1666, in the house of Samuel Pepys in Seething Lane, two weeks before the Great Fire of London. The London optical-instrument maker Richard Reeves was the man who lit the 'lanthorne'. It seems likely that some of the images were of ghosts, since Huygens designed a sequence of images for projection – the images were of dancing skeletons.[9]

In Leipzig, a coffee-house owner named Johann Schröpfer used to project his images on to smoke, a technique that perhaps gives us the phrase 'smoke and mirrors'. This technique was originally pioneered in the mid-eighteenth century by a Frenchman, Edme-Gilles Guyot, and the shows tended to be labelled 'phantasmagoria'.

Schröpfer's *Gespenstermacher*, or 'ghost maker', seems to have sprung in part from his interest in the more theatrical aspects of the Masonic,[10] and he was the first person we know of who liked to use such new technology to deceive: he wanted the audience to believe that he had magus-like powers to raise the dead. Dressed in wizard garb, he would conduct necromantic séances, with his wife and a team of assistants creating atmospheric and sinister noises offstage. It seems he also mastered the art of throwing voices as a ventriloquist, a full century before Victorian mediums were doing the same. And it also seems that among the incense thrown on to the hot coals to make the smoke there were opiates, creating a highly susceptible audience on the verge of hallucination.

These largely private shows before too long became lucrative public spectacles. Étienne-Gaspard Robertson (1763–1873), who had originally trained for the priesthood, set up a show in the crypt of an abandoned Capuchin convent near the Place Vendôme in 1797. To make the skeletons appear to come close and then withdraw, he would 'dolly' his camera on four wheels behind a hanging screen, maintaining the focus, much as a skilled lens puller would do on a movie shoot now. Robertson very much thrived on the unease abroad in society after the French Revolution; instances of ghost-belief seem to become more widespread in times of social stress. He was closed down only after some of his shows were presumed to be anti-revolutionary in nature, and he left France for England.

In 1801, a phantasmagoria production by the German innovator

Paul Philidor (also known as Paul de Philipsthal) opened at London's Lyceum Theatre in the Strand. Philidor too had thrived in Paris, though a perceived anti-revolutionary message in his work had seen the authorities come down hard on him after his shows in 1793. It was Philidor who invented moving back-projection, a technique still occasionally used in the movies. As the *Britannic* magazine noted, 'With the aid of his broken English, and a most sublime interpreter, he indeed converts his shadows rapidly into substantial English guineas.'

The best example of this effect is 'Pepper's Ghost'. It was the first 3D illusion. It was invented by a retired Liverpool engineer[11] and featured an actor in a hidden pit in front of the stage; his live image would be projected on to a sheet of glass positioned at the same angle. It's a technology still in use today in places, for example the haunted-house 'ride' in the Disney theme parks.

First shown to the public in 1863,[12] it became a box-office

30. An engraving (circa 1865) of 'Pepper's Ghost', the first 3D illusion – used in theatres. This optical effect using mirrors was invented by Henry Dircks and later (more famously) developed by John Henry Pepper.

sensation, even drawing the royal family, who attended Windsor Theatre for the first time since George III was on the throne. Over the pond, the technology was used in the melodrama *True to the Last* at Wallack's Theater in New York, in which the entrepreneur who staged it tried to keep the secret by pasting brown paper 'over all the keyholes in the theater'.[13]

One ghost, a skeleton called 'The King of Terrors' was a bag of bones of horrible purpose; the first mechanical ghost to haunt the New York City stage. It was considered poignant under the circumstances since, offstage, many of the Civil War dead remained unburied on the battlefields.[14] When the ghost appeared, the lights dimmed, the orchestra played what is called in the trade 'sneak music' and the props man lightly cranked the wind machine into a low howl. In 1876, a travelling showman was prosecuted for using the patented technology in a show in Old Street, Shoreditch, not far from the old Shakespearean theatre in Curtain Road, where *Romeo and Juliet* had premiered. His open-air twenty-minute show, which featured a headless man having his head restored, was accompanied by an organ and the occasional tinkling of a triangle.

'Pepper's Ghost' became a cultural meme, sneak music for a certain kind of vanishing act. In 1864 a horse named Pepper's Ghost ran at Ascot, and in London cabbies adopted the term as slang for those who absconded without paying their fares.

It's difficult to imagine now how disturbing radio was for those who first encountered it, but it was: deeply disturbing. That a machine could channel a human voice from the ether, a tone from silence, seemed uncanny beyond reason. In 1894 spiritualist Sir Oliver Lodge invented the 'coherer', which became an essential component in the early radio sets of Marconi. The idea of people themselves being akin to radio sets, able to tune in to etheric voices, suddenly did not seem implausible and, suddenly, medi-

ums who claimed to do so as a kind of 'mental radio' no longer
seemed as ridiculous as they had done only a decade earlier.

Much of the early technology that led to the cathode-ray tube
and the use of cables and radio waves to broadcast disassociated
voices started its journey in the brains of men like Lodge and
William Crookes,[15] men who believed that science might be
used to contact the dead or, at the very least, once and for all to
clear up the matter of whether it could be done. No wonder a
ghost crawls out of a television in the horror film *Ringu*, when
you think of Crookes' dalliance with young, dead women[16]
in full-figure apparitions. No wonder the white noise of the
television in the film *Poltergeist* is where the entity nests most
comfortably.

In the 1930s, the research became about the living and breathing,
not the dead. The supernatural officially became the paranormal.[17] In 1930, a young academic who as a 23-year-old sergeant in
the Marines had won the President's Match (a sniper contest in
which all branches of the US armed forces compete)[18] set up the
world's first parapsychology laboratory at Duke University. How
did the best shot in America come to be the most respected paranormal researcher there has ever been?

J. B. Rhine was a maverick in the tradition of the better-known
Alfred Kinsey, the sexologist who also began life as a botanist, one
of the best foundations in taxonomy it was possible to have.

Rhine had become interested in the evangelism of Conan
Doyle, but took what was essentially the SPR and ASPR (American Society for Psychical Research) line: ghosts were the product
of live brain tissue using as-yet-unknown processes to gather and
communicate information. In 1934, he published a monograph
detailing 90,000 trials he had conducted on the subject of ESP,
deploying for the first time specially-produced Zener cards, a now
very familiar set of designs including circles, rectangles, 'plus plus'

signs and wavy lines. Some of the experiments involved injecting the test subjects with sodium amytal.

In 1943, Rhine published a paper on 'psychokinetic effects'. As time went by, these tests and their methodology became increasingly automated, but their importance lay in the efficient collation of vast amounts of data, something that had never been done in the field of the paranormal before.

In the end, though, Rhine became a slave to his laboratory, doomed to repeat what were essentially the same experiments over and over again, even if they did become more sophisticated and automated. And, in some senses, Rhine had a touch of the showman about him also. He sent his book on extra-sensory perception (1934) to four hundred individuals he had picked out from *Who's Who*. Despite an invitation from the Lutheran priest at its centre to visit a 1949 instance of 'possession' – it became the basis of the 1973 film *The Exorcist*, though it involved a young boy rather than a girl – Rhine failed to take his technology out into the field. This has to be one of the great 'what-ifs' in this area.[19] Fieldwork was to be left to the American public to carry out, many decades later.

If the 1890s was the decade of spooky technology and the 1930s that of the laboratory, then the 1960s was the decade of Bell's Theorem. Are ghosts quantum events? In 1964, John Stewart Bell published work on the 'Interconnectedness Theorem', which sought to answer something which Einstein himself had called 'spooky action at a distance' (*spukhafte Fernwirkung*). The essence of Bell's theory is that two particles that have become 'entangled' carry on acting as if they are linked at very great distances. This theory, called 'non-locality', seems to the layman at least to overturn every known law of physics, even if physicists will tell you it doesn't. There was also a further aspect: observed particles behaved differently from non-observed particles, thereby indicating that the act of looking, of consciousness lapping onto an object beyond the body, seemed to alter the way that object behaved.[20]

In 1994, the anaesthesiologist Stuart Hameroff at the University of Arizona proposed that 'cytoskeletal tubules', mysterious nanometre-sized particles found within neurons, might be a possible site for registering quantum effects in the brain. Perhaps the ghosts that resemble time-slips, the ghosts that seem trapped in a repetitive loop, are thereby cytoskeletal shadows. Perhaps this is why we're more likely to see the ghosts of people we know, because we are entangled with them. (Until the eighteenth century, in England, people only ever really saw ghosts of people they knew.)

Perhaps this is why when, in one report, wooden panelling from an Elizabethan hall is sold, the ghost travels with it, entangled in the fabric of the wood. Recent experimentation has shown that diamonds become quantum entangled,[21] thus indicating that larger objects may also be prey to these forces. Ian Walmsley at Oxford University has managed to make lattice-like 'phonons' vibrate in sympathy after separating two entangled diamonds, and all large objects can have these phonon structures, although the effects can be measured only in picoseconds. No wonder so many jewels are cursed. Their phononic qualities have been washed with human blood.

Also in this decade, when news broke in 1961 of a parapsychology lab at the University of Leningrad, the possibility that Russia had developed applications for ESP seemed to be on the cards. The Russians had been calling ESP 'biological radio' since 1916. The CIA and US army were to spend money on similar projects during the sixties, and even the seventies, but the anticipated paranormal Manhattan Project, a massive US government-funded research expenditure envisaged by J. B. Rhine, never happened.[22]

Experimentation with sleep states and telepathic states also took place in the sixties, and again seemed to indicate that the heart of the ghost was the live brain of the person looking at it.[23] The brain waves of separated twins were first posited as being interconnected in 1965, the year in which J. B. Rhine retired from Duke University. But perhaps the biggest coup of the sixties fell under the aegis of the famous anthropologist Margaret Mead: parapsychology was officially recognized as a science by the AAAS (American Association for the Advancement of Science) and the Parapsychological Society was admitted to its ranks. The date was 30 December 1969, and suddenly all the ghost stories in the world had come true, just hours before the decade ran out.

There are still active parapsychology laboratories (two main ones in the UK, one in Liverpool and one in Edinburgh, plus parapsychology centres, including one at Northampton and an 'anomalistic psychology unit' at Goldsmiths in London). Despite a succession of elegantly written books by Dean Radin looking at the discipline in 2012, it's hard not to feel that the J. B. Rhine project has failed. There are now eighty years of data to draw on and, despite cautious acceptance of aspects of it by scientists including Carl Sagan and sceptic Richard Wiseman, parapsychology has never become interdisciplinary and has failed to take the scientific establishment with it.[24]

The literal-minded have a tendency to discount an entire source forever if one instance of fraud is detected, and so when, only four years after the science of parapsychology was accepted, Rhine's successor at the Parapsychological Association was revealed as a fraud, the high summer was over before it even began.

With brain mapping advancing every year, could it be that the thirty- to forty-year cycle of paranormal positivity is about to crank up again? Could the next paranormal decade be connected to the science and understanding of the brain?

Once parapsychology had proved reluctant to move out of the laboratory, an interesting democratization of technology occurred. Ordinary, untrained enthusiasts started looking for ghosts – but they were, to the parapsychology establishment, an embarrassment, since their vulgar enthusiasm seemed to be undoing all the painstaking work of parapsychologists seeking establishment respectability. In this, the (usually middle-class) scientists were conforming to a Western model of social attitudes hundreds of years old.[25]

One of the few US parapsychologists interested in apparitions, Loyd Auerbach,[26] was unusual in this respect. Using a 'Trifield' meter, he once followed what he claimed was a 'moving electromagnetic field' through a house, thus returning, full circle, to the idea that ghosts act similarly to some 1890s concept of electricity – or, more precisely, a folk version of electricity.

No US ghost hunter is equipped these days without a whole host of electrical detection gadgets, sold on specialist internet websites. A complete ghost hunter's kit costs $109, and includes EMF readers, Gaussmeters programmed to cut out powerline interference, and the all-in-one Trifield ('This is our meter of choice for affordable pricing and fast, reliable measurements of AC Magnetic Field, AC Electric Field, and Radio/microwaves,' states one website.)[27] Watching a TV show such as *TAPS*, with its extraordinary emphasis on detecting and surveillance technology, modern American ghost-belief is a mixture of Dan Aykroyd's[28] *Ghostbusters*, English Jacobean Protestant theology and a Halloween whizz of Irish Catholic and pagan tradition.

The American love affair with ghost-detecting technology dates back to the 1970s, when a strange phenomenon became a kind of craze. That craze was EVP – electronic voice phenomenon. In 1971, a book was translated from Swedish claiming that if you left a tape recorder recording on its own somewhere and listened carefully to the playback, you would hear the dead whispering to you. The man behind the book, Konstantine Raudive (1909–74), was a clinical psychologist in Uppsala, and had been inspired by an eccentric artist called Friedrich Jürgenson. In 1959 Jürgenson had been recording birdsong only to find that ghosts had left him messages, among them direct communications from his wife, mother and father. Working with Jürgenson, Raudive assembled tens of thousands such communications, often under controlled and electronically screened conditions and usually consisting of one word or one short phrase. These Raudive recordings have most recently been heard in public again in London at the art exhibition of Susan Hiller at the Tate Britain Gallery[29] in May 2011.

It's not hard to see the appeal. Sarah Estep, who founded an American Association for EVP in 1982, observed that you didn't need to be a 'psychic superstar' to experience the uncanny; in other words, not only were scientists done away with but the mediums as well. It was a true and profound democratization. Thomas Edison, Nikola Tesla and Alexander Graham Bell all believed that the soul survived death and travelled to another state, possibly as a para-electrical force. It is often pointed out that the father of modern electrics, Michael Faraday, was a professional sceptic – he invented a table that couldn't be pushed to test mediums who were table-tipping with their toes – but what is less well known is that he was a sceptic for fundamentalist Christian, not scientific, reasons. Edison had no such scruples. In his *Diary and Sundry Observations*, he mentions being engaged in the design of an apparatus that would enable 'personalities which have left this earth to communicate with us'. However, no such plans were found among his effects when he died.[30]

These days, ghosts communicate through any number of technological channels, including the spellchecker[31] on your laptop's document program. There is a whole genre of apparently true mobile-phone ghost stories, especially texts from the dead, silent phone calls from people who have been buried with their phone in their coffin, and so forth. These weird phenomena coming at you via everything from phone texts to illuminated LED alarm clocks have a name: 'instrumented transcommunication'.

Some would call the use of EVP and similar technology to overhear ghostly murmurs as pareidolia (vague and random phenomenon perceived as significant). But one thing is clear: the use of the technological – cold technology with cold bones – as a form of haunting is very far from being over in the history of human experience. The haunting of virtual reality is not that far away.

Most Haunted

'For when they shall see that haue been falsly taught, and that they were not the soules of men whiche appeared, but eyther falsehood of Monkes, or illusions of deuyls, franticke imaginations, or some other friuolous and vaine perswasions, they will think it profitable . . . as to saue their money from such greedy caterpillars.'

– Lewes Lavater, 1572

The business of ghosts has never been far away from the *business* of ghosts. There always seems to be someone profiting from a good ghost story. Horace Walpole noticed how Smithfield pubs cashed in on the crowds craning to see a glimpse of the nearby Cock Lane ghost. The Victorian flashmobs were, in the opinion of the London Metropolitan police, often created by gangs of pickpockets looking to create distracted crowds of the gawping and the credulous. Outside London, on the coasts of Devon, Sussex and the Isle of Wight in the eighteenth century, ghost stories were often spread by cross-Channel smugglers trying to conceal their illicit late-night activities.

As the early press discovered with Cock Lane, a good ghost story sells a lot of papers. That fascination continues today. Shows about contacting, experiencing and even pursuing the supernatural dominate some cable and satellite channels – in the UK, for example, the ironically named Living TV. The long-running British TV show *Most Haunted* generated a tidy income for its producers simply by popularizing the ghost hunt and making it financially lucrative.[1]

In 2010, a property sale in Portsmouth gathered national press attention when an estate agent claimed it to be the 'most haunted house in England'. It was no such thing, but since the *Most Haunted* team had staked it out in their seventh series, the estate agent believed that its ghosts were a selling point. Similarly, in 1936, *The Times* offered a haunted house for sale with the clear motivation that this was an extra selling point, like a conservatory, or central heating. Such a practice can go both ways, of course. In 1947, the Luton Assessment Committee was asked to lower the local rates on a domestic property for the sole reason that it was haunted.

If nothing else, this demonstrates the power of Harry Price's marketing tag, 'The Most Haunted House in England'.[2] Why is it necessary that we should find and define the 'most' haunted? The answer is almost certainly money – in what location can you be guaranteed a ghostly experience? If such a place could be pinned down, it would be immensely valuable, in all sorts of ways.

As early as 1858, ghost hunting was seen as a leisure activity. In her *Guide to the Lake District* published that year, Harriet Martineau mentions haunted locations with the clear implication that they would be of particular interest to her readership. In 2002, York promoted itself as the most haunted city in England with an eye to boosting tourism. On its webpage, the Golden Fleece ('York's Most Haunted Pub') flags up ghosts[3] as a way of promoting its four guest rooms, and at the time of writing includes a link to a psychic investigator, should you experience anything from the grave before your full English breakfast. At hauntedrooms.com you can pick the haunted hotel or pub where you'd like to stay and subscribe to newsletters. Pluckley, in Kent, so prides itself on being the 'most haunted' village in England that it has been the subject of a travel piece in the *Telegraph*.[4]

Owners of crumbling stately homes are increasingly seeking income from renting out their properties for evening ghost hunts. All this attention has speeded up the evolution of ghost stories. In the 1970s, Appuldurcombe House on the Isle of Wight was barely regarded as 'haunted' at all: all it had was the ghost of a monk, a classic folkloric invention. However, due to a visit by *Most Haunted* to the house two decades later and the existence of a local ghost-hunting tour, this picturesque ruin, a largely roofless English Baroque house with a scandalous past, now open to the public, has triumphed simply because it looks the part and has some history. Now, it is commonly regarded as the Isle of Wight's most haunted house.

But the idea of the 'most haunted' is not a new one. 50 Berkeley Square in Mayfair was notorious for almost a century as the 'most haunted house in London'. In November 1872, in *Notes and Queries*, a correspondent first raised the subject of its ghosts. The query was replied to by George, the melancholic 4th Baron Lyttelton.

'There are strange stories about it,' he wrote, 'upon which this deponent cannot enter.' When, three years later, he committed suicide by throwing himself down a staircase, without having revealed the nature of any of these stories, it served only to heighten the Victorian press's increasingly hysterical interest in the house.

In 1879, the weekly magazine *Mayfair* took up the story of the 'House in Berkeley Square', which had been the residence of prime minister George Canning and then his spinster daughter. In 1865, it was taken on by a man named Myers, and it was at this point that the property acquired its sinister reputation; he was a recluse, and it was said that he was jilted by a fiancée and withdrew from all human contact, living in a small room at the top of the building and opening his door only to receive food from a single servant. Myers had a habit of wandering the building at night with a candle burning, glimpses of which terrified passers-by walking through the dark streets. In 1873 he received a court summons for not paying his taxes, but the judge was lenient, commenting that the house in question was known locally as being haunted.

As a magazine in tune with its readership, *Mayfair* knew how to set the scene:

If there be physiognomy in bricks and mortar, one would say that house has seen murder done . . . a valuable house left seemingly to decay, with windows caked and blackened by dust, full of silence and emptiness, and yet with no notice about it anywhere that it may be had for the renting. This is known as 'the haunted house in Berkeley Square'.

It also mentioned the popular story that was circulating about (the now late) Lord Lyttelton: that he had kept a vigil in the haunted attic room, armed with two hunting guns loaded with silver sixpences (silver being a prophylactic against the unholy). During the night, he discharged one at something that immediately 'dropped like a rocket'.[5] But morning revealed nothing more than shot-damaged floorboards.

Notes and Queries developed a regular correspondence on the issue, in December 1880 publishing a letter addressed to the late Bishop Thirlwall which described the house's evil room, where a housemaid had been struck dead with fright, and where a subsequent male guest, 'his eyes fixed upon the same spot where hers had been fixed the night before', was found in a state of shock, leaving the house without ever having revealed his experience.

Stories continued to generate. A Mr Bentley took the house with his two teenage daughters, who complained of a musky, feral smell, as if an animal was prowling the house. A maid found one guest, a Captain Kentfield, screaming, 'Don't let *it* touch me!' as he cowered in horror in his bedroom, and later, after foolishly returning to the room, he was found dead of fright. Later stories include the wraith of a sobbing child either tortured or frightened to death in the nursery, and the ghost of a woman who fled the embraces of a lecherous uncle by throwing herself through the window. Another dating from the 1920s told of sailors breaking in and being frightened to death by the same ghost,[6] usually described as being formless and smoke-like. In 1975, the house's status as the most haunted in London was reaffirmed by Peter Underwood in his *Gazetteer of British Ghosts*, where he calls it, carefully, the 'most famous of all London's hauntings'.

Online, there are still people claiming that the house is haunted, that, as you go in, there is on the wall a framed police notice forbidding anyone to use the upper floor; but a quick email to Maggs Brothers, the antiquarian booksellers who have been in residence at the address since 1938, brought the following response: 'There are absolutely no first-hand accounts of ANYTHING at all. It's fiction reversing into reality – similar to what folklorists call ostension.'

At 50 Berkeley Square, the stories themselves had taken over. It seemed so odd to passers-by to see an empty house in such an exclusive part of London that the public imagination rose up to explain. It's one of the best examples of the viral haunted-house story in the literature; pepped up by magazine columns and authors selling books, as with Arthur Machen and the Angels of Mons, a fiction that started life in a newspaper or (in this case) a periodical became eventually considered 'true', and was added to by the public who walked by it every day and shuddered at its blank windows and peeling door. The process continues to this day on the internet, with websites claiming new incidents and embellishing and changing the old stories, and its reputation gets darker and darker with each story. There's a long tradition of houses which, left empty for a while, attract a reputation which is filled in with ghosts. In his memoir of working-class life in Salford, Robert Roberts mentions that houses 'rarely stood vacant for longer than a fortnight before the ghosts got in'.[7]

Back as a ghost-obssessed school boy in the 1970s I never reached any conclusions about England being the most haunted of nations, that claim I read in so many of the books on the subject.

There's no objective way of testing it. It was a proud boast, if rather forlorn under the circumstances. Economically, everything seemed in a state of decay and dereliction, but at least we had an impressive theme-park array of grey ladies, headless coachmen and poltergeists. England may well be the most haunted country simply because more people in England believe in ghosts. Belief in the paranormal has become a form of decayed religion in secular times: ghosts are the ghosts of religion itself.

A very specific set of circumstances has made England extraordinarily haunted. Across medieval Europe, it was fully accepted that the dead might sometimes return to haunt the living. The Catholic Church rationalized (and to a large extent took over) the ancient belief in ghosts by teaching that such apparitions were the souls of those trapped in Purgatory, unable to rest until they had expiated their sins. Most of the medieval ghost stories that survived were used by the clergy for teaching purposes and are of a genre known by scholars in this area (M. R. James among them) as *miracula*. In one of the earliest, the Venerable Bede (672–735) tells of a nun called Tortgith who has a relationship with a dead abbess, who returns to help her negotiate on what day the sickly nun wishes to leave the earthly world, with all its snares and sins. Other ghosts include the ghostly monk Boisil from Melrose Abbey,[8] who instructs those who will heed him to go to Ireland and not Germany on their pilgrimages. In this, one sees the hand of the Church drumming up business more locally. Here again, it's all about the money.

Many early ghost stories were explicit morality tales in which the dead returned, burdened with the weight of their sins, to warn the living. Their punishment was often apposite, such as the story of the alcoholic who, in death, had to drink from an eternally full cup of sulphur and brimstone.

In medieval times, the Church clamped down on ghost stories. People who reported seeing the ghosts of their dead relatives were prosecuted by Church courts for 'occasioning scandal'. Any attempt at ghost-hunting was seen as highly improper, but it obviously went on, since regulations for some medieval guilds included a clause banning any attempt by the night watchmen to amuse themselves by summoning up ghosts during the hours of darkness. The existence of ghosts was so self evident that it was never disputed.

The violent abolition of Roman Catholicism in the late sixteenth century changed everything. As Christina Hole observed, 'The transfer of Church property to secular owners at the Reformation left a trail of hauntings behind it, both because the violently ejected monks returned to their lost homes after death and because such property was supposed to carry its own curse with it.'[9] The colourful churches were whitewashed, the statues of the saints taken away and destroyed, the rich communities of nuns and monks scattered. The spiritual landscape of England was changed for ever.

Unchecked by Church courts, slowly the ghosts crept out of the abbeys and churchyards. Some ghosts foretold the future (at St James's Palace, the Duchess of Mazarin returned to assure her friend Madame de Beauclair that there was an afterlife and that she would die that night); others were doomed to repeat the past, such as the ghost at the Battle at Edgehill, where the Catholic-leaning Royalist soldier clashed swords with the Puritan soldier. With no rite of exorcism available, people (for example, a Canvey Island farmer in 1709) increasingly turned to cunning women and renegade priests to help with a haunting, thus reinforcing the general notion that ghosts were an aspect of witchcraft.

This wasn't helped by one of the fundamental tenets of the early Protestant reformers being the denial of Purgatory: that, at the moment of death, all souls proceeded straight to Heaven or Hell. The question of whether one believed in ghosts now marked the difference between Catholic and Protestant as strongly as belief in the transubstantiation of the host or the infallibility of the Pope. Many saw the ghost stories of the past as the Catholic Church's attempts to exploit popular credulity in order to enhance its own wealth and position. No true Protestant could believe in ghosts.

So, when people kept seeing ghosts after the Reformation, against all reason, they were taught not to take them at face value. Those apparitions that were still being encountered were not to be recognized as the souls of the departed but as spirits, usually evil ones sent by the Devil. In *Religion and The Decline of Magic* Keith Thomas cites the example of Lady Fanshawe, who, when she saw a ghost[10] in Ireland in November, 1650, sat up for the rest of the night with her husband, discussing why such apparitions were so much more common in Ireland, coming to the conclusion that the Irish were much more superstitious and lacked a faith strong enough to protect them from the attacks of the Devil.[11]

Anne Boleyn is sometimes pictured as a frivolous figure, but her religious beliefs were serious and deeply held. She was, if anything, more committed to the Protestant Reformation than her husband, the king. Catholics, now obliged to follow their faith in secrecy on pain of death, considered the queen their mortal enemy, and thus there was a certain grim justice in having multiple copies[12] of her headless ghost[13] wander the land, in direct defiance of the beliefs she had fought so hard to impose. It's interesting, likewise, that the ghostly re-enactment of the Battle of Edgehill was later seen only by the Catholic-leaning Royalist side.

Lewes Lavater's *Of Ghosts and Spirits Walking by Night* was published in 1572, and appears to have been familiar to Shakespeare. It's very clear that this author considers the encouragement of belief in ghosts a papist plot.

But the rigour of the early Protestant rejection of ghosts proved hard to maintain. They were just too popular. *Hamlet* (1601) opens with the sensational sighting of the dead king. Like Marcellus, any firm Protestants in the audience would have seen

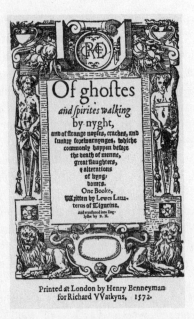

Of ghostes
and spirites walking
by nyght,
and of strange noyses, crackes, and
sundry forewarnynges, whiche
commonly happen before
the death of menne,
great slaughters,
& alterations
of kyng-
domes.
One Booke,
Written by Lewes Laua-
terus of Tigurine,
And translated into Eng-
lyshe by R. H.

Printed at London by Henry Benneyman
for Richard VVatkyns, 1572.

31. The frontispiece of Lewes Lavater's *Of Ghosts and Spirits
Walking by Night* (1572).

this ghost as a demon and the resulting carnage as the result of
listening to the Devil. Yet Hamlet's ghost is no hallucination –
this ghost is quite clearly and physically there, and the audience
sees it too.[14]

Joseph Glanvill and the circle of thinkers at Ragley in 1665 were
all good Protestants who, a century before, would not have dared
to try directly to experience ghosts and chronicle all manner of
hauntings. In *Saducismus Triumphatus* (its title referred to the triumph over the Sadducees, who, like the Epicureans and the
Diggers, denied the existence of the soul and the possibility of life
after death), Glanvill defended his attempts to obtain scientific evidence of the existence of witchcraft and ghosts in order to offer
incontrovertible proof of the existence of the soul. Atheism had
now become a bigger threat to true religion than Catholicism,

and a belief in ghosts, however much it pained strict Protestants such as Thomas Hobbes, did at least constitute some kind of belief in a spiritual world. To gather proof of their existence was to make Christianity itself stronger – or at least that was the plan. But without the structure medieval Catholicism had supplied, these ghosts were much more troublesome and frightening.

To the early Reformers, the experience of ghosts was akin to that of witchcraft. Unlike the Catholic Church, they did not seek ownership of ghost stories (as an important way of making moral messages much more vivid to an uneducated congregation; also picked up on later by the Methodists), they rejected them outright. So when ghost sightings continued apace, they were pushed farther and farther into the hinterlands of folklore and urban legend.

32. A drawing of a ghost from Pierre le Toyer's *A Treatise on Spectres*, (1658), showing a spirit holding a taper, a cheap kind of candle, as they were customarily envisaged to do.

By the time the laws against Catholicism were finally lifted in the eighteenth century, ghost belief was being openly acknowledged once more. The cheapness of printing presses and the production of books and pamphlets meant that stories of sightings were now being written down for the first time. The sheer number of pamphlets that survive today show how hugely popular tales of these sightings were.

All were sold as true stories. Obviously, whoever told the tale put their own spin on it, whether to curdle the blood or to impart a moral message, but the key thing was sales. The makeover Defoe gave the story of Mary Veal meant that his version of events was enjoyed by a fascinated middle class who might not normally have stooped to buy the more sensational pamphlets that were everywhere. His pamphlet went through several editions, and its success may well have inspired him to return to ghosts with his *Essay on the History and Reality of Apparitions* in 1727.

Belief in ghosts never became respectable, but its popularity was bolstered further by a new form of Christianity that also tacitly espoused a belief in spirits and ghosts – Methodism. In his youth, Methodism's founder, John Wesley, had been strongly influenced by the haunting at his family home in Epworth, and these experiences were carried through to the religion he founded, which was regularly criticized by the Church of England for its interest in witchcraft and magic. Even after his death, Wesley was active. In 1846, a tract was published exhorting Methodists not to backslide, to hold true to the beliefs of their founder. Intriguingly, Wesley is depicted as a ghost, appearing in a white sheet to a believer sitting by the fireside, an iconography of ghost depiction which by that time was nearly two hundred years old.

Although far from a united religion, in its early years, evangelical Methodism became almost synonymous with a belief in the supernatural. Several of the great figures of the Age of Reason were similarly keen to experience direct evidence of a spirit

33. Wesley's Ghost: a pamphlet from 1846.

world: Samuel Johnson often spoke of his yearning to see the ghost of his dead wife, and was among the committee who disappointedly declared the Cock Lane poltergeist a hoax. Another on that committee was the Methodist William Legge, Lord Dartmouth, whose family connection to Hinton Ampner[15] may also have encouraged his beliefs.

The European revolutions of the late eighteenth century, with their brisk rejection of the traditions and superstitions of the past, proved hostile to ghosts. The rapid industrialization of Britain and the gulf between country folk beliefs and city materialism acted as another powerful modifier. And, as Methodism became increasingly respectable, its former tolerance and interest in ghosts was jettisoned and, to a large extent, written out of its history. It was a general social change unconfined to Methodism. By 1830, belief in ghosts had virtually collapsed in England and, not for the first time, it was predicted never to return.

But, less than twenty years later, the growing German fascination with ghost lore caught on in England, when Catherine Crowe published *The Night Side of Nature* in 1848 (the same year the Fox sisters invented the séance in America). Britain's new royal family was German too, and the Hanoverian / Saxe-Coburg-Gotha fascination with ghosts proved second only to that of the Stuarts – who had pressed for up-to-date reports on, among others, Mother Leakey's Ghost[16] in Minehead in 1636, the Tedworth Drummer, and the ghost of Mrs Veal.

For many years, Queen Victoria lived in a sepulchre. After the death of Albert in 1861, she elaborately mourned his death for over forty years, dressing in black every day and keeping their home exactly as it was the day he died. A bust or painting of the prince was prominently displayed in nearly every photographic portrait of the royal family. Each morning, servants set out Albert's clothes, brought hot water for his shaving cup, scoured his chamber pot and changed the bedlinen. Victoria was, in a real sense, living with a ghost.

There has been much speculation as to whether the queen was ever involved with anything as unrespectable as séances. Officially, she wasn't. For many years, a watch, known as 'Vicky's Ticker', was on display at the College of Psychic Studies in London. It bore the following inscription: 'Presented by Her Majesty to Miss Georgiana Eagle for her Meritorious and Extraordinary Clairvoyance produced at Osborn [sic] House, Isle of Wight, July 15th, 1846.'

The watch was stolen in 1963, but its origins have been the source of speculation ever since. The granddaughter of a Shoreditch publican baptized in St Leonard's Church and daughter of a stage magician, Georgina Eagle was a stage clairvoyant who would have been only eleven years old in 1846. At this time, child clairvoyants were unusual, but not unknown.[17] However, as

'Osborn' is a misspelling (it should be 'Osborne'), the watch is very unlikely to have been a genuine gift from the queen and much more likely to have been used as a guarantee of authenticity.

Belief in ghosts had become almost respectable by the late Victorian period, when many scientists felt confident they were about to prove that – once and for all – on this particular scientific quest, Britain led the world.

The Society for Psychical Research was set up by socially well-connected men and women in 1882. Its purpose was to investigate the paranormal, with the understanding that ghostly phenomena were aspects of as yet not understood science. But even they were surprised by what they unleashed. When they published the 'Census of Hallucinations', the 17,000 responses, collected between 1889 and 1894, proved that ghost belief was widespread. Yet the expected scientific breakthroughs proving, or definitively disproving their existence never came.

The Edwardians were treated to the arrival of M. R. James's ghost story in 1904. This scholarly and private man seemed, in some mysterious way, to have some affinity to J. M. Barrie and Lewis Carroll. Although he is not thought of as a children's writer, it is often forgotten that he wrote several of his ghost stories especially for children. As provost of Eton, just after the end of the First World War, he knew the schoolboy on whom Peter Pan was partly based, and hosted Barrie in his own school chambers on the annual school holiday on 4 June. His *Lost Hearts*, a story he cordially and mysteriously disliked, involves a murdered ghostly boy and girl with revenge on their mind.[18]

The huge number of fatalities of the First World War stunned people once again into belief in the supernatural. The phenomenon of table rapping, which had been on the verge of dying out, suddenly became popular again. Even the British establishment clutched at ghostly propaganda, in turning the fictional story of the Angels of Mons into a witnessed phenomenon. The poet

Robert Graves thought it almost a commonplace to see ghosts of the freshly killed still stumbling around, as if they hadn't quite grasped their predicament, and people at home in the Shires saw them too. The same thing happened in the Second World War. By June 1944, sales of ouija boards, almost zero in 1943, went up to 50,000 in one New York department store alone.[19] After the war, there was a return to the attempt to turn ghost-hunting into a science. Suddenly, poltergeists were in vogue.

In the 1930s, plenty of people we would now call 'cultural commentators' made an implicit connection between the poltergeist and the rise of Nazism in Germany, as National Socialism was, among other things, a force of inchoate destruction that fed on the energies of the young. This wasn't helped by the quite public interest of certain senior Nazis in creating a new scientific discipline studying the paranormal as essentially Anglo-Saxon in its origins.

Despite decades of character assassination, many years on, Price had left his greatest legacy in his pioneering of live broadcasts. The canny media manipulator conducted his first broadcast from the 'most haunted house in England' in 1936 and, well, the rest is history.

There are three things that constantly mediate our belief in ghosts – religion, the media and social status. Since these are things that change, our ghosts have changed in accordance with them.

Where a Babylonian saw a dusty, maudlin underworld shadow, a Jacobean might have seen a white figure in a shroud, and a Victorian a dead murderess in black satin and long gloves. For centuries, the ghost was recognized, and it always had a purpose. After the Reformation, the *shim* (an old Isle of Wight word) of strangers was seen, through it seemed to have no obvious purpose in coming back from the grave. By the early nineteenth century, it was only servants who saw ghosts – at least in the view of the middle classes. It seems quite plausible to me that among the many reasons for the arrival of the English Christmas ghost story is that – as happened with the Epworth poltergeist – house servants were traditionally hired at Martinmas, in early November. At Christmastime they would have just moved into a house they didn't know and, if they were young, might have been away from their families for the first time.

Today, sightings are much more complicated and broad-ranging. Until the publication of Aldous Huxley's *The Devils* (1952) and William Peter Blatty's *The Exorcist* (1971), the belief in possession had all but died out in America. It is now extraordinarily widespread, as is the belief in angels – a reconnection to a Jacobean mindset so direct it should wear a stiff plain collar and ribbons at the knees.

When I began this journey back to my childhood, I chose the title *A Natural History of Ghosts* as something of a provocation. But I've found that there is, indeed, a natural history of ghosts. There is an Aristotelian form of classification; or, if ghosts can be held as, generally, a form of organic entertainment, different genres.

It's not much of a science though, and attempts at 'measuring' seem to get us nowhere. Generations of scientists have tried to catalogue and pin down the details, but the best evidence for the natural history of ghosts remains in the ordinary, the unconsidered and the everyday. It's a lonely business being a parapsychologist, although recent advances in the understanding of the brain are offering new hope. Dean Radin, who has spent a great deal of time researching PSI (telepathy, telekinesis), gives this insight into his average week:

On Monday, I'm accused of blasphemy by fundamentalists, who imagine that PSI threatens their faith in revealed religious doctrine. On Tuesday, I'm accused of religious cultism by militant atheists, who imagine that PSI threatens their faith in revealed scientific wisdom. On Wednesday, I'm stalked by paranoid schizophrenics who insist I get the FBI to stop controlling their thoughts. On

Thursday, I submit research grants that are rejected because the referees are unaware that there is any legitimate evidence for PSI. On Friday, I get a huge pile of correspondence from students requesting copies of everything I've ever written. On Saturday, I take calls from scientists who want to collaborate on research as long as I can guarantee that no one will discover their secret interest. On Sunday, I rest, and try to think of ways to get paranoid schizophrenics to start talking to the fundamentalists instead of me.

As I've noted, one of the few parapsychologists who goes ghost-hunting is Loyd Auerbach. One ghost told him that, when she knew she was drawing her last few breaths, she was suddenly deeply afraid of going to Hell. She concentrated on being back home and, almost instantly, she was back in her house. She didn't have much to say about the 'other side', simply because she'd never been there, and described herself as a 'ball of energy' without form, projecting her appearance on to the minds of those looking at her.

And seeing is the thing. No one asks whether you have *heard* a ghost; people ask whether you have *seen* one – for apparitions do not exist unless there is someone to see them.

We love ghost stories not just because they explain what happens at the end of our lives but because they take us to the beginning, and we reconnect to our childhood, pleasurably. The deliciousness of mediated fear is a great attraction, one that many do not want to grow out of. Secret ghost-belief is a pleasure, a thread of light back to our childhood selves. Children are now taught from a very early age not to see ghosts, since believing in ghosts violates natural law, and there are no sterner guardians of this law than the middle-class scientist or university review-writing polymath. Ghosts are no longer to be feared, but belief in them surely is. Still, the sightings and the hauntings continue.

Statistically, you are most likely to see a ghost while you are dozing in bed, recently bereaved, have some limited brain damage or a history of temporal lobe epilepsy, or take drugs that interfere with your dopamine levels (such as amphetamines and cocaine). You might have been in a library working with old books during the day, in which case you might have ingested the hallucinogenic spores of a mould.[20] It helps if there is sun-spot activity, if there's some kind of low-frequency noise from geological strata moving deep, deep beneath your bed, and if you are in a place saturated by leaking electrical fields. Oh, and if you aren't French. The French, who have also firmly separated the secular and religious, consistently score as the most cynical among Europeans about ghosts.

During the writing of this book, I found myself talking to all kinds of people about ghosts. Quite often, there's an initial hoot of embarrassment, but then something else appears. I'm now very familiar with, the sudden, shy, serious look that comes on to someone's face when they've worked out they can trust you and that you are willing to believe their story. I've been confided in by all sorts of people, from successful lawyers and directors of large public and private organizations, to the security guards at the British Library. They've shown me photographs of ghosts on their phones and told me about hauntings in their houses that only their wife and daughter can see.

Two friends who were benignly sceptical about my rediscovered interest in the subject admitted they saw a spirit walking in broad daylight on London Fields. These tales are everywhere, and there's something intensely private and intimate about them. I've been told stories that haven't been shared with husbands or wives.

In the introduction, I mentioned one of the folkloric ghost stories I learned as a child, about a Roman centurion haunting a wood outside Bembridge. We used to drive through it on the way to the beach, to visit my grandmother. During the course of my research for the book, I discovered the name of this wood: St Urian's. St Urian was the name of a church and village wiped out by the Black Death. It was not rebuilt and became covered in woodland. St Urian became 'centurion'. The name made the ghost story.

*

34. An obviously manufactured photograph splicing together a sententious
Houdini and the spirit of Abraham Lincoln. Houdini's plan to prove or
disprove the spirit world's existence was equally ambitious.

Someone who tackled the human complexities of ghost-belief
head-on was Harry Houdini. Like Harry Price, he had experienced the world of ghosts both as poacher and as gamekeeper. In
his early career, Houdini and his wife, Bess, had made a living
conducting fake séances. During these séances, Houdini made
tables float and played musical instruments while tied to a chair.
In 1899, when he turned these skills towards escapology, he left
the medium business behind. Distraught at his mother's death
in 1913, he went to a vast range of psychics and mediums but,
enraged by their obvious faking, he became a committed cam-
paigner against spiritualism. He took to attending séances in
disguise: his training in stage magic and trickery gave him the
edge in exposing frauds. He wrote a book about his experiences,

A Magician among the Spirits (1924), ending his introduction bluntly: 'Up to the present time everything that I have investigated has been the result of deluded brains.'

Despite his cynicism or perhaps because of it, Houdini made a pact that, if the afterlife did exist, he would come back. He left his wife with a code that no one would be able to guess or bluff.

After some years of séances held on the day of his death (appropriately enough, Halloween), something electrifying happened: in 1929, a professional medium, Arthur Ford, came forward with the secret message. It suddenly seemed that mediums were right and Houdini was wrong.[21] But Bess's overwhelming excitement was soon dashed. It was a hoax, a set-up; on investigation, it seemed that she had inadvertently revealed the code to a journalist some time earlier.

Bess persisted with these séances for another seven years. But, in 1936, she announced to America (the séance was held live on radio): 'Houdini did not come through. My last hope is gone. I do not believe that Houdini can come back to me, or to anyone . . . The Houdini Shrine has burned for ten years. I now, reverently . . . turn out the light. It is finished. Good night, Harry!'

Her disbelief hasn't stopped the Houdini séance from continuing as a kind of institution. It has been held every 31 October ever since.

The agreed message, full of personal and sentimental touches, ran 'Rosabelle – answer – tell – pray, answer – look – tell – answer, answer – tell.' Bess Houdini's wedding ring was inscribed with 'Rosabelle', the song she sang in her act when they first met, and the other words correspond to a secret spelling code used to pass information between a magician and his assistant during a mind-reading act.

After establishing the Rosabelle identity, the Houdini secret signal would have spelled out one clear command from beyond the veil.

That command was, simply, 'Believe.'

A Chronology

AD 100–09:   Pliny writes his account of the haunted house in Athens

AD 731:   The Venerable Bede publishes *Historia Ecclesiastica Gentis Anglorum*, with its tale of the ghost of an abbess visiting the nun Tortgith

1534:   The Act of Supremacy, Henry VIII's final break with Rome and the effective outlawing of the Roman Catholic Church in England

1536:   Anne Boleyn executed

1612:   The 'Devil of Mâcon' haunts the house of a Calvinist priest

1642:   The Battle of Edgehill, followed by its ghostly re-enactment over Christmas

1661:   The Drummer of Tedworth is investigated by England's first ghost-hunter, Joseph Glanvill

1665:   Joseph Glanvill journeys to Ragley, where he meets Lady Conway and becomes part of her extended circle, who discuss theology and ghost-belief

1705:   Daniel Defoe writes 'The Ghost of Mrs Veal', the first formal English ghost story, set in Canterbury, based on an apparently true story

1716:   A poltergeist wreaks havoc and feeds on family discord at Epworth Rectory, the childhood home of John Wesley

1734:   Franz Mesmer born

1762:   The poltergeist at a working-class household in Cock Lane in the City of London attracts large crowds and celebrity witnesses; the first media circus

1765:   Mary Ricketts moves into Hinton Ampner, Hampshire, with her family, and soon comes to regret it

1778:   Great Britain passes the Catholic Relief Act, paving the way

	for full legalization of the practice of Roman Catholicism for the first time since the Reformation
1788:	Elizabeth Bonhôte warns middle-class parents not to let their children listen to the ghost stories of their servants
1791:	Berlin bookseller Friedrich Nicolai sees ghosts, and wonders whether there might be a medical explanation for ghost-seeing
1803:	Hysteria in west London over the Hammersmith Ghost
1813:	The Mancunian physician John Ferriar publishes *An Essay towards a Theory of Apparitions*
1816:	Byron and the Shelleys make up ghost stories at their villa in Geneva, inspired by a book of German tales
1829:	Walter Scott publishes a short story, 'The Tapestried Chamber', the first modern British ghost story
1843:	Dickens publishes *A Christmas Carol*
1848:	Catherine Crowe publishes *The Night Side of Nature*, which brings German folklore and the word 'poltergeist' to Anglo-Saxon culture. It becomes a bestseller. In the US, the Fox sisters invent the séance
1852:	The new American fashion for the séance arrives in London; séances are hosted by the wife of a newspaper editor from Boston, Mrs Hayden
1856:	Sir David Brewster publishes *The Stereoscope*, which reveals for the first time the possibility of the faked ghost photograph
1861:	William Mumler claims accidentally to have photographed a ghost in Boston
1863:	The illusion 'Pepper's Ghost' is first shown on stage in London and then New York
1868:	The most famous medium of them all, D. D. Home, is prosecuted for fraud in London
1871:	First account of the haunting of Hinton Ampner is published
1872:	In France, Charles Richet first witnesses the use of hypno-

tism, and changes his medical career to one that encompasses his interest in the paranormal. The magazine *Notes and Queries* first mentions the haunted house at 50 Berkeley Square

1873–4: Sir William Crookes studies the teenage medium Florence Cook amidst rumours they are conducting an affair

1874: Mobs of over 5,000 people gather every evening in Westminster hoping to glimpse a churchyard ghost at Christ Church, on Broadway

1878: Crowds gather when the ghost of the murderess Mrs Manning is seen at a window in south London

1882: Society for Psychical Research founded in London

1885: The American Society for Psychical Research is founded

1894: George du Maurier publishes *Trilby*

1895: The Archbishop of Canterbury tells Henry James over dinner the core story for what turns out to be *The Turn of the Screw*

1896: X-rays, cinema and radio arrive in London within months of each other. Science seems to have breached new levels of the unearthly

1897: Georges Méliès makes an early ghost film, *The Vanishing Lady*

1904: M. R. James publishes his first collection, *Ghost Story of an Antiquary*

1911: *An Adventure* published by Eleanor Jourdain and Charlotte Moberly

1914: Ethel Hargrove witnesses the time-slip apparition of Knighton Gorges on New Year's Eve. Arthur Machen publishes a short work of fiction, 'The Bowman', in a London newspaper, launching the legend of the Angels of Mons

1916: Electrical and radio pioneer Sir Oliver Lodge publishes *Raymond, or Life and Death*, concerning his attempts to contact his son beyond the grave

1917: German submarine U65 launched in Hamburg

1929:	Harry Price first visits Borley Rectory, a house he was later to dub the most haunted in England
1930:	J. B. Rhine sets up a parapsychology department at Duke University. Upton Sinclair publishes *Mental Radio*
1936:	The first live broadcast from a haunted house is unveiled by the BBC, and is conducted by Harry Price. In Norfolk, Indre Shira and a colleague take a photograph of the famous Brown Lady of Raynham Hall. In the US, Houdini's widow concludes her final public séance for her late husband
1937:	Nazi-run Bonn University announces parapsychology to be a new Nordic science. Harry Price takes the rental of Borley Rectory for six months
1944:	Sales of ouija boards go through the roof in the US
1959:	Swedish opera singer turned painter Friedrich Jürgenson records mysterious voices while trying to record birdsong
1961:	A parapsychology lab is unveiled at Leningrad University, thus initiating a decade-long paranormal phoney Cold War
1969:	Parapsychology is formally recognized as a science by the AAAS (American Association for the Advancement of Science)
1971:	Dr. Konstantin Raudive (1909–74) publishes *Breakthrough*, with its extensive descriptions of Electronic Voice Phenomenon
1973:	William Friedkin's *The Exorcist* released
1977:	The Enfield poltergeist in situ
1984:	Ivan Reitman's *Ghostbusters* released

Notes

My Haunted Houses

1. The Isle of Wight was the last region of England to be converted to Christianity, in AD 686.
2. King Bran. The ravens in the Tower are his, it is said.
3. *Notes and Queries*, 8 August 1860.
4. The clergy always had an interest in Knighton Gorges and its last owner, George Maurice Bisset, since he is referenced in one of the bestselling religious tracts of the Victorian era, *The Dairyman's Daughter* by Legh Richmond. Richmond was a deacon at Brading, also on the Isle of Wight, who came to Knighton to visit one of Bisset's servants, a consumptive girl named Betsey Wallbridge who was in the process of becoming a kind of saint – her goodness and poverty held up as a beacon of pre-Victorian godliness. At the time of Knighton Gorges' destruction, Richmond was chaplain to the Duke of Kent, father to Queen Victoria.

    It has been estimated that Richmond's Baptist tract has sold approximately 4 million copies, and been translated into nineteen languages. Devout tourists who visited Betsey Wallbridge's grave may well have gone on to gaze at the remains of Knighton and thought hard of the wickedness and worldliness of its last owners and the vanity of the rich. Betsey is also almost certainly the model for the selfless Little Nell in Dickens' *The Old Curiosity Shop*; Dickens mentions the tract by name in his later Christmas story, 'Dr Marigold', published in 1865.
5. This enormous bed, mentioned by both Shakespeare and Byron, and recently removed from the Victoria and Albert Museum and sent back to a special museum in Ware, was reputedly made for

Edward IV. It is said that anyone not of royal blood who dares to sleep on it receives a visit from its irate maker, Jonas Fosbrooke.

A Taxonomy of Ghosts

1. The folklorist Christina Hole (*Haunted England*, 1940) would say that this is proof of ancient fairy belief: where you would never dare look upon a fairy as it passes by. You would cover your face with an apron or whatever was to hand. Curious though it may seem to the modern individual suffused with pop culture, fairies and elves were considered extraordinarily dangerous in the past. A film like *Paranormal Activity* is much closer to the lore of fairy folk than *Lord of the Rings*.
2. The likelihood is the one-time prime minister Arthur Balfour, since he was at one time the Secretary for the Society for Psychical Research.
3. The *draugr* can be found in Icelandic sagas. They usually emerge as reanimated corpses from their burial mounds at night. M. R. James, a medievalist familiar with Northern Europe and Scandinavia, would have been familiar with the tradition that these entities are capable of 'wrestling' with humans; many of his stories come down to a wrestle with a corpse.
4. Although parapsychological purists will dispute that they are ghosts at all.
5. Now in her forties, the girl at the centre of the case, Janet Hodgson, has recently been speaking to the press on the news that Hollywood is to make a film about the case. The photograph of her levitating above her bed, David Soul posters behind her, is almost totemic. Inhabitants of 284 Green Street still report phenomena, including the sense of being watched, and hearing someone talking downstairs, as reported in the *Daily Mail* (28 October 2011)
6. Seventeen books have been written and two films made about this case, including *An American Haunting* (2006). One of the witnesses is supposed to have been General (later President) Andrew Jackson and it's one of the few stories in which a ghost appears to kill some-

one, by administering poison. This, however, would go against every other poltergeist case reported, where even heavy objects thrown against someone seem only to touch them as lightly as a feather; there seems some immutable law that poltergeists can threaten but never harm.

7. 'I had gone down to my cabin thinking to write some letters. I drew aside the door curtain and stepped inside and to my amazement I saw Wilfred sitting in my chair. I felt shock run through me with appalling force and with it I could feel the blood draining away from my face. I did not rush towards him but walked jerkily into the cabin – all my limbs stiff and slow to respond. I did not sit down but looking at him I spoke quietly: "Wilfred, how did you get here?" He did not rise and I saw that he was involuntarily immobile, but his eyes which had never left mine were alive with the familiar look of trying to make me understand; when I spoke his whole face broke into his sweetest and most endearing dark smile. I felt not fear – I had none when I first drew my door curtain and saw him there – only exquisite mental pleasure at thus beholding him. He was in uniform and I remember thinking how out of place the khaki looked amongst the cabin furnishings. With this thought I must have turned my eyes away from him; when I looked back my cabin chair was empty . . . I wondered if I had been dreaming but looking down I saw that I was still standing. Suddenly I felt terribly tired and moving to my bunk I lay down; instantly I went into a deep oblivious sleep. When I woke up I knew with absolute certainty that Wilfred was dead.' *Journey From Obscurity*, 1963

8. See '*The Visible Couch: A Brief History of Ghost-Hunting*'.

9. The ghost-hunter Hans Holzer found a haunted rocking chair at Ash Lawn, Virginia, though I would argue that it is not possible to define furniture as haunted unless it repeats its behaviour in a new location.

10. The Prince's ruby is a 170-carat spinel which was taken from the lifeless body of Moorish prince Abu Said. The Koh-i-Noor had a similarly troubled and violent history, and is supposed to be unlucky for men but not for women.

11. The companion hound of Odin perhaps, with eyes as large as saucers.
12. The Pendle Witch trial in 1612, which so influenced the later Salem witch trials in the US, involved evidence of a familiar spirit called Tibb appearing as a brown dog, a hare and also as a cat. Of the witch Elizabeth Demdike: 'the said spirit seeming to be angry, therefore shoved or pushed her into the ditch, and so shed the milk which she had in a can or kit: and so thereupon the spirit at that time vanished out of her sight: but presently after that, the said spirit appeared to her again in the shape of a hare, and so went with her about a quarter of a mile, but said nothing to her, nor she to it'. This collision of spirit and animal is an ancient watermark in human culture.
13. I don't believe this has been generally mentioned before, since the orb on digital images is a relatively new development, but the idea of the soul as a sphere is a very ancient one. Those who write about it include the theologian Origen (c. AD 185, probably in Alexandria, Egypt – c. AD 254)

The Visible Couch: A Brief History of Ghost-Hunting

1. O'Donnell was proud of his self-considered royal Irish blood and expressed his interest in ghosts as part of his national identity. He wrote over fifty genre books and seems very much the fantasist; it was reported in 2009 that a biography of the man was in the process of being written, but it is yet to appear. In 1898, O'Donnell witnessed a particularly revolting elemental plop from the trees in Greenwich Park: 'a figure half human and half animal – stunted, bloated, pulpy and yellow. Crawling sideways like a crab, it made for a bush opposite and disappeared.'
2. Marianne Foyster. See 'Murder at the Parsonage'.
3. A hybrid of the detective, horror and science genres, these stories were written by William Hope Hodgson, something of a cult figure among genre enthusiasts. They involved people being summoned to a house in Cheyne Walk and stories being told around the fire.

4. For twenty minutes, beginning at 8 p.m., Price describes the scene and his preparations – including his use of microphones and a demonstration of electric contacts which gave an alert were a door to open. A camera and a thermograph (to record temperature changes) were also in use. From 11.45 p.m. until midnight, listeners tuned back in; the broadcast seems to have been a mix of pre-recorded and live moments. Nothing of note happened.

5. Joad (1891–1953) proposed that ghosts might be a hybrid being, a dis-embodied spirit of a dead person combining with some 'piece of matter' to produce a temporary, though very elementary, intelli-gence. Many have noticed this fractured aspect of ghosts. 'Based on the things that people report them saying, ghosts strike me as quite senile,' writes Mary Roach in *Spook* (2006).

6. There's no actual evidence of him faking anything, rather of putting a lot of very significant spin on various incidents. The photograph of a 'flying brick' in the ruins of Borley Rectory published in one of his books, and his inference that it 'might' have been thrown by a poltergeist, when he knew perfectly well it had been lobbed by workmen, was typical of this.

7. Among his formal papers read to the Royal Society were an explor-ation of the healing waters of Bath and another concerning the lead mines nearby.

8. Reports of early ghost sightings would remark on the hair and clothes of ghosts having been singed by their Purgatorial status; they had been rather too close to the fires of Hell.

9. Nobody who was in Heaven would return. Why would they?

10. The best known is the witch of Endor, who raises the ghost of the prophet Samuel in the first book of Samuel in the Old Testament.

11. Hilary Evans, *Intrusions: Society and the Paranormal* (1982).

12. It could be Winston Churchill, but the more likely is Arthur Balfour. His role in the creation of Israel led conspiracy theorists to assign an occult meaning to his actions as prime minister because of his sister's role as a parapsychologist (and his own membership of the SPR) – all of which, it goes without saying, is nonsense.

13. He also discovered why the sky is blue, the perennial favourite question of children. The theory behind it is now known as Rayleigh Scattering.
14. It reads quaintly now but is still full of sound advice, especially on the state of mind of the investigator, which is something no one seems to consider these days.
15. This late and very disreputable cash-in on a haunted-house scenario is remarkably akin to events in the career of Harry Price. In the case of Amityville, the story has been comprehensively debunked.
16. Tobe Hooper's *Poltergeist* (1982) and the novels of Stephen King, such as *Pet Sematary* (1983), are two very good examples.
17. Obituary, *New York Times*, 29 April 2009.
18. *Where the Ghosts Are: The Ultimate Guide to Haunted Houses*, Hans Holzer (1997).
19. *TAPS* in the US and *Most Haunted* in the UK.

The House That was Haunted to Death

1. The Ricketts and Jervis families were to have strong links with the Royal Navy over a considerable period, ending with one of Mrs Ricketts' descendants, Robert St Vincent Sherbrooke, being awarded the Victoria Cross for his role in the defence of a Baltic convoy in 1943.
2. *The Hinton Mystery*, British Library MS collection 30011.
3. Silk is a recurrent ghostly motif over the ages, going back as early as 1587, when a ghost described as 'a bright thing of long proportion without shape, clothed as it were in silk' appeared to the wife of a Hertfordshire labourer with instructions concerning the safety of the queen.
4. This is possibly the Miss Parker who was later to marry John Jervis, Mary's brother.
5. In the marriage settlement between George William Ricketts and Letitia Mildmay on 2 November 1791, the New Canaan Estate register includes a schedule of 200 slaves.
6. Streeter seems to have been targeted by the spirits. Having not heard the sounds before, she 'rashly expressed a wish to hear more of

them, and from that night till she quitted the house there was scarce a night passed that she did not hear the sound as if some person walked towards her door, and pushed against it, as though attempting to force it open'.

7. Lady Stawell had by this point remarried, to the Earl of Hillsborough, then acting as American Secretary in the British Cabinet, George III's go-to man in the lead-up to the American War of Independence.

8. By the time Frances Williams Wynn gets to tell her version many years later, Captain Jervis lingers on to help his sister pack up the house; she sits down to rest in the housekeeper's room (downstairs between the parlour and the kitchen) and leans against 'a large press which had just been emptied of its contents'. They are suddenly 'both startled by a noise close to their ears, which she compared to that of dry bones rattling in a box. Sir John threw open the door of the press, exclaiming, "The Devil is here, and we shall have him": however, nothing appeared.'

9. They were close for brothers-in-law – indeed, they had done business together, in 1766 buying 20,000 acres each in Florida on St Johns River, no doubt with the intention of setting up sugar plantations to be carved out of the virgin territory. Had the American War of Independence not happened when it did, Jervis could well have ended up a substantial slave and plantation owner in the Deep South. Slavery lurks in the background of this story.

10. Jervis even records the interest the Duke of Gloucester took in the case during the long sea-voyage to Italy; he mentions how the duke was becoming an expert on the details of the story, eagerly demanding updates via Jervis in letters sent by Royal courier.

11. The correspondence was forwarded to Lady Hillsborough while the family were on their summer holidays in Ireland (just weeks before one of the very few occasions on which Hillsborough entertained his nemesis, Benjamin Franklin, with any civility). Franklin was a sceptic but interested in ghosts, writing about them in American publications. It is curious that his enemies were at one remove from

the owner of Hinton Ampner and his friends at one remove from the tenants of Hinton Ampner. But there is alas no evidence he ever heard the story.

12. In fact, the practice of exorcism had been explicitly forbidden under Canon Law of the Church of England since 1604. Article 72 stated that no ministers were to 'attempt on any Pretence whatsoever . . . the cast out any Devil or Devils'.

13. The Bishop of St Asaph was one of the few members of the House of Lords who deplored the punitive measures taken against the colonies after the Boston Tea Party. It seems possible he had heard of the Ricketts ghost; it is said that the bishop's support for the North American rebels cost him the post of Archbishop of Canterbury. Benjamin Franklin stayed in his house not far from Hinton, and wrote part of his autobiography there.

14. Mary Ricketts spent a long time widowed, since her husband died in 1799 in Jamaica, aged only 62. She herself died in Bath in 1828. She seems to have been close to her daughter and surviving son, giving up her house for her daughter and frequently staying there.

15. Mary does what nearly all the participants in this narrative do, which is to muddle up Mr Legge and Lord Stawell; Mr Legge never became Lord Dartmouth, but his brother did. It's clear that both men were equally disliked by their servants, and both had an unsavoury local reputation.

16. Frances Williams Wynn: *Diaries of a Lady of Quality* (1864).

17. There are few detailed descriptions of dreams of this period, let alone one connected to the ghostly.

18. This seems to be an account written down by Mary some years later, and she had her son, Edward Jervis, witness it.

19. The skull has never been located, but Harry Price decided to highlight it in his book, calling the whole story, with his vaudevillian eye for the selling point, *The Hinton Ampner Skull*. It seems another red herring when it comes to this story; there's no evidence one way or another that it even existed.

20. Revd Hughes has another connection to this story: he tutored the

Duke of Cumberland as a young man and both his Uffington parish and Hinton Ampner were partly owned by the Abbey of St Swithun's in Winchester.

21. She was also the author of *Letters and Recollections of Sir Walter Scott*, published posthumously in 1904.

22. The reality behind this could be as simple as the aged cleric simply feeling that the subject was not suitable for either his wife or his children. As an indicator of sexual impropriety among the upper classes, and a breakdown in the barrier between upstairs and down-stairs, it was not a topic that would have been relished by the Victorians.

23. The behaviour of his two brothers in secretly marrying obliged George III to pass the Royal Marriages Act the following year, 1772. It has recently been amended to allow any future eldest daughter of Prince William to become queen.

24. Hillsborough was at the time Secretary for America, in essence the Viceroy of America, since the powers he managed to pool for sev-eral years were greater than any but those of the king himself. It was Hillsborough who first sent in the Redcoats, against Benjamin Fran-klin's counsel, and Hillsborough whose astonishingly high-handed treatment of Franklin caused, between them, one of the great feuds of history. The American historian Hiller Zobel said of him, 'only the impossibility of one man's having lost America saved Hillsborough from that distinction.'

25. This hardly seems credible, but there it is, in black and white – which if it can be any way verified would suggest that smallpox inocula-tions were taking place in Hampshire at least one year before the otherwise first-ever account of an inoculation, in Yetminster, Dorset. They did own a cattle herd, after all. Hoadly writes on 12 May 1773, 'We rejoiced not a little at the happy event of inoculation of your dear little boy. I wish my child could have shared with him the distemper. She is well and jolly notwithstanding her situation but a melancholy one, for I dare not carry her abroad nor no visitors agreeable to her . . . everyone in this part of the world expresses as

much fear from a hooping cough as from any other infectious dis-temper.' However, the simplest explanation is that the 'inoculation' was a natural process of gaining immunity through ordinary disease vectors.

26. The last of her direct male first-born descendants, then on anti-psychotic medication, committed suicide aged only twenty in 2001, with his father's shotgun, and the earldom has reverted to an eighth cousin related to a relative who preceded Mary Ricketts. It remains one of the oldest Scottish peerages.

27. He stopped a mutiny on board HMS *Marlborough* in its tracks by ordering his ships to surround that ship and, if necessary, to pound it with cannon fire, in November 1797. After he had forced the muti-neers to hang their own leader, Jervis was heard to observe to his officers, 'Discipline is preserved.'

28. Pisa, 18 November, 1771 British Library.

A Kind of America

1. Some recent scholarship has in fact moved this date to 1666.

2. He certainly wasn't a puritan of the Plymouth stamp – witness the accounts in the diary of Samuel Pepys from exactly this period of time. Between September and November 1665, Pepys was in Glan-vill's London house on several occasions, and indeed met one of his sexual partners, Mrs Pennington, there, and he found himself drink-ing, carousing and flirting by the fire in high Restoration style.

3. No doubt under the eye of her female librarian, Sarah Bennet, a companion as early as 1651. Bennet travelled with her to France in 1656, where Lady Conway, in extremis with her headaches, was ser-iously considering an operation to saw open her head without the use of anaesthetics. One wishes one knew more about Miss Bennet.

4. Mainly thanks to the profound effect it had on Cotton Mather, the driving force behind the trials. Mather's *Wonders of the Invisible World* is largely modelled on this book and its persuasions.

5. The diarist John Evelyn describes Lady Conway's childhood home in 1666 as 'standing to a very graceful avenue of trees'. The original Jacobean building she knew remains, within the wings and additions designed by Wren. The house is now most associated with Diana, Princess of Wales, and with its emphasis on the display of dresses and treasure hunts, Kensington Palace these days has little time for the true daughter of the house, Anne Conway, author of the posthumously published 1690 *Principia Philosophiae Antiquissimae et Recentissimae*, which had a great influence on the philosopher Leibniz. At the time of writing, on the Palace website you can 'vote for your favourite princess' but not, alas, for your favourite advocate of theodicy and monadology.

6. To give an impression of how debilitating these migraines were, in 1658, her husband wrote, 'it was seven weeks last Sunday since she was confined to her chamber, and goes very little out of her bed, being unable to set one foot before another, but as she is held up, by t[w]o persons . . . she is so dismally melancholy; and her sighs and grones come from so deep from her, that I am terrifyed to come neere her.'

7. Being a wealthy doctor, he used medical instruments made out of silver, which, without knowing it, gave him an antibacterial advantage over other doctors, with their iron instruments, and thereby probably increased the survival rates of his patients.

8. As the king's physician, he had examined Jennett Hargreaves and Mary Spencer for bodily evidence of witchcraft – usually the skin tags then supposed to be false teats for the suckling of devilish creatures. With the assistance of no fewer than ten midwives and a doctor assistant, he dismissed the notion that these were functional nipples, and so four of the seven accused women were pardoned. Hargreaves had, as a 10-year-old child, accused her mother of witchcraft, setting a legal precedent that was followed closely by the judges at Salem.

9. Not long after joining the Ragley salon, Glanvill published his first work on the subject of witchcraft; with a rather delicious irony,

almost the entire edition was burnt in storage during the Great Fire of London in 1666.

10. There's a fictionalized account of Lady Conway's psychic salons at Ragley in the trashy Victorian period novel by J. H. Shorthouse, *John Inglesant* (1881), depicting her as credulous, superstitious and 'crotchety'. It's considered an outrage by the philosophy and feminist academe currently trying to rehabilitate her forgotten intellectual legacy.

11. Hearing of the story, Glanvill also notes that the Bible was not only open, but open at a relevant place: at St Mark III, which concerns unclean spirits.

12. I have to say that this image of a spirit in a white linen bag reminds me forcefully of the seminal J-Horror film *Audition* (1999) by Takeshi Miike.

13. The Drummer of Tedworth reappears in America in 1730, as it happens, courtesy of the *Pennsylvania Gazette*. In a satiric exchange of letters almost certainly written by Benjamin Franklin (who was a friend of the same Bishop of St Asaph who helped Mary Ricketts), a correspondent notes the tale of two clergymen assailed by a spirit 'not a whit less obstreperous, than the Tedsworth Tympanist'. The clergymen, sharing a room in an inn, were kept awake all night by a ghostly drummer first on one side of the bed and then the other.

14. It's often forgotten that London had a long tradition of transporting criminals to the American colonies, and probably would have carried on doing so; these far predate the better-known transports to Australia.

15. See Michael Hunter's *New Light on the 'Drummer of Tedworth': Conflicting Narratives of Witchcraft in Restoration England* (2005) on Birbeck ePrints.

16. I marvelled, when I read this statement, at its similarity to Dean Radin's introduction to his book *The Conscious Universe* (1997) and his experience of always having to explain to sceptics that one hundred years of constant laboratory testing has, in fact, proven the existence of PSI, as reviewed by the statistician Jessica Utts from the Univer-

sity of California in 1995. 'No one likes a lecture, so instead I wished I just had a book I could hand to them that would explain all this for me . . . this is that book.'

17. It is my earnest hope that country-music artist Conway Twitty might be proved, one day, to be part of this connection.

18. Robert Boyle heard it first-hand as little more than a schoolboy since, shortly after leaving Eton College, where he was educated, he embarked on the Grand Tour, and in 1644 was in Geneva on the way home from visiting Galileo in Florence. It's a fairly classic poltergeist haunt, all flying kitchen pans and sheets ripped off beds, plus a noise like a fusillade of muskets from beneath the floorboards that very much recalls the Hinton Ampner ghost.

19. *Cock Lane and Common-Sense*, Andrew Lang (1894).

20. There's a touch of Glanvill in a story such as 'The Tractate Middoth', one of the first of James's to be adapted for an American audience (as 'The Lost Will of Dr Rant' in the 1951 TV show *Lights Out* starring Leslie Nielsen), set in a library amidst ancient texts; and in 'The Rose Garden' and 'The Ash Tree', with their spidery imminence of seventeenth-century witchcraft. *Lost Hearts* is set in a house much like the modern Ragley, and the evil scholar Mr Abney, who collects the hearts of children to prolong his life, is described as owning 'neo-platonic' books of the Ragley style.

The Devil of Mâcon

1. Gauld and Cornell's analysis of nearly two hundred English and North American poltergeist cases where there was an obvious individual focus for manifestations revealed that, of these individual foci, nearly 75 per cent were female and 78 per cent were under the age of twenty.

2. David Parsons, *The Supernatural at War*, quoted in the *Guardian*, 25 July 1941.

3. I can't help wondering whether this identification of the Nazis with

the poltergeist is one of the reasons why the word is not in common usage in Germany.

Entering the Epworth Scale

1. Alongside another brother named Charles Wesley, who wrote the hymn 'Hark the Herald Angels Sing'.
2. Her forced marriage is said to have been the inspiration for the Samuel Richardson novel *Clarissa*.

The Ghost of Mrs Veal

1. All modern Halloween aesthetics come from these itinerants, who were mostly from Ireland, and who consequently took their rituals with them to the US on a tide of emigration.
2. 'Some Remarks on Ghost Stories', M. R. James (1929).
3. Although it is now generally accepted that Defoe is the author of this story, and has been listed as such since 1790, there are dissenting voices. George Starr in 2003 argued in an academic journal that Defoe wouldn't ever have written such a thing, for the simple reason that he didn't believe in ghosts – though this seems to leave aside what this perennially indebted writer hounded by creditors might be prepared to do for a little ready cash.
4. Among the many other curiosities of the Mrs Veal story is that it includes mention of a Dr Sherlock and a Captain Watson. There would, after all, be no detective fiction without the ghost fiction that preceded it, something that ardent spiritualist Arthur Conan Doyle knew only too well. Sherlock Holmes is all about the rational explanation of the uncanny; he is awfully like a ghost-hunter.
5. Defoe's tombstone can be seen in Hackney Museum.
6. Henry More believed that the dampness of the night-time air helped ghosts coalesce and find their form.

7. This letter survives in manuscript form in the correspondence of John Flamsteed.

8. There are some additional handwritten notes from an unknown hand, which don't appear to have been noted before in the literature. The crabbed hand of a dissenter, much as Defoe was, adds from some unknown source, 'Something was also mentioned in this conversation of former times when dissenters were persecuted by King Charles II 'at which says Mrs Veal:' people should not persecute one another whilst they are all are upon the road to eternity.'

9. Sasha Handley, *Visions of an Unseen World* (2007).

10. Crusoe is not above the following meditation: 'I know not to this hour whether there are any such things as Apparitions, Spectres, or Walking of People after they are dead . . .'

11. *Ghosts and the Japanese: Cultural Experiences in Japanese Death Legends* by Michiko Iwasaka and Barre Toelken (1994).

12. Latterly best known for the crop circles that appeared there in the late 1980s.

13. Incidents which seem to indicate a scenario where servants are playing tricks on their employers and blaming it on ghosts include the Stockwell poltergeist, and the hauntings of Borley Rectory and that by the Drummer of Tedworth.

The Ritual of the Ghost Story

1. On top of this there was a global weather effect at a high watermark: the Dalton Minimum had another fifteen years to run during a period of unusually diminished solar activity.

2. 'Manfred, distracted between the flight of Isabella, who had now reached the stairs, and yet unable to keep his eyes from the picture, which began to move, had, however, advanced some steps after her, still looking backwards on the portrait, when he saw it quit its panel, and descend on the floor with a grave and melancholy air.'

3. She was the child of a Holborn shopkeeper, and so was born in

similar circumstances to the twentieth-century psychic researcher Harry Price.

4. Most recently, Peter Ackroyd in *Albion* (Vintage, 2004).

5. The Newcastle curate Henry Bourne observed as late as 1725 that it was 'common for the present Vulgar to say, none can lay a Spirit but a *Popish Priest'*.

6. The 3 p.m. Ceremony of Nine Lessons and Carols was introduced the year before M. R. James left, in 1918, and it seems he didn't much approve of the innovation – which, incidentally, was invented by E. W. Benson at Truro Cathedral in 1880. If we recall, E. W. Benson later became Archbishop of Canterbury, and it was he who told Henry James what may have been the seed story for *The Turn of the Screw*.

7. On the other side of the whistle is inscribed '*Fur, Flabis, Flebis*' meaning 'O thief, you will blow [it], you will weep.' James always used to refer to the story as '*Fur, Flebis*', rather than the title given above, which is taken from a Rabbie Burns song.

8. Gildersleeve and Lodge, 1867: 'the person *at* whom one speaks or points'.

9. That boy is Monty James, or rather a simulacrum of his childhood self who saw the ghost from the window, though this time he is standing in the ghost's position.

10. The letter was addressed to Gwendolyn McBride, and his correspondence with her was published in 1958 as 'Letters to a Friend' (Edward Arnold). One of the great revelations of these letters was M. R. James's very great interest in cats, and his tendency to work on the edge of a chair while his cat, Job, took up most of the seat. Was James's storytelling infected with the *Taxoplasma gondii* parasite passed from cats to humans? According to an issue of the *New Scientist* (27 August 2011), one of the effects of this invidious protozoan, the subject of an episode of the TV drama *House*, is to make fear 'pleasurable'.

11. Mark Bond became a President of the Dorset Natural History and Archaeological Society (1972–5). You can be sure he never forgot that evening listening to M. R. James, whose procession of ghostly bar-

rows and ancient landmarks perhaps lodged in his mind. James, at least, would have approved.

Miss Fanny's New Theatre

1. Horace Walpole to Horace Mann, 29 Jan 1762.
2. Curiously, Parsons had a position which is referred to early in the annals of English literature; in *Piers Plowman* (*c.* 1362), Langland talks of 'Clarice, of cokkeslane, and the clerke of the cherche'.
3. A sister publication of the *Old Bailey Proceedings*, this periodical pamphlet contained biographies of the prisoners executed at Tyburn.
4. See 'Entering the Epworth Scale'.
5. Douglas Grant, *The Cock Lane Ghost* (St Martin's Press, 1965).
6. Paul Chambers, *The Cock Lane Ghost: Murder, Sex and Haunting in Dr Johnson's London* (Sutton, 2006).
7. Of the same family, the Legges, who owned Hinton Ampner, by strange coincidence.
8. And incidentally destroyed the house of Lord Mansfield, who happened to be the judge on the Cock Lane case and also presided over the lawsuit brought against Captain Bisset of Knighton Gorges.

Bloodletting and the Brain Mirror

1. Amazingly, Nicolai's house is one of the few eighteenth-century domestic structures still standing in modern-day Berlin.
2. A TV producer who makes programmes for Sky TV has suggested that something similar is true of the British stage magician Derren Brown.
3. Strictly speaking, he won the Nobel in the category Physiology or Medicine.

4. He financed Louis Charles Breguet (1880–1955), with whom he created the first helicopter; the gyroplane Breguet-Richet took to the air in 1907.

5. As the summer of 1838 wore on, however, the medical aspects of the whole enterprise became lost, and the suspicion grew that the O'Key sisters were faking the whole thing. A rumour circulated that they were members of an apocalyptic evangelical church at Islington Green whose congregation was given to speaking in tongues, but the aristocrats who attended their evening 'show' seemed charmed by their girlish impudence and tendency to fall asleep on their well-tailored laps. Elliotson was forced to resign from the hospital in disgrace.

6. Max Dessoir, in *The Psychology of Legerdemain*, is of the opinion that the well-educated investigator is in fact far more credulous. 'The uneducated person is far more difficult to deceive than the cultivated; for the former sees at every turn an avowed mistrust of his intelligence, and attempts to dupe him, against which he contends with all his strength, while the latter surrenders himself without resistance to the illusion, for has come with the sole purpose of being deceived.'

7. Studies including one by the neurologist Peter Brugger in Zurich suggest that those with raised dopamine levels (an effect of ether abuse) have a greater belief in the paranormal. Dopamine is the neurotransmitter involved in the 'feelgood' factor and a tendency to find meaning in patterns. Studies on rats at the Russian Academy of Medical Sciences in Moscow in 1999 concluded that 'female rats are more liable to reinforcement from ether vapour than males'. By this same token, Sherlock Holmes's use of dopamine-affecting injected cocaine would have enhanced his ability to see patterns.

8. *Testifying in Court as an Expert Witness*, Andrew M. Colman, University of Leicester. Notzing's pioneering appearance as an expert witness is a role that's now a staple part of US prime-time shows.

9. Walter Randall and Steffani Randall, 'The Solar Wind and Hallucina-

tions – A Possible Reaction Due to Magnetic Disturbances'
(*Bioelectromagnetics* 12, 1991).

10. Dr Blackmore went along as a guest of the BBC science programme
    Horizon. She writes: 'In the end, however, these observations are
    nothing more than correlations. They don't prove that neural activ-
    ity in the temporal lobes causes psychic experiences – or even that it
    is an effect of psychic experience. What has been missing is a direct
    demonstration that specific experiences can be created by specific
    firing of neurons in this part of the brain.' Amazingly, this may soon
    be technologically possible, thanks to the work of Professor Ed
    Boyden at MIT. His Synthetic Neurobiology Group has managed to
    imprint algae proteins, using a programmed virus, on actual brain
    neurons, which can then be individually fired by using a light-source.
    In other words, he can turn bits of the brain on and off like a light.

11. The lines were to inspire T. S. Eliot: 'Who is the third that walks
    always beside you / When I count, there are only you and I together /
    But when I look ahead up the white road / There is always another
    one walking beside you.' (*The Waste Land*)

12. A fleeting, uncontrollable episode of sleep which may last from a
    fraction of a second up to ten seconds. It is a natural, physiological
    reaction to fatigue, which can be very dangerous when the recipient
    works with heavy machinery.

On the Vulgarity of Ghosts

1. Legend has it that her liking for satin, and the satin of her black
   dress, made the material unpopular for decades. Her biographer,
   Albert Borowitz, however, discovered that satin remained fashionable for decades afterwards; at the Great Exhibition two years later,
   seven black satins won textile prizes.

2. Though he was only nine at the time, and did not actually see the
   execution, the image of that dress and the execution haunted
   Thomas Hardy. He described a much later hanging of a labourer's

wife, Elizabeth Martha Brown: 'I remember what a fine figure she showed against the sky as she hung in the misty rain, and how the tight black silk gown set off her shape as she wheeled round and round.' The dress had been imposed by his imagination, itself a kind of ghost.

3. She has most recently been incarnated as Miss O'Brien in *Downton Abbey*.

4. She was lady's maid to the Duchess of Sutherland, who happened to be Mistress of the Robes in the court of Queen Victoria, a detail which perhaps emphasized the fabric and dress element of this particular ghost. *Punch* called her outfit a *'corsage à la condamnée'*.

5. Patrick O'Connor was murdered for his money and possessions by Mrs Manning at Minver Place; she then buried his body in quicklime under the kitchen floor. The police description of her after she absconded has her at 5 foot 7 inches tall, 'stout' and with a scar on the right side of her chin extending towards the neck.

6. In many ways, the black colour of her dress served to emphasize to the English mind that Manning was foreign.

7. At the time of writing, the London show at the Fortune Theatre is about to celebrate its 9,000th performance, after 23 years and a total audience estimated at 7 million.

8. See 'The Tedworth Drummer', 'The Ghost of Mrs Veal', 'The Cock Lane Ghost', the Hinton Ampner case and the 1634 case of Mother Leakey's Halloween ghost in Minehead, Somerset, into which Charles I's Privy Council ordered an investigation.

9. At least one of Acorah's performances was assumed to be fraudulent: on-call parapsychologist Ciarán O'Keeffe fed him information about a fictional character and, on cue, Acorah became possessed by this fictional character.

10. This reached a conclusion after the show was investigated for alleged regulatory breaches by Ofcom in 2005. Ofcom cleared *Most Haunted*, concluding that it demonstrated 'a high degree of showmanship that puts it beyond what we believe to be a generally accepted understanding of what comprises a legitimate investigation'. Thereafter the programme always referred to itself as an entertainment show.

The Thrilling of the Tables

1. I'm not clear why the Red Sea loomed with such potency in the theology of Protestant ghost-belief. I assume it is a clear resonance with Old Testament stories, including the flight from Egypt, where the Red Sea was parted and the ungodly were relegated to its depths.

2. The ability to crack toes and joints was noted as a cardinal feature of the fakers. Betty Parsons, the girl who was found to be faking the Cock Lane ghost, was accused of this.

3. These days, it is more commonly rendered in Gaelic: *Buaidh no bas*.

4. Professor George Bush's first book, on the life of Muhammad, which was not sympathetic to the founder of Islam, became a flashpoint in the Arab world in 2004, when it was suggested that a disregard for Islam clearly ran in the family. The US State Department quickly had to cobble together a press release to confirm that he was only a distant relative of the then serving President – a cousin five times removed from George W.

5. Cox's Hotel was also the workplace of the second wife of the almost completely forgotten Maharajah Duleep Singh, the owner of the Koh-i-Noor diamond. Ada was a chambermaid there before the glamorous Indian potentate married her in the 1880s.

6. After, it was said, being jailed in Mazas prison, Paris, France, it seems he immediately married a god-daughter of the Tsar of Russia, called Sacha. Alexandre Dumas was his best man.

7. Home warned the young soldier about the hideous ghosts who were stalking there but, infuriatingly, none of his descriptions seem to have been recorded. Home, having described 'several spirits at the Tower in the most graphic language', told Lindsay that he would shortly be treated to an encounter himself. Lindsay later confirmed that this came to pass, without leaving any record as to what the ghost was.

8. When scientific organization the Dialectical Society analysed the incident some time later, things became complicated when Lord

Lindsay said that the event had taken place at a different address, and
by disagreements as to whether there was a ledge outside the window.

9. Varley's understanding of electricity was mystical, but unsurpassed
until the arrival of Nikola Tesla. For example, see this description:
'An iron wire is to an electrician simply a hole bored through the
solid rock of air so that electricity may pass freely.'

10. Peter Lamont in *The First Psychic* (2005) puts it at £60,000 at
unadjusted value.

11. His successful Malvern Spa hydrotherapy practice is featured heavily
in the film *Creation* (2009) about Charles Darwin, which is structured
around his visits there in 1851.

12. There has been some controversy about Florence Cook's age, but
the Society for Psychical Research has confirmed her birth date with
public records as 3 June 1856 (Medhurst and Goldney, 62).

13. After Blackburn's wife died, Florence's sister Kate and their mother
moved in with him to care both for him and his clinically insane
daughter. This is held by at least one biographer as proof of a criminal conspiracy by the Cooks to get their hands on the Blackburn
fortune.

14. Now Mornington Terrace, in Camden.

15. Two years later, in 1876, Gully's name was dragged through the dirt
during the inquest into the death by poisoning of Charles Bravo of
Balham, when it emerged that Gully had conducted an illicit sexual
affair with the very much younger Florence Bravo. Gully was
stripped of his medical affiliations after it transpired he had performed the abortion on her subsequent pregnancy; the identity of
the poisoner of Charles Bravo was never established.

16. It wasn't only women who made use of body cavities; the Australian
apport medium Charles Bailey secreted live jungle sparrows in his
anus for a Grenoble séance in 1916.

17. *The Darkened Room*, Alex Owen (1989).

18. Edmund Gurney (1847–88) was a founder member of the SPR, thus
becoming the first full-time psychical researcher in history. A fellow
of Trinity, Cambridge for a while, he later studied under the physicist

Oliver Lodge, who derived his interest in the supernatural from his pupil. In 1886, he was the lead author of *Phantasms of the Living*, a ground-breaking study of 'telepathic' hallucinations. It is said he was the model for George Eliot's Daniel Deronda. He died in a Brighton hotel, having overdosed on chloroform, possibly to treat neuralgia.

19. The son of a clergyman and another Trinity, Cambridge man, Myers (1843–1901) was one of the founders of the SPR. Some sources call him 'The Father of Psychical Research'. William James thought Myers had a 'genius not unlike that of Charles Darwin'. Myers is also increasingly seen as a pioneer in the psychiatric field.

20. There is something about Shaker furniture that seems to beg for poltergeist attention.

21. Claude Henri de Rouvroy, Comte de Saint-Simon (1760–1825) was a utopian socialist.

22. When the test involved gripping a handle rather than having coins strapped on, she simply put one of the handles beneath her knee and used her free hand to strum a guitar and cut shapes from paper. When one of Crookes' galvanometers was recently discovered in the Science Museum in London, tests showed it to be child's play to fool – tucking it into your sock was one way.

Angels in the Skies and Demons in the Deep

1. A few years after having this ghost story published, he wrote a book defending the British police force, *The Thin Blue Line*, in 1965.

2. There is a comment pencilled in the margin of the British Library edition of this book, drawing attention to the fact that sixty-five is five times thirteen!

3. The USS *Hornet* is another warship with a long history of being haunted.

4. *Many Inventions*, 1893.

5. This inspired Cecil B. DeMille's *Joan the Woman* (1916) and helped lead to her eventual canonization after five centuries, in 1920.

6. Helen de G. Verrall, 'An Enquiry Concerning "The Angels at Mons"', *Journal of the Society for Psychical Research*, December 1915.
7. Imperial War Museum, 'The Angels of Mons', Information Sheet, no. 24, Booklist no. 1256A. London: Imperial War Museum, undated.
8. K. McClure, *Visions of Angels and Tales of Bowmen*, 1994.
9. As it happens, I found myself at Woodchester mansion for the *Most Haunted* midsummer special. The experience was the strangest combination of cut-price TV production and careful marshalling of its invited audience, but if you could get away from the nonsense, it was the most unnerving of locations.
10. The three other types of Greek ghost were the plaintive *aôroi*, mostly children and babies; the troubled *ataphoi*, who had not received proper burial; and the spiteful *agamoi*, those who died without being married. If female, they were bitter, spinster ghosts.
11. Despite these reports, it remains a subject of controversy among classical scholars as to whether there were any horses at the Battle of Marathon at all.

The Brown Lady of Raynham Hall

1. There's a further interesting point about Philip, Duke of Wharton. The year in which he was impeached on a charge of high treason by the king and Dorothy's brother, Robert Walpole, and all his titles and estates confiscated, was 1729. This was the year Dorothy died. Could the family legend be true – that she starved herself to death as a result of Wharton's complete ruination at the hands of her own brother?
2. One of these children, Edward, became Dean of Norwich.
3. The idea of a portrait whose eyes follow you about the room, so popular especially in supernatural comedies, seems to originate in a short story, 'The Yellow Gown' (1858), by G. J. Whyte Melville, in which the narrator is struck by the 'strange optical delusion' of the painted woman watching him.

4. Most sources have him down as a Colonel Loftus, but since Gwladys calls him a major and she was, after all, a relative, I follow her example.

5. A favourite of Hemingway and praised by Joseph Conrad, the now-forgotten Frederick Marryat was an influence on Patrick O'Brian in his seafaring books. Captain Marryat (1792–1848) wrote *Mr Midshipman Easy* and *Children of the New Forest*, and his sketch of Napoleon on his death-bed is one of the best-known images of the age. In 1820, Marryat had commanded the sloop *Beaver*, which was responsible for bringing news of Napoleon's death on St Helena back to England. He did write about the supernatural: his *The Phantom Ship* (1839) is very *Pirates of the Caribbean*.

6. It does indeed show a pale translucent shape hovering above the thirteenth step of the staircase, and many since have commented on its 'Marian' appearance – that is, it looks like a conventional image of the Virgin Mary. This seems especially interesting since Lady Townsend was a Catholic and had a particular interest in one of the most venerated of all Catholic shrines, nearby at Walsingham.

7. Tom Ruffles, 'The Brown Lady of Raynham Hall', nthposition.com, January 2009.

8. There's a persistent story that Lady Townsend had actually hired Indre Shira, in which case, *cui bono*, it seems more than possible that this was a sophisticated publicity stunt for the book, which opens with the Brown Lady story. I must say that Lady Townsend comes across in her book as quite lively and slightly mischievous, more of a Bright Young Thing than the gloomy Catholic grande dame implied by some; in one story, in telling of the Monmouth Room, she says that at one of her house parties the 'loveliest debutante of the year' had insisted on sleeping there in the hope of seeing the cavalier. She didn't, but only two days later, an old lady who had slept there did.

9. There was a similar denouement with William Hope (1863–1933), a carpenter turned photographer, who in 1920 produced a spirit photograph of someone very much alive.

10. The term 'thoughtographs' was later replaced by 'nengraphs'.

11. In 2007 an interview with the mathematician Persi Diaconis in the *New Scientist* again threw up doubts about the whole procedure, with Persi claiming he had seen Serios cheat. This does not entail the conclusion that all he ever did was cheat, however.

Murder at the Parsonage

1. Smith never did get his report.
2. I remember a similar explanation at Knighton Gorges (see 'My Haunted Houses'), and the small dilapidated garden cottage that survives. I was told with some confidence by a local expert that the reason there were no windows looking out on to the garden of the old house was because an owner 'did not like the things he saw at night' when the ghosts grew busy, to borrow a Jamesian word. In reality, in such cases, it is usually so the servants couldn't gawp at their employers while they were taking tea on the lawn.
3. He did return once during the Foyster incumbency to examine some more writing on the wall, but that was it. Once again, his connection to Borley had ended barely as it began.
4. In a letter to Ian Greenwood many years later, Marianne observed that 'Fisher got caught . . . he thought I had money, and I got caught, I thought he had.'
5. It is also claimed that, in 1941, Marianne duped another man named Davies, a widowed GP, by pretending to channel the spirit of his dead wife, Tweatie, especially at climactic moments while they were having sex. She extracted money and gifts from him over a six-month period. After she broke up with him, she returned his wife's clothes, twisted into 'doll-like shapes' and accompanied by pieces of cardboard on which 'cabbalistic symbols' were written. Davies felt she was putting a curse on him (*The Widow of Borley*, 1992).
6. Marianne abandoned all but two of her three adopted children at some point, keeping only the last one, Vincent O'Neil. Similarly, an

evacuee she briefly looked after was one day, without warning, simply marched to the station and put on a train back to London. O'Neil learned of his mother's connection to Borley only after her death in 1993, and for a while ran a pioneering website, about the case, before refusing any further connection to the Borley story after 2004.

7. Marianne went to such lengths to cover up her bigamy, including false names, ages and addresses on official documents, that her domestic arrangements are not altogether clear. In the 1950s Trevor Hall tried to unravel the whole skein of deception, but it seems she lived with Fisher and passed off Lionel Foyster as an aged father in Ipswich and Rendlesham after leaving Borley. It's quite possible that husband number two really thought that husband number one was his wife's invalid father.

8. 'A Kind of America'.

9. My thanks to the genealogist Robert Barret, who looked into this matter and can find no evidence that the two are related.

10. Ellic Howe was an author with an interest in the occult movement known as the Golden Dawn, and his skills in graphic design were key to forging authentic Nazi documents for the British war effort while working for SOE master forger Sefton Delmer in 1942.

11. Price later wrote to the vicar, Revd Henning, about the coat: 'Mr Henning informed me that he knew nothing about the coat, had never seen it in the Rectory, and had no idea how it could have "appeared" there. Furthermore, he made enquiries in the village, and no one had lost a coat or knew anything about it . . . the coat was left where I found it. During my year's tenancy of the rectory, it disappeared completely for one week, according to our observer's report.' (Harry Price, *The Most Haunted House in England*). Unfortunately, the house was not as secure as Price seemed to think it was.

12. Roger Glanville was to join the RAF – during the Second World War he became a squadron leader.

13. A form of ouija board that involves a wooden triangular or heart-shaped pointer instead of a glass. There was a craze for them,

especially in the US, in the 1860s. Most recently, they have been used in the *Paranormal Activity* films.

14. Although, to be fair to Price's supporters, the brick is a great distance away from the only visible workman.

15. At the end of August 1878, 18-year-old Esther was raped by a man she knew, which triggered mysterious knockings, bangings and rustlings in the little house in which she lived. Visited by many, including clergymen, the words 'Esther Cox You Are Mine to Kill' appeared above her bed, and she began to suffer seizures and swellings on her body.

16. The anthropologist Dr Eric J. Dingwell (1890–1986) was no fan of Harry Price; as well as being the SPR's intellectual attack-dog, his professional life was mostly spent cataloguing in the British [Museum] Library as 'Honorary Assistant Keeper', where he, among other things, was in charge of its 'private case material' of erotica. One of his donations to the library included 'Prospectuses and advertisements for erotica in various languages, dating from around 1890 to 1970'.

17. It can be found in the British Library, where he once worked as a librarian.

18. Great Livermere, where M. R. James spent his childhood, is only twenty miles from Borley; with his love of East Anglian churches he almost certainly visited Borley at some point.

19. The script survives in the Harry Price Collection at the University of London, and it never went into serious development. Sinclair is best known these days for writing *There Will Be Blood*, which was made into a movie with Daniel Day-Lewis in 2007.

20. This may or may not be the manuscript called 'The Ghost That Kept Harry Price Awake'.

The King of Terrors and Other Tales of Technology

1. After her cremated ashes were tested for radioactive residues, there is now evidence that Marie Curie died not of exposure to the radium she worked on, but exposure to early X-ray machines.

2. You can glimpse a version of it in the latest filmed adaptation of the Susan Hill novel, *The Woman in Black* (2012).

3. Technically, the first ever projected screening in the UK was by British pioneer Birt Acres on 10 January 1896 at the Lyonsdown Photographic Club in High Barnet, but the Royal Photographic Society screening in Marlborough Hall appears to have been the first public show.

4. 'To the house whose entrants are bereft of light/where dust is their sustenance, and clay their food/They see no light and dwell in darkness/they are clothed like birds in wings for garments/and dust has gathered on the door . . .' Ištar's Descent to the Netherworld. Transliteration provided in R. Borger, *Babylonisch-assyrische Lesestücke* vol. 1 (Rome, 2006).

5. https://www.youtube.com/watch?v=K4MnFACzKfQ

6. https://www.youtube.com/watch?v=8ZrATNzuksQ

7. Abraham Lincoln was assassinated at Ford's Theater, Washington, DC while watching this actor perform on stage. Lincoln remains one of the most supernaturally charged of all the presidents, supposedly haunting the White House and appearing in a Mumler spirit photograph. Lincoln believed in prophetic omens, once looking into a mirror and seeing a double image of himself, and dreaming of himself lying in state. General Ulysses Grant and his wife, Julia, had been supposed to accompany the president to Ford's Theater, but that morning Mrs Grant had felt the urgent conviction that they should leave Washington and return home to New Jersey. Grant at first refused; only a few days earlier he had accepted the surrender of General Lee and was due to be feted that evening. But his wife was insistent, sending messages during the day begging her husband to leave the Capitol immediately. Only after the assassination, in which Grant was to have been sitting in the box with Lincoln, was it discovered that he was also on Booth's list of intended victims.

8. His proposal of a 'sympathetic telegraph' in his *Magiae Natralis* in 1585 involved a needle swinging around letters of the alphabet – rather more ouija board than telegraph, perhaps.

9. They were inspired by Holbein's *Dance of Death*.

10. It seems he also created his own Masonic order.
11. Henry Dircks.
12. Some accounts have a performance on Christmas Eve, 1862.
13. *Herald*, August 1863.
14. Lucy E. Frank, *Representations of Death in Nineteenth-century US Writing and Culture*, 2007.
15. Röntgen discovered X-rays using the Crookes tube in 1895.
16. See 'The Thrilling of the Tables'.
17. The two words have opposite meanings, which is why the title of the movie franchise *Paranormal Activity* is completely incorrect. The paranormal is simply a nod to as yet unregistered physical laws of science. The supernatural defies science. Demons are not paranormal.
18. A heavy thunderstorm erupted during the event, but he never flinched, scoring 289 out of 300 on the target.
19. The Revd Luther Schulze of Washington, DC wrote to Rhine about the 13-year-old son of a Maryland congregant in 1949. The possession seemed to get worse when Catholic priests became involved; the boy would masturbate in front of priests and writhe suggestively on the bed. Once, an arrow appeared like a red welt on his skin, pointing to his penis. In Schulze's account, a mental-health professional gave their opinion that the boy 'did not want to grow up'. The phenomena finally died out without fanfare. Rhine met Schulze only after the whole incident was over.
20. Though there has been some experimental evidence of non-locality taking place with organic matter – tetraphenylporphyrin ($C_{44}H_{30}N_4$) – science still seems very far away from explaining how such exalted physics could possibly interact with our perceptions. See *Multiscale Methods in Quantum Mechanics: Theory and Experiment* by Philippe Blanchard and G. F. Dell'Antonio, 2004.
21. *Science*, December 2011.
22. It wasn't until 1995 that the US army and other US governmental bodies officially distanced themselves from these paranormal special projects.
23. Some of these were conducted under the fashionable influence of drugs, including LSD.

24. It is true that much of the scepticism levelled at parapsychology is biased, but even so, you can produce all the data you like, but if no one is prepared to read it, it is in essence meaningless.
25. See 'On the Vulgarity of Ghosts'.
26. Parapsychologists in Europe seem readier to get out of a chair these days – Ciaran O'Keeffe is one who springs to mind.
27. www.lessemf.com
28. 'People often ask me how I came to write *Ghostbusters*,' Dan Aykroyd wrote in a foreword to his father's book, *A History of Ghosts*, in 2009. 'The truth is that in the early 1900s my family was part of a world-wide cultural and social phenomenon driven by a wish to make contact with spirits of the dead whether the dead wanted it or not.'
29. *Magic Lantern*, 1987; 35mm slide projection with sound.
30. Unless it resides in the TV show about haunted artefacts, *Warehouse 13*.
31. The SPR investigated a case in Staffordshire at Westwood Hall in 1998 in which the caretaker was writing a document on Lady Prudentia Trentham, who was supposed to haunt it. When the spellchecker highlighted 'Prudentia', its alternative spellings were 'dead', 'buried' and 'cellar'.

Most Haunted

1. To involve the viewer at almost every turn was a canny move. Online viewers for the live shows were encouraged to participate by accessing the locked-off camera feeds in dimly lit rooms and corridors in real time, reporting anomalous activity back to the production team.
2. Which he applied first to Dean Manor and then to Borley Rectory, depending on which would generate more press.
3. www.thegoldenfleeceyork.co.uk
4. As with Borley, though the locals do get fed up with ghost-hunters haunting the churchyards at night.
5. This story is almost certainly a folkloric incursion from the Captain Marryat incident at Raynham Hall, discussed in 'The Brown Lady of

Raynham Hall'. This habit of borrowing hauntings, and translocating them to other situations, is very typical of the way that ghost stories are told and passed on, their details always changing. See also the tale of the Tower of London sentry bayonetting an advancing ghost in the first chapter of this book.

6. Fabricated in December 1924 by ghost-hunter Elliott O'Donnell for his book *Ghosts Helpful and Harmful* (1924).

7. *A Ragged Schooling* (Fontana, 1979).

8. Melrose Abbey was a great preoccupation of Sir Walter Scott, whose haunted-bedroom story is the first modern ghost tale. The heart of Robert the Bruce and the body of occultist Michael Scot are buried at the abbey. Michael Scot was a kind of Celtic John Dee, who invoked spirits to bring him dishes from the royal courts of France and Spain and was written of by both Dante and Boccaccio. After 1,200 years, the abbey is still associated with the uncanny. Once a building is haunted, it remains haunted, it seems, almost forever.

9. *Haunted England: A Survey of English Ghost Lore*, 1941.

10. It was a pale woman with red hair who leant in through the window; 'to me her body looked more like a thick cloud than substance'.

11. *Memoirs of Lady Fanshawe*, 1830.

12. Her ghost is associated with several country houses, including Blicking Hall, Hever Castle, Bollin Hall in Cheshire and the church at Salle, Essex. Her pleas for justice can be heard in the cellar of the Archbishop of Canterbury's house at Lambeth Palace, and she also appears on a spectral boat on the Thames for her last journey by river to the Tower.

13. Although headless ghosts are traditional throughout Europe, and some Saxon cemeteries in England show evidence that bodies were decapitated to stop them rising from the grave, stories of headless ghosts in England do not much predate that of Anne Boleyn.

14. The eighteenth-century actor David Garrick, who made his name playing Hamlet, had made for himself a mechanical wig which allowed the strands of metallic hair to stand in fright on cue.

15. See 'The House That was Haunted to Death'.

16. Just before Christmas, and only six weeks after her death, there was heard 'knocking and noise in the chamber and about the bed, which went away like a drove of cattle'. Then came Mother Leakey's full apparitions, one after another, with the ghost dressed in black but with a white stomacher. When asked whether she is in Heaven or Hell, she disappears with a groan.

17. If little Georgina had come to Osborne House, Prince Albert would still have been alive. The most likely situation is that she performed in front of the queen during one of their many tours of English theatres, and that her father, always with an eye on self-publicity, had the watch made up himself.

18. Contrary to what many people think, there have been very few recorded ghost-children in the United Kingdom, compared to, say, Scandinavia and the Baltic states, regions of Europe with which M. R. James was familiar.

19. The ouija board was originally sold as a children's board game. William Fuld patented it as the product of 'involuntary muscular action of the players, or some other agency'.

20. Dr R. J. Hay, writing in the *Lancet*, has composed just such a paper on the hallucinogenic properties of fungi lurking in old books. He is one of the UK's leading mycologists and a professor of dermatology at Guy's Hospital.

21. There was later a somewhat hysterical claim made that the Spiritualist Church had organized Houdini's death.

Further Reading

Abbot, G., *Ghosts of the Tower of London* (David & Charles, 1986)

Ackroyd, Peter, *The English Ghost, Spectres Through Time* (Chatto & Windus, 2010)

Adams, Paul, with Brazil, Paul Eddie, and Underwood, Peter, *The Borley Rectory Companion* (History Press, 2009)

Aykroyd, Peter H., *A History of Ghosts: The True Story of Séances, Mediums, Ghosts, and Ghostbusters* (Rodale Books, 2009)

Babbs, Edward, *Borley Rectory: The Final Analysis* (Six Martlets Publishing, 2003)

Baldwin, Gay, *Ghosts of Knighton Gorges* (Baldwin, 2010)

Blum, Deborah, *Ghost Hunters: William James and the Search for Scientific Proof of Life after Death* (Penguin Press, 2006)

Bywater, Hector, *Their Secret Purposes: Dramas and Mysteries of the Naval War* (Constable, 1932)

Chambers, Paul, *The Cock Lane Ghost: Murder, Sex and Haunting in Dr Johnson's London* (History Press, 2006)

Clarke, Andrew, *The Bones of Borley* (www.foxearth.co.uk)

Clarke, David, *The Angels of Mons: Phantom Soldiers and Ghostly Guardians* (Wiley, 2004)

Cox, Michael, *M. R. James: An Informal Portrait* (Oxford University Press, 1983)

Crowe, Catherine, *The Night Side of Nature* (T. C. Newby, 1848)

Davies, Owen, *Ghosts: A Social History* (5 vols.) (Pickering & Chatto, 2010)

—, *The Haunted: A Social History of Ghosts* (Macmillan, 2009)

Felton, D., *Haunted Greece and Rome: Ghost Stories from Classical Antiquity* (University of Texas Press, 1999)

Further Reading

Folklore, Myths and Legends of Britain (Various Authors, The Reader's Digest Association, 1973)

Finucane, R. C., *Ghosts: Appearances of the Dead & Cultural Transformation* (Prometheus Books, 2006)

Gauld, Alan, with Cornell, A. D., *Poltergeists* (Routledge & Kegan Paul, 1979)

Geiger, John, *The Third Man Factor: Surviving the Impossible* (Canongate, 2009)

Green, Andrew, *Ghosts of Today* (Kaye & Ward, 1980)

—, *Ghost-Hunting: A Practical Guide* (Mayflower, 1976)

Haining, Peter, *The Mammoth Book of True Hauntings* (Robinson, 2008)

Hall, Trevor, *The Spiritualists: The Story of Florence Cook and William Crookes* (Helix Press, 1973)

Handley, Sasha, *Visions of an Unseen World: Ghost Beliefs and Ghost Stories in Eighteenth-Century England* (Pickering & Chatto, 2007)

Hole, Christina, *Haunted England: A Survey of English Ghost Lore* (Scribners & Sons, 1941)

Hood, Bruce, *Supersense* (Souvenir Press, 1980)

Horn, Stacy, *Unbelievable: Investigations into Ghosts, Poltergeists, Telepathy, and Other Unseen Phenomena, from the Duke Parapsychology Laboratory* (Ecco Press, 2009)

Irwin, Henry J., with Watt, Caroline A., *An Introduction to Parapsychology* (McFarlane, 5th edn, 2007)

Iwasaka, Michiko, with Toelken, Barre and Hufford, David J., *Ghosts and the Japanese: Cultural Experience in Japanese Death Legends* (Utah State University Press, 1994)

Jones, Andrew, *Medieval Ghost Stories: An Anthology of Miracles, Marvels and Prodigies* (Boydell Press, 2001)

Lamont, Peter, *The First Psychic: The Peculiar Mystery of a Victorian Wizard* (Abacus, 2006)

Lang, Andrew, *The Book of Dreams and Ghosts* (Longmans, Green & Co, 1897)

Lavater, Lewis, *Of Ghosts and Spirits Walking by Night* (1572)

Mackenzie, Andrew, *Hauntings and Apparitions* (Heinemann, 1982)

Marshall, Peter, *Mother Leakey and the Bishop* (Oxford University Press, 2008)

Maxwell-Stuart, P. G., *Ghosts: A History of Phantoms, Ghouls and Other Spirits of the Dead* (History Press, 2007)

McBryde, Gwendolen, *M. R James: Letters to a Friend* (Edward Arnold, 1956)

McCorristine, Shane, *Spectres of the Self* (Cambridge University Press, 2010)

Melechi, Antonio, *Servants of the Supernatural: The Night Side of Victorian Nature* (Heinemann, 2008)

Morris, Richard, *Harry Price: The Psychic Detective* (Sutton, 2007)

O'Hara, Gerald, *Dead Men's Embers* (Saturday Night Press, 2006)

Oppenheim, Janet, *The Other World: Spiritualism and Psychical Research in England, 1850–1914* (Cambridge University Press, 1988)

Owen, Alex, *The Darkened Room : Women, Power, and Spiritualism in Late Victorian England* (University of Chicago Press, 2004)

Playfair, Guy Leon, *This House is Haunted: The Investigation of the Enfield Poltergeist* (Souvenir Press, 1980)

Price, Harry, *The End of Borley Rectory* (George Harrap & Co, 1946)

—, *Poltergeist over England: Three Centuries of Mischievous Ghosts* (Country Life, 1945)

—, *The Most Haunted House in England: Ten Years' Investigation of Borley Rectory* (Longmans, Green & Co, 1940)

Radin, Dean, *Entangled Minds* (Pocket Books, 2006)

Roach, Mary, *Spook: Science Tackles the Afterlife* (W. W. Norton, 2006)

Sitwell, Sacheverell, *Poltergeists: Fact or Fancy* (Faber & Faber, 1940)

Smajic, Srdjan, *Ghost-Seers, Detectives and Spiritualists: Theories of Vision in Victorian Literature and Science* (Cambridge University Press, 2010)

Steedman, Gay, and Anker, Ray, *Ghosts of the Isle of Wight* (Steedman/ Anker, 1978)

Tabori, Paul, with Underwood, Peter, *The Ghosts of Borley* (David & Charles, 1973)

Further Reading

Thomas, Keith, *Religion and the Decline of Magic* (Weidenfeld & Nicolson, 1971)

Underwood, Peter, *Gazetteer of British Ghosts* (Souvenir Press, 1971)

Weisberg, Barbara, *Talking to the Dead: Kate and Maggie Fox and the Rise of Spiritualism* (Harper Collins, 2005)

Westwood, Jennifer, and Simpson, Jacqueline, *The Lore of the Land: A Guide to England's Legends, from Spring-heeled Jack to the Witches of Warboys* (Penguin, 2006)

Wood, Robert, *The Widow of Borley* (Duckworth, 1992)

Acknowledgements

I'd like to thank my agent and old friend Piers Blofeld from Shiel Land Associates for his very great support, wisdom and encouragement. I'd also like to thank my wonderful editor, Georgina Laycock, who juggled benign patience and significant enthusiasm in equal measure, whilst also starting a family. I couldn't have done it without either of them. Many thanks to my long-suffering copy-editor, Sarah Day, for her methodical attention to the smallest detail. Thanks very much to Tom Ruffles for reading through the manuscript; few people know more on this subject than he does. Thanks to my very long-suffering other half, Simon Su, who takes on the subject of ghosts with great and honest Chinese sanguinity. Thanks to Tom Blofeld and Robert Barret for always being there, especially to Tom for lending me the eighteenth-century Library at Hoveton, where the proposal for this book was written. Thanks to Iain Smith for buying the laptop on which most of this was written; it was eventually stolen from a Soho pub along with all my research notebooks. Thanks to Adam Roberts for always being so supportive. Thanks to Johnny Mains for being Johnny Mains. Thanks also to security guard George Prosser at the British Library, who lent me a book including the story of the U65. I've read a great deal to research this book, but I'd like to pay particular homage to the *sans pareil* expert on this subject, Owen Davies, whose *The Haunted* and magisterial five-volume overview, *Ghosts: A Social History*, are essential reading. Thanks to Sarah Hutton for advice on Lady Conway, George Malcolmson of the Portsmouth Submarine Museum for his help on the haunted U65 submarine, and Ed Maggs of Maggs Brothers on the subject of the haunted house in Berkeley Square. Thanks to the late Andrew Green and the late Tony Cornell for their kindness towards my teenage enthusiasms, and to Peter Underwood, who took my interest seriously when I was only fourteen.

Picture Credits

The author and publishers have made every attempt to track down the original images and copyright holders and are happy to incorporate any emendations. They would like to thank the Bridgeman Art Library for permission to reproduce William Faithorne's engraving of the Tedworth Drummer (7) and Look and Learn/The Bridgeman Art Library for the haunted U-boat (21) and Archives Charmet/The Bridgeman Art Library for the Brown Lady of Raynham Hall (23); Fortean/Top Foto for the engraving of Epworth Rectory (9) and the flying brick photograph (28); Topham Picturepoint/TopFoto for the Bowmen of Mons (22) and TopFoto for Borley Rectory writings on the wall (29); the Hulton Archive and Getty Images for the photograph of M R James (11) and Time Life Pictures/Getty Images for Gerald Brimacombe's photograph of Ted Serios (25) and Archive Photos/Getty Images for the picture of Pepper's Ghost (30); the Mary Evans Picture Library/Harry Price for the photograph of 'Katie King' (19) and the photograph of the hall at Borley Rectory (26); and the University Librarian and Director, The John Rylands Library, The University of Manchester for Wesley's Ghost (33).

Index

Index

Index

Index

Index

Index

DISCARD